I0824439

CUT TO BLACK

A Legendary Life in Sports (and Maybe a Few Beers)

ROD BLACK

with **JIM LANG**

PUBLISHED BY SIMON & SCHUSTER

New York Amsterdam/Antwerp London
Toronto Sydney/Melbourne New Delhi

A Division of Simon & Schuster, LLC
166 King Street East, Suite 300
Toronto, Ontario M5A 1J3

This Simon & Schuster Canada edition May 2026

SIMON & SCHUSTER CANADA and colophon are trademarks of Simon & Schuster, LLC

Simon & Schuster strongly believes in freedom of expression and stands against censorship in all its forms. For more information, visit BooksBelong.com.

For information about special discounts for bulk purchases, please contact Simon & Schuster Special Sales at 1-800-268-3216 or CustomerService@simonandschuster.ca.

Interior design by Ruth Lee-Mui

Manufactured in the United States of America

1 3 5 7 9 10 8 6 4 2

Online Computer Library Center number: 1543018598

ISBN 978-1-6680-3455-2
ISBN 978-1-6680-3456-9 (ebook)

My Dream Team: Nancy, Tyler, Brody, Jesse, and Sienna

Contents

Foreword

THE WAY THAT ROD CARRIED HIMSELF, I THOUGHT OF HIM AS THE BOB COSTAS OF Canada. To me, Bob Costas was the premier, eminent play-by-play guy. Not just for baseball, but for every sport. Costas was heavily involved, from the Olympics, to football, to baseball and everything else. I looked at Rod as that type of broadcaster in Canada. Rod did figure skating, football, basketball, baseball, the Olympics. Rod was a jack-of-all-trades.

I first met Rod when I was playing for the Blue Jays. I remember him interviewing me in 1992 and 1993. Those were the times I remember him the most; Rod was always on the scene at all the big sporting events.

It wasn't until after I retired, and Sportsnet came to us with the idea of Rod and me calling Blue Jays games, that we became friends. During my playing career, we knew each other on a professional level. When we worked together, I really got a chance to sit down and get to know Rod.

Rod and I played golf almost every day on the road. We would golf in the morning, then call the games in the evening. It was fine to do back then, because after we golfed, I didn't have to go back and play a baseball game—I just had to talk about the game. It was a lot of fun for me, and I didn't have to exert too much energy on the telecast.

Rod and I are basically the same type of person. One, we enjoy being around people. Two, we love to have fun. And three, what we do, hopefully, pleases a lot of other people. We just get along. When we are together, we talk baseball, we talk sports, we talk family.

I loved that his son Tyler got drafted by the Milwaukee Brewers. The night before Tyler was born, Rod stayed at my hotel because he couldn't go back to his place that night. We did so much on the road. We were two people who both love sports. We hit it off, right from the first time we started working together.

When Tyler was called up to the big leagues, one of the first people Rod called was me. You talk about a proud dad—he was so excited that day. It is great to share those dreams and moments with your family and your friends, and Rod does that.

When I started my annual charity golf tournament, I called up Rod and said, "Hey, buddy, you got to do this." The thing is, I can call Rod in a split second and say to him, "I need this," and he is right on it. And then Rod will call me up at the last minute and tell me that he needs me to tape a video. Usually when Rod calls me for something, he needs it yesterday. But for Rod, I put everything aside and I get it done. Because Rod is that type of guy, and he has helped us out tremendously.

Rod has hosted my golf tournament for over sixteen years. Rod always comes up with great questions and great stories and videos on each celebrity. The way that Rod interviews these athletes at the tournament is phenomenal. One of the hardest things you can do, as I found out as a broadcaster, is interviews. You don't want to sound stupid with the questions that you ask. I watch sports all the time, and I see sideline reporters' questions and I know that it is tough. But Rod always had some interesting questions for the athletes at the golf tournament. He always came up with these questions and stories that nobody else had talked about before. Rod is clever and quick on his feet when he is talking to these athletes.

Rod is also a dedicated family man. When I worked with him, Rod and Nancy had a dog named Barkley, after Charles Barkley. It is a perfect reflection of his love of family and sports.

One thing you have to understand: Rod Black is always on the go. I don't think I have ever seen him sit and be still. I have seen him five minutes before the opening broadcast of a Blue Jays game and he is sitting there, figuring out the intro. During those five minutes, Rod's mind would be going a thousand miles a minute as he worked out what he was going to say. Then, when the broadcast started, he would come up with these awesome openings. I still don't know how he did it. It was a pleasure to watch him work. The only thing that he liked about working with me is that I was able to get restaurants to bring us free food for the seventh-inning stretch. The Chicago Cubs have their seventh-inning stretch; well, Rod and I had our seventh-inning meal break.

Usually when I call Rod, his number will come up as "unavailable." I'll leave a message: "Rod, I don't know how to get in touch with you. I don't know which phone to call. Is this your work phone? Is this your personal phone?" I always tell him, "Rod, you are not that important that you have to hide your phone number." It isn't like he is the prime minister or the president. But other than that, Rod is one of the most down-to-earth guys I know.

Rod and his wife, Nancy, and their kids, they are a great family. Rod is one of the best people—not only on the air, but off the air as well—that you could ever meet. I can't say enough kind words about Rod Black. I am proud to call him a friend.

Joe Carter, November 2025

Introduction

I HAVE A CONFESSION TO MAKE: I'M OBSESSED. YES, TOTALLY OBSESSED.

For those who know me, this may come as a shocking admission, but the truth is, I've learned to deal with this condition. That's because I've been living with it for as long as I can remember. It's an unrelenting, powerful obsession that has bounced around in my brain and pounded away at my heart for over six decades.

No, it's not booze. It's not drugs. It's not sex or gambling. But it's definitely an obsession. It's in my blood. It is untreatable and it is incurable.

And I love it that way.

That's because I'm obsessed with *sports*.

That is why I am writing this book. I want to share the great stories from all of my experiences. I have been lucky enough to be around the greatest in the game at their respective sports, and I want to share those moments with everyone. To this day, I learn something from these legends.

Even now, I get excited to call sports. Whether it is an NCAA game down south, the Allan Cup—the national championship for senior hockey—or the Canadian Elite Basketball League, I love it all. People ask me what my favourite event is that I have done, and I always tell them, "The next one." Whatever tomorrow brings make me excited. I pride myself on being as excited for a high school game as I am for the Olympics.

For me, the key is to match the moment—don't be too big on something that is small, and don't be too small on something that is big. But no matter what sport or event I am calling or hosting, it all means something special to me. I am doing what I love, and I am getting paid for it. It doesn't get much better than that. In the end, I've learned it's never really about where you're going; it's about the ride. The people you meet, the moments that catch you off guard, and the lessons you only understand once you've already lived them.

Thank you for hopping onboard this wild broadcast journey. But fair warning: There are going to be some highs and lows along the way, a number of twists and turns, more than a few bumps, a ton of laughs, and yes, even a few beers.

So, buckle up.

Let's go.

CUT TO BLACK

1

THE TRANSCONA KID

I AM SERIOUS WHEN I SAY THAT SPORTS IS AN OBSESSION. TO SOME, BEING OB-sessed with something can be viewed as being unhealthy. However, to me, sports has been my life for as long as I can remember. I have been hooked on sports since I was a young kid growing up on the cold Canadian prairie in Winnipeg, Manitoba.

How did this love affair with sports begin? Was it was somehow embedded in my DNA, or passed along at a young age? I would probably say that neither was the case. The more likely reality is that I didn't find sports—sports found *me* in the 1960s in a sleepy, yet quirky little suburb in the east end of Winnipeg called Transcona. Known as the Park City because of the abundance of green space, it had a bigger reputation because of its history with the national railways, including the National Transcontinental Railway, which gave the town its name. Everyone, it seemed, worked for the railway or at least knew someone who did. Transconians worked hard and they played even harder.

For whatever reason, Transcona was also endlessly suburb-shamed by people who lived in other regions of the city. Some mockingly referred to it as "Trash-cona," as it wasn't exactly high on the economic scale, or they called it "Flamingo City," since a lot of houses in the area displayed plastic pink flamingos on their front lawns. That flamingo lingo has been part of Transcona lore for decades. Despite all the trash talk, Transcona was and always will be one thing to me: home.

It was my neighbourhood. It's where I grew up, made friends, went to school, played games, got my first job—and, more than anything, learned to dream.

Like many kids, I dreamed of being a pro athlete. The goal was to become a hockey player like my father, who was born with the given names Henry John, but to everyone he met was forever known as Jack. Yep, that's right, *Jack Black*, who, decades before a Hollywood actor made that name famous, was a junior hockey star in Flin Flon, Manitoba, and earned a tryout with the New York Rangers.

Unfortunately, debilitating knee injuries and bad timing ended his pro career before it started, but he never looked back with regret. He did keep some scrapbooks of his hockey memories, but he hid them in the bottom drawer of a dusty dresser and rarely, if ever, brought them out. He wasn't someone who bragged about his playing days, but it was clear from the pictures, old newspaper articles, and write-ups that "BlackJack," as he was nicknamed, was a big deal and had a legitimate shot to make the NHL. And while he didn't get an opportunity to live out that dream, my dad never lost his love of the game and passed that passion down to me and my younger brothers, Derrick, Sean, and Ryan. He never made it to the big leagues, but make no mistake: Jack Black was my first true sports hero.

My dad was my coach growing up. He did the typical parent thing and drove us all around to rinks. My dad coached me for a couple of years, then he moved on and coached my younger brothers. He was big on volunteering, and he did a lot of stuff in the community. My dad wasn't one of these parents who pushed sports on you. When we were growing up in Winnipeg in the 1960s and 1970s, playing sports was just part of the culture. Everybody was outside all the time, playing some sort of sport, and we mainly learned how to play on our own. Growing up, we were outside playing, morning, noon, and night. I was lucky enough to be in a neighbourhood that had so many kids. We would arrange games every day and we even kept stats! Invariably, there would be some fight that would happen, mainly brothers against brothers. But the next day, we would all be there, and we would all get back to playing.

Dad was an everyday hero, too. A friend to anyone he met. The only issue he had: The dude just loved to talk—to everyone, everywhere, anytime. He talked and talked and talked (I guess the apple doesn't fall far). He even talked in his sleep, but he never, *ever* talked about himself, and what I admired most was how much he listened and how much he cared.

He cared mostly about his family and then his community. He became a local coach, a volunteer for charities, and a champion of first aid, where he saved lives and received a Governor General's Medal.

Before my dad became the safety coordinator for the Manitoba Highways, he worked down the street from our house at a construction company called BACM, which in the early 1970s had an ownership stake in the Winnipeg Jets of the new World Hockey Association.

That wasn't my dad's favourite job, but it soon became mine—as in *gold* mine. As a valued employee, he got tickets to almost every single Jets game, and we in turn got great seats to see so many of hockey's biggest names who had made the jump over to the WHA.

I was too young to know the impact that this new rebel league would have, and at the time, I honestly didn't care. All I wanted to do was see all those familiar stars that I had watched on *Hockey Night in Canada*. That's where my dream began. Every Saturday night, I was transfixed by the black-and-white TV set in our living room, cheering and hoping that someday I might be the next Jean Béliveau, Gordie Howe, Bobby Orr, or Bobby Hull, who just happened to be my favourite.

Yep, to me, Bobby Hull was a hockey god. So, you can imagine my nine-year-old excitement when my dad, at the dinner table on June 26, 1972, told me that he had heard a rumour in his workplace that the man nicknamed "The Golden Jet" was about to leave the NHL's Chicago Blackhawks to sign with the Winnipeg Jets. My dad looked at me and said, "Apparently, Bobby Hull is flying in tomorrow and then coming to BACM before he heads over to Portage and Main [the most famous intersection in Winnipeg] to sign the richest deal in hockey history."

I remember that moment just like yesterday. My dad looked at me sternly with his dark eyes squinting, and then, breaking into a little grin, added, "Whatever you do, keep it a secret."

I didn't know what to think. At first, I thought he was joking, but why would he joke about that? I couldn't believe what I had just heard. I wanted to jump out of my chair and scream to the moon, but I held it together because I suddenly had a plan.

I quietly nodded to my dad, scoffed down my Kraft Dinner, left the table, and then sprinted to my younger brother Derrick's room, shut the door, and put a finger to my mouth.

"*Shh* . . . listen, I got some big news," I breathlessly whispered to Derrick, who was only seven years old at the time and, like me, was absolutely infatuated with hockey. "You are not going to believe this. Dad just told me that Bobby Hull is coming . . . to Winnipeg . . . tomorrow . . . to sign with the Jets . . . and he's going . . . to Dad's work."

Derrick looked at me like I was an alien . . . but then, in unison, we started jumping up and down like we had just won the Stanley Cup—or at least the Bobby Hull Cup. When we stopped celebrating, I grabbed him with both hands and said, "Listen, we can't tell anyone. Put your pyjamas on. Go to bed and I will wake you up bright and early."

He looked at me quizzically. "Why?"

I looked back towards the door, and, in an even lower whisper, told him, "Why? Because we are going to see Bobby Hull."

I slowly crept back to my room, where I set my alarm clock for 6 a.m.—but that really didn't matter because I don't think I even went to sleep. I was so jacked.

When morning came, I tiptoed back to Derrick's room to wake him up. I made sure that our parents and baby brother, Sean, were still sleeping as we quickly got some clothes together, grabbed our baseball gloves, and made some peanut butter sandwiches to take with us. I threw all our supplies for the "Bobby Hull Mission" into a bag I attached to the end of a stick, like Tom Sawyer, and out the door we went.

The sun was just peeking over the horizon as we made our way down the back lane of our street—Ravelston Avenue West. There we were, two cute but nervous little hockey fan fugitives, hand in hand, big brother trying to console his little brother, who had tears in his eyes because he thought we were "running away from home."

"No," I assured him. "We are '*walking* away from home'—to meet Bobby Hull."

When we got to my dad's work, the parking lot was empty and the doors to reception were locked, since we had arrived a few hours before the offices opened. It was early, but it was already smoking hot outside, and I was starting to sweat even more when I realized that I might have screwed up the timing of our adventure.

I wouldn't have worried if I had been by myself, but I had Derrick with me, and he was getting more and more distressed knowing that we were going to be in big trouble when our parents woke up and found out we weren't in our beds.

So, I did what any good big brother would do. I played the distraction game. I took him on a tour around the office buildings to see the trucks and machinery. We got our ball gloves out and played catch. We sang songs. We played rock paper scissors. We looked for four-leaf clovers. We had a picnic and ate our sandwiches.

Then, around eight thirty, just when we had run out of food and I was running out of games to play, cars started to pull into the parking lot and people started arriving for work. Quickly, we both lunged into surveillance mode, finding a perfect hiding spot just outside the reception area.

Our operation was twofold: First, to keep our eyes out for any Golden Jet sightings, and second—and maybe more importantly—make sure we didn't bump into our dad, who we knew would go ballistic, derail our mission, and likely send us home with sore butts.

So, we both ducked down and waited . . . and waited. One hour became two, two became three, and as the sun kept beating down on us, I was starting to seriously worry. Still no luck, still no Bobby, and Derrick at this point was losing it.

"Please, I just wanna go home," he cried.

Finally, just after noon, I decided to listen to him and abort the mission. Holding back tears, I picked up the backpack and started to head home. I don't know what made me more upset: the fact that we didn't get a chance to see one of my hockey heroes or the fact that my dad had let us down—and, even worse, lied to me.

That's when the big corporate doors suddenly opened, and a very nice receptionist beckoned us to come inside out of the heat and grab some water. Unbeknownst to us, she had been watching us all morning, making certain that we were staying out of trouble.

Hesitantly, we walked inside, sat down on the lobby couch, and grabbed our glasses of water. Then—*whoosh*—a side door burst open and in walked a couple of older gentleman in suits, followed right behind by . . .

My hockey god—Bobby Hull, right there in front of me, and I absolutely couldn't believe it.

(Now, I would be overdramatizing it if I said there was a bright light and some heavenly entrance music, but back in 1972, in a nine-year-old's impressionable mind, it certainly seemed like that was the case.)

I don't remember exactly what happened next, since I was frozen in shock, but I do recall that he came over, shook our hands, sat down, and talked with us for about twenty minutes. I couldn't stop staring at him. His blond hair, blue eyes, and big smile framing the battle scars over his chiselled face. He looked exactly like his hockey card.

That's when another door opened from the employee side of the lobby and in walked . . . my dad, who looked like he was ready to kill someone until he realized who we were sitting with.

My dad's face brightened as he walked over, shook Bobby's hand, told him that we were his sons and that we had been waiting all day long to meet him. Bobby laughed and signed some autographs, including a four-by-six-foot piece of plywood that he inscribed to our whole family.

I was so nervous meeting Bobby Hull. I asked him, "How do I improve my slapshot?" He looked at me, and in his gravelly voice he said, "You don't! You want a great wrist shot, kid. Make sure you have a great wrist shot." Then he said, "I hope to see you at the Jets games and see you at the arena."

Years later, when I was in broadcasting, I had a chance to work with him. I wore the number 9 in hockey because of him. I thought Bobby Hull was the ultimate hockey hero. He lit up every room he was in. And he never shied away from an autograph seeker, and he never denied anyone an autograph. Bobby had his faults, and he had his demons off the ice. Near the end of his life, even after all of the negative stories that had come out, I would watch Bobby Hull walk into a room at an event and people would line up to see him.

Looking back, I really wish the cellphone had been invented at that time, because Bobby and I would have taken the best selfie ever, but the next-best thing was that piece of plywood that would end up hanging on a garage wall fifty years later.

That day was so memorable for so many reasons.

I'll never forget that feeling of fulfillment from seeing a plan come together, the thrill of meeting someone you idolized and realizing that that person is as human as you are—a fact that was really crystallized for me a few years later, when I got a chance to work alongside Bobby and started to discover his shortcomings. Yes, he lit up every room he entered—but he also had a serious dark side, including some anger management and domestic abuse issues that made headlines everywhere and tarnished his so-called golden image. To this day, I've had a difficult time processing how my boyhood hero could be so seriously flawed, but the best lesson learned was that even those you worship can disappoint you.

I'll also never forget how Derrick and I got into so much trouble when we finally got home and had to face the music. It wasn't pretty for both of us, especially when we found out that the police had been called and there was an APB out for two runaway boys in West Transcona. Oops.

But the biggest memory I cherish of that day is the look on my father's face when he saw us in that lobby. In one moment, he was steamed, absolutely infuriated with us, but then, only a moment later, his mood had changed completely—not because Bobby Hull was sitting there, but because he was so proud that his boys would have the balls to do something so crazy, yet so cool.

I knew right then that my dad would always be my true hero, but I also came to the realization that the guy who talked too much would never tell me a secret again. Dad took me to a lot of Jets games during their WHA days. One of the proudest moments I had with my dad took place during this era. I knew he was a good hockey player, and we had a scrapbook at the house. One time, BACM had a charity game against the police all-stars. Bobby Hull had practised earlier and then joined Dad and the BACM team for the game. My dad was playing with Bobby Hull! I was never so proud of him.

While my father was the goal scorer and captain of "Team Black," it was our mother, Bonnie, who was the stay-at-home defenceman. She was an amazing mom. She was a beautiful lady, incredibly compassionate, with an infectiously boisterous giggle that set decibel records.

Bonnie was kind and she had a heart of gold, but she was also stubborn, feisty, and fiercely loyal. If you pissed her off, or if anyone said something about one of her boys or someone in her family, her Irish blood would boil and blue flames would shoot from her aqua-blue eyes. Just ask a few local referees and umpires who felt the wrath of Bonnie. If she didn't like a call, she either let them know right away or confronted them after the game and gave them an earful.

In her mind, her boys could do no wrong—even though we often did.

Bonnie would also be the voice we heard—in fact, the whole street heard—at dinnertime, or as we called it, supper hour. Almost every day of the year, we would be outside, playing road hockey, baseball, or football, when the clock approached 6 p.m. Suddenly, my mom would appear on her front step and scream at the top of her lungs, "ROD, DERRICK, SEAN . . . BOYS . . . SUPPER!"

And that was it—game was over. No overtime or extra innings. We'd bust our asses to get to the dinner table, stuff our faces, sometimes slip the food we didn't like to our dog, and then scurry back out into the street or onto the field to finish the game before sunset and the inevitable second appearance of Bonnie, who would then scream, "ROD, DERRICK, SEAN . . . BOYS . . . BEDTIME!"

My mom had a kind heart and, more than anyone, taught me about the importance of giving back to the community. She loved kids in general, not just her own. My mom was big on keeping everyone together and keeping the family together. Every Sunday, she made sure that we were all together. My mom was a professional mother. Everything she did was geared towards the kids and the house. We didn't have much growing up, but what we did have, we all had the same. My mom was insistent on fairness. If one person got something, nobody else could get more. She also hated bullies, and my mom was a real character. Later in life, when I was older, I really understood her attitude about fairness and why she did what she did. Even though my brothers and I went our separate ways later in life, I think we are all still close. That is all because of the lessons our mom taught us.

We lived a simple life, managing to squeeze six bodies into a small house in a modest lower-income neighbourhood, and we never complained. No fancy cars. No fancy clothes. No fancy anything. We were far from wealthy, but man, we were rich because we all had each other and our parents. Through the best of times and worst, our mom and dad were our constant guiding lights.

Mom and Dad taught us right from wrong, emphasized academics before athletics, and made us understand that family always came first. They could be doting and overprotective at times, and while I often hated the Black "shield" they put up around us while we were growing up, I'm so glad they did, because we always felt safe and we knew they had our backs. They never stood in our way in pursuit of our individual dreams. They were never judgmental, nor did they push us in a direction we never wanted to go. Like most great parents, they took time to listen and genuinely gave good, sound advice, but whatever we believed in, they believed in, and they encouraged us to reach for the stars.

Those stars, however, seemed galaxies away when I was that impressionable kid in Transcona. It wasn't that I didn't believe in my dreams. It's just that I had so many of them.

I loved every sport, and I tried to play them all. I would watch games or events on TV and immediately go outside and replay what I just saw—or pretend that I was playing in those games, that it was *me* who was scoring the winning goal for Canada, like Paul Henderson did on my tenth birthday (September 28) in the 1972 Summit Series. Or that I was Reggie Jackson or Pete Rose winning a World Series, or perhaps Canadian quarterback Russ Jackson capturing the CFL's Grey Cup. I had so many games going on in my head, I soon started to hear voices.

Voices like the announcers I heard on the TV and radio. Legends like Foster Hewitt, Danny Gallivan, Vin Scully, Howard Cosell, Don Chevrier, Johnny Esaw, and so many more. I would mimic their voices, not because I wanted to be like them, but because they were suddenly doing play-by-play in the theatre of my mind while I was play-dreaming. Whatever sport, whatever game, and whatever day—these voices lived in my head rent-free.

Night after night in the frosty winter, I would put my skates on at home and then glide down our back lane to the outdoor rink, where I would freeze my ass off taking shot after shot, the ice cracking under my feet, snot streaming out of my nose, skating lap after lap under the light of a Winnipeg moon.

Just me, myself, and all my announcer friends.

"There's Orr, over to Hull, over to Béliveau, back to Black—there's a cannonading shot," I would shout out in my best Gallivan before morphing into a Foster: "HE SHOOTS—HE *SCORES!!!*" I would be out there for hours and hours, but it didn't seem like it. That's because time flies when you're playing games in your mind. I also had one rule: My imaginary buzzer would sound only if one of my favourite players scored in overtime or my toes were burning from frostbite. Whatever came first. That's when I'd take my stick and puck and skate all the way back home, celebrating another victory.

It may sound like crazy stuff, but I did that almost every day with every sport. I'd be on the rink, in the field, on the diamond, or in the street and I'd find my special place, tune in to the broadcast booth in my brain, and then do what every kid should be able do—play and dream.

The voices would subside as I got to my teenage years, but my insatiable love for all things sport never dissipated. Little did I realize that those impromptu imaginary games would be invaluable practice sessions aiding me in my pursuit of becoming a better athlete. The more games I played, the more I developed and the more success I had in whatever sport I transitioned to.

But with all that came a big negative. By playing so many different sports for so many different teams, I barely had time for anything else. It was a whirlwind that made it extremely difficult for my parents to manage the schedules, especially when there were inevitable conflicts. From hockey, baseball, football, and lacrosse to school sports like basketball and volleyball, not to mention tennis and golf tournaments—it was insanely wonderful. I lived in a blur.

I was so gloriously intoxicated with the circus of sports that I don't think I even considered the importance of winter, spring, summer, or fall. To the young me at that time, the changing of the seasons only meant one thing—a game change. Trade your skates for sneakers, your helmet for a cap, a puck for a ball, put on a different uniform, and let's get right back on the roller coaster to keep the dream alive.

Funny thing is, I was starting to find that my own voice, and my career path in sports would soon steamroll in a straight line, only towards a different profession—one I really didn't see coming.

2

THE ROD CASTER

WHEN I WAS ABOUT NINE YEARS OLD, I WOULD SNEAK A SMALL TRANSISTOR RADIO into bed and try to quietly listen to games at night. I would listen to the Jets' away games on that radio. At night, I could pick up WGN out of Chicago and KMOX out of St. Louis. In Winnipeg, their signal would come in crystal clear. I would hear broadcast legends on these stations, calling baseball and hockey and other sports. My mom would get mad, and my dad would tell me to turn it down. I was fascinated by the announcers. I didn't listen to music as a kid; I would listen to these games.

Sports was my life 24/7, and 365 days a year. No, that isn't a promo for a TV sports network. That was the motto of my early childhood growing up in Winnipeg. I lived it, breathed it, played it, and then replayed it over and over in my head. Day after day, playing games with my community teams or with my brothers and my neighbourhood buddies, and then night after night, planted in front of the television set in our tiny Transcona home, watching whatever team, game, or sport that happened to be on at the time.

Problem was, back then, there were only three local channels on the tube, and most of the time, there was nothing on except local news, soap operas, game shows, or sitcoms like *Gilligan's Island*, *The Brady Bunch*, or *Get Smart*. Don't get me wrong: Like most kids at the time, I used to love those shows, but when it came to sports, they all finished a distant second. When there was a game on—*any* game on—I would make sure I had a front-row seat and would follow every pass, every shot, every move . . . basically everything. Until it was time to get up and leave the real broadcast, sometimes way before its conclusion, and either go outside or march down to the basement to continue with the imaginary "Rod Games," where the only rules were that I was the "Rod-caster," and my favourite players *always* decided the outcome. Every game was always a win.

Then I'd head to bed, turn out the lights, slip under my covers, and turn on my AM transistor radio. I'd make sure the volume was turned down low so my parents would think I was sleeping, and through the static I'd follow the late games—whoever was playing whatever, wherever—until I finally dozed off or the batteries in the radio died. And, of course, all those games and voices would continue playing in my dreams. Until I woke up and then actually went on the radio for real.

You have to understand, I was a mimic as a kid, and I would imitate the teachers. I loved *The Carol Burnett Show*, *The Dick Van Dyke Show*, and shows like that at night. I loved Rich Little and other impressionists. There was a comedian in the 1970s named Bill Saluga, and he did a character called Mr. Johnson. I was around twelve years old, and I would do a perfect version of his routine. I also did Wolfman Jack, among others. I decided to share my talent with others. I would call in to Winnipeg's most popular radio morning show and do these impressions.

Funniest thing of all was that no one, not even the host, knew who this impressionist was, nor did they have any idea that he wasn't even a teenager yet.

Yep, sounds crazy, but there I was as a twelve-year-old, waking up bright and early almost every morning, and then appearing live with legendary disc jockey Don Percy, known in the 'Peg as the "Master of the Morning."

Appearing as what? A twelve-year-old sports announcer? Not a chance. As a twelve-year-old disc jockey? No way. But there I was, a few times a week, live on the radio, doing impressions.

Not only was I a sports addict but I was also an aspiring Rich Little, imitating broadcasters, actors, celebrities, teachers, friends, and even family members. Some of the voices were spot on, others were a bit of a reach, but trust me, no one was immune from my mimicry, which probably developed because of all the voices spinning in my head.

I'd wake up around 5:30 a.m. and tiptoe down the hallway, making sure not to wake anyone. I'd cover myself with a blanket to buffer the sound, and then I'd dial in to the station. When someone finally picked up on the other end, I would start riffing with whatever voice of the day I came up with. Next thing you know, I was live on the air.

One day it would be the stuttering actor Jimmy Stewart. The next it could be a burger-eating Elvis Presley. Some days it would be the bumbling secret agent Maxwell Smart, or it could even be that "wascally wabbit" Bugs Bunny.

They never knew who was coming or what was coming. And in those days, the fact there was no caller ID meant I was always the mystery guest. Sometimes my routine was a little too loud, and I would hear my mom or dad shout out from their bedroom, "Rod, what are you doing? Get back to bed!"

They had no idea. It was just me and my voices.

But my go-to voice was Mr. Johnson. Luckily for me, Bill Saluga's character appeared on a variety of talk shows and his shtick was simple, funny, and mostly obnoxious. Any time the host or interviewer would refer to him as Mr. Johnson, he would break into this long-winded staccato spiel: "*Noooooooo*, you doesn't hasta to call me Johnson. My name is Raymond J. Johnson Jr. Now, you can call me Ray, or you can call me J., or you can call me Johnny, or you can call me Sonny, or you can call me Junie, or you can call me Junior, or you can call me Ray J., or you can call me R. J., or you can call me R. J. J., or you can you call me R. J. J. Jr. . . . but you doesn't hasta call me Johnson."

Saluga would then crack a smile, take a long puff of his cigar, and continue the interview until the next time the host said "Mr. Johnson," which would set him off on his rambling rant once again. This went on and on and on . . . until they cut him off or gave him the hook.

The bit was both hilarious and insufferable, but Mr. Johnson soon found his way onto Winnipeg radio after a twelve-year-old in Transcona channelled his inner Saluga. In other words, I ripped him off, and it was dead on.

Don Percy would answer the phone and say, "Good morning, KY-58."

I would say, "Good morning, this is Mr. Johnson . . ."

He would say, "Mr. Johnson . . . how are—?"

And then I would "Johnson" him. Over and over and over again. Until he cut me off.

I did this off and on for about a year or so. Same thing every time.

"You doesn't hasta call me Johnson" became a morning staple. Some loved it. Others, as I would find out, not so much. One Sunday, we were out at a family barbecue north of the city when one of my aunts, who was a regular Don Percy listener, blurted out that she couldn't stand when Mr. Johnson was on the show.

"He drives me nuts, If I hear that guy one more time doing that 'Ray J., R. J., R. J. J.' thing, I am going to lose it," she ranted.

That's when one of my uncles chirped in and said, "I love him. That guy is hilarious."

My mom, who only heard the skit from another room or if it was previously recorded, added her two cents.

"I don't know who that guy is . . . but I do know he's crazy."

Everyone laughed and kept talking about this rude, rambling dude who seemed to invade the Percy show.

That's when my brother spilled the Johnson beans.

"Don't you guys know who he is?" Derrick interjected.

I'd never realized that he also was waking up very early in the morning and had been eavesdropping on all of my radio appearances.

"He's right here," he announced and pointed right at me.

I sheepishly grinned. My face went scarlet red, and I had only one thing to say.

"*Noooooooo* . . . you doesn't hasta call me Johnson. You can call me Ray, you can call me Jay . . ."

Completely in character, I did the whole Johnson.

When I was done, everyone started laughing uproariously. Not because it was particularly funny, but because they couldn't believe that I was Mr. Johnson.

I'll never forget the shocked look on my mom's face, followed by the trademark Bonnie cackle.

"What? When did you do this? How did you do this?" The questions came fast and furious.

I smiled as I told them the story of how I would get up before the roosters and basically live a secret life as the kid who did "voices" on the radio, unbeknownst to everyone except my younger brother.

My auntie who was anti-Johnson quickly apologized.

"By the way, Rod, you know I was only kidding," she said. "I actually do think he—I mean *you*—are pretty funny."

And so, my secret was out. The jig was up. But the show went on.

I kept waking up early, doing Mr. Johnson on the radio; the only difference was that everyone in my family was now tuned in, and I no longer had to do it undercover since my parents would sit in the kitchen to watch, listen, and laugh—until, of course, I got cut off.

As surprised as my family was after the big reveal, no one was more stunned to discover who the real Mr. Johnson was than Don Percy himself.

I'm sure he probably thought this nauseating intruder on his show was some older guy who was getting his "Johnson" off, but it wasn't until he was doing a live breakfast show from downtown Winnipeg that Don realized who he was talking to all of those early mornings.

It was a special charity event, and Percy had invited all his morning show "friends" to join him at the Eaton's store. My dad accompanied me for my guest appearance, and I remember being very nervous as I walked into a food court area full of people watching a radio show.

Right in the middle of the room, behind a desk with a microphone, sat the Master of the Morning.

It felt like everyone was looking at me—and they probably were—since I'd decided to come dressed in character with a fedora, fake moustache, and chocolate cigar.

I somehow summoned the courage to walk right up to the broadcast area, where Percy gave me this awkward glance.

I'm sure he thought, *Who the hell is this kid?*

That's when my dad stepped in. "Hey, Don, I'd like to introduce you to Mr. Johnson."

Percy, who was on the air, practically choked and yelled out, "What? *This* is Mr. Johnson?"

That's when I burst into the "*Noooooooo* . . . you doesn't hasta call me . . ." And I went full Johnson.

The crowd roared. He roared . . . and then, of course, he cut me off.

My dad was beaming.

When the segment ended, the audience applauded, while Don shook my hand and laughed at how this young kid had been calling him and duping him for such a long time.

It may not have been the most memorable moment in morning show history, but that day was a huge thrill for a young, impressionable impressionist who found a way to shake off his nerves and feel right at home behind a mic and in front of a crowd.

Being there, being on air, it was intoxicating. I was way too young to do drugs, but it was such a buzz.

Best of all, I also recognized that Don Percy, the morning show legend who seemed larger than life, was just like you and me—a normal, down-to-earth guy who loved his job. He had a great sense of humour and a greater sense of the moment, and he left me with some words I've never forgotten:

"Good luck, kid. I hope to hear you on the air someday."

When I got home, I wrote those words down on a piece of scrap paper and kept it on my desk for a long time. Percy would often joke that he was the guy who gave me my start. In some ways, he did. I never had a chance to tell him that day, and I never had a chance to tell him in later years.

But I will now. Thank you, Don Percy. You lit the spark.

3

HOT ROD AND THE ROLLER RINK

NOW, DON'T GET ME WRONG: DOING IMPRESSIONS AND CHARACTERS ON A RADIO show is still a long way off from launching a career in broadcasting. Being Mr. Johnson was not a precursor to becoming the next Ernie Johnson of *Inside the NBA*, but it did ignite the fire of possibility.

The dream of being a pro athlete was still very much alive, but this broadcasting stuff was really starting to creep from the shadows. It really emerged when I turned fifteen and got my first part-time job—in, of all places, a roller rink.

Back in the late 1970s, roller skating was so popular that people would line up for hours to strap wheels on their feet and gather for good, clean exercise and entertainment in a building that was more than just a rink—it was a nightclub or discotheque.

You can imagine my excitement when I learned that my 'hood was about to get one of these new entertainment facilities—the Saints Roller

Rink—and even more exciting, I was lucky to be hired as one of its first employees.

I don't know how or why I got the job, especially since hundreds of other teenagers my age had applied, many of whom didn't do what I did during the interview.

I lied. When asked if I had skated before, I said yes, of course I have, not mentioning that I had only skated on ice and not on a floor. Regardless, I got the job and was assigned to be a "skate boy," which meant I handed the customers their skates, fixed the skates, and later in the day, put all the skates away. It wasn't the most glamorous job, but it kept me on my toes, and hey, I was finally getting paid.

Opening night was insane—it was a circus. People everywhere, music pounding, lights flashing, disco ball spinning, bodies flying, bodies falling, and through all of this roller craze haze, everyone was hopped up, hyped up, and having a blast.

The skate counter I was attending to was just starting to settle down when the boss, a really cool middle-aged man with an English accent named Ethan James, came over and asked me if I could help out on the floor. With so many people out there, he said, we need another skate guard.

So, I said sure, no problem.

But there *was* a problem. A *big* problem. I had told the bosses that I could roller-skate.

So, with severe trepidation, I laced up a pair of wheelies and slowly walked on the red carpet towards the aqua-coloured, plastic-covered floor. *Not too bad*, I thought. *Seems good so far. Really, how hard can it be? I've ice-skated my whole life. I got this.*

But I hadn't got this. I hadn't got any of this. All those positive thoughts racing through my brain were instantly zapped when I took my first step on the rink and fell like a ton of bricks. I quickly got up, took a stride, and then tumbled again, and again, and again. I don't know what was hurting more, my banged-up body or my bruised pride from looking like a crash test dummy while bratty six-year-old kids were whizzing by, laughing at me.

When I finally started to get the hang of it, I picked up a little speed, started grooving to the sweet sounds of "Stayin' Alive," and then crashed right into the back of some older lady, who dusted herself off, shot me a dirty look, and flipped me the finger.

I squinted through the disco lights to apologize and realized—it was my mom!

My parents were my opening night guests and, like me, were having the same navigational challenges. Only difference was they hadn't told anyone they had skated before.

"Oh, Rod, sorry. I didn't know that was you." Bonnie laughed, and then wobbled back into the rolling mass.

I tried to keep up with her, but I couldn't dodge enough bodies and once again ended up falling flat on my face. It was about the tenth time I had hit the deck; however, this fall was very different. This one was a game changer.

When I scrambled to my feet, I found myself standing right smack in front of the DJ booth, and as I looked up, I was mesmerized by the silhouetted figure that seemed to be hovering above the entire rink. He was wearing a bright cherry-red sweater and was holding a microphone while pointing his finger at the crowd with his other hand. It seemed like such a cool job. The dude was having such a blast, and at that moment, all I wanted to do was take off my skates and be *that guy*.

Eventually, I would become that guy. But it didn't happen overnight. It took a few weeks of handing out skates, working the concession stand, cleaning the carpets, and occasionally practising my skating skills before a co-worker named Sharon Marks, whom I had been practising all my voices on while working the skate counter, looked at me and said, "You know, you'd be a great DJ."

Little did I know that Sharon had already put the wheels in motion. A few days later, I was called to the office to speak with the manager, Mr. James. I remember being so nervous as I sat down across from Ethan and thought I was about to get shit for not cleaning up properly or messing up the skates. Then he looked me straight in the eye, took a drag on his cigarette, and in that thick British accent, said, "I'm sorry, Rodney. I've got some bad news for you."

My heart sank. For Christ's sake—I just got this job.

"Unfortunately, we can't let you work the skate counter anymore," he said dryly.

I could feel the tears welling in my eyes.

"That's because you are now going to be our new disc jockey."

I was stunned. I jumped out of my chair, shook his hand, and through a mile-wide smile, shouted out, "Thank you, sir. That's the best decision you've ever made."

I couldn't believe I'd said that, but it didn't matter. I sprinted out of his office and put my hands in the air like I had just won the Stanley Cup.

Ethan James didn't realize it then, but that day changed my life. Forever.

I had just scored my first real dream job: a roller DJ.

Yep, that's what got the ball rolling. Rock and rolling, you might say, even though most of the music we played at the Saints Regent Roller Skating Centre in the late 1970s was dance or disco.

Might seem strange nowadays to think that the biggest night on the town back then was to strap on some wheeled skates and glide around in a circle like a massive herd of rolling sheep under some flashing lights, bopping along to the thumping music while some gangly, pimply-faced teenage dude was spinning records.

All we had were our records, two turntables, a mixing board, and a microphone. Very simple, but also very stressful. It wasn't rocket science by any stretch, but trust me, it could get chaotic in the booth, especially when you're trying to energize a crowd and keep the session flowing, mixing song after song, trying to fulfill every request, finding the next track, cuing it up quickly, making sure not to scratch the vinyl as you delicately drop the needle to find that perfect moment to blend it into the previous song. Sometimes my hands would sweat and my heart would pound—not from music but because I was left scrambling. There I was, trying to look composed, keeping my eyes out on the rink to make sure there were no mishaps, while frantically trying to set up the next song, all the while wearing a pair of roller skates and trying my best to look cool. Did I really say this was my first dream job?

But there I was, not old enough to drive yet, all eyes and ears on me and handed the responsibility of keeping the show rolling. Certainly didn't seem like a scenario that would spawn a successful broadcast career, but that thought wasn't even remotely in the back of my mind back then. I was more jockey than disc jockey—just trying to grab the reins and stay on the horse, hanging on for dear life. It was challenging. It was crazy. It was pressure-packed. It was intoxicating.

It was perfect.

I was a bit of a rebel DJ, too, trying to occasionally impose my love of rock music onto the playlist. There were times when I'd put on a song—probably something from Led Zeppelin, Rush, AC/DC, or my favourite, Kiss—pump up the volume, and go out for a lap. Then one of the acting managers, who didn't like the tune, would jump into the DJ booth and, much to my frustration, change the song in midstream to something that was more in tune with what was being played on pop radio—the Village People, the Bee Gees, or Michael Jackson.

Didn't matter to me, though. I just kept playing the music, learning to cue things up quicker, managing the pace of the show, and most of all, using my voice to help entertain a jam-packed crowd night after night. Hard to believe, but this non-ice rink was suddenly the hot spot of the community. People were lining up around the block, sometimes in minus-thirty-degree weather, to get in on the roller craze. It was nuts. All of us high school students who worked there were treated like local celebrities. It was like we were all characters of the TV show *Cheers*. We weren't working at a bar, but we knew we were in a special place where everyone knows your name.

Of course, it helped that we had name tags, but that didn't matter; we all were enjoying the popularity, not to mention the pretty good money we were all making as kids in a business that was seemingly booming.

We were also becoming great friends. Friends like Donnie, John, Tim, Ken, Colleen, Neil—and, of course, Sharon, who gave me that first nudge to the DJ booth.

And then there was Graeme. Graeme McGinnis, another Transcona dude who not only worked at the rink but quickly became one of my best teenage friends. I didn't have an older brother, but Graeme certainly filled that role at that time in my life.

We hung together a lot in those days, mostly because he had a car and I didn't, and I bummed a lot of rides from him. He really was my first Uber driver. He drove me all over the place—to and from work, to and from McDonald's, to and from my games, to and from everywhere. Graeme was a couple of years older than me, but it didn't matter. All that time spent together, we became pretty much inseparable.

He first worked as a skate guard at Saints while I was a DJ, and we worked a lot of shifts together. He was the guy who always looked out for me, telling me to take my role to a different level. He said, "Rodney, don't just play music, play your personality." He told me to use the microphone more, use my own voice more, but also use the imitations that I had been practising in my prepubescent radio appearances. He said: "Don't just be another DJ—be *the best* DJ."

I was a little skittish at first, but I took his advice and decided to run with it . . . or, I guess, run my mouth with it.

The spark suddenly became a fire.

I started using the microphone more, using the voices in my head more, and most importantly, using the DJ booth as my own personal stage. Instead of just spinning discs and making rink announcements, I started introducing songs like a radio DJ, injecting my own brand and personality and inciting the skaters to sing along with the music. Suddenly, Saints was more than just the bar from *Cheers*—it was transforming from a roller rink into a party palace.

It didn't stop there.

We were getting pretty good on the wheels, so we started doing skating tricks and incorporated routines into the sessions. We added more lights and some sound effects, and, crazily, I began wearing costumes—from outlandish masks to ridiculous wigs to the Steve Martin arrow-through-the-head contraption. It was wild and crazy.

Our bosses—Ethan James, who gave me the job, and his assistant, John Sawatzky—didn't necessarily love all the hijinks, but they tolerated my creative ideas and let me roll with them.

Mr. James would stand up near the booth, looking bemused, take a deep drag on his cigarette, and just shake his head. Any time he thought I had crossed the line into stupidity or bad taste, I would skate away from the booth or put on my headphones until Graeme, my own personal skate guard, rolled to my rescue. He always had my back.

On one occasion when I might have "accidentally" pulled a silly stunt—speed skating through the crowd, swerving, weaving, zigging, and zagging while wearing a bright yellow helmet with a siren and flashing beacon on it—Mr. James sprinted like an Olympic runner to the booth, where he waited until both Graeme and I sheepishly skated up to face the music. This wasn't going to be good. His nostrils were flaring and there were flames shooting out of his eyes—or at least it seemed like it.

"Rodney, do you have any fucking idea how dangerous that is?" Ethan screamed with my beacon light shimmering in his face.

That's when my partner in crime, Graeme, stepped in and said, "Mr. James, he's not dangerous . . . he's the *Hot Rod*."

Shaking his head, Ethan looked at us like we were madmen and said, "Well, then . . . *Hot Rod*. I like the helmet. I like the siren. But slow the fuck down or I'll give you my own ticket. This isn't fucking roller derby. Do you both understand?" He then smiled and, before walking away, extended his hand to us. "Now keep up the good work and keep this place hot . . . Rod."

It was one of those moments that remains crystallized in my memory for a number of reasons. I didn't get hurt. I didn't get fired. I was told to slow things down. At the same time, I was being told to heat things up. And a nickname was born.

Even though I was uncomfortable with it as first, the "Hot Rod" thing stayed with me for a long time. Longer than I had hoped. Every regular who visited the rink started to use that moniker, but the only other people I knew with that handle were race car drivers or porn stars, and I was clearly too slow for one and too fast for the other.

That nickname carried me through the roller-days craze and then stayed with me when I turned seventeen and took my DJ talents a few kilometres east down Regent Avenue to a hotel bar called the Golden Oak. The owner and manager, Chris Ledohowski, had visited the rink a couple of times and had seen first-hand how much fun we were having entertaining the crowd. One night, he stopped by the booth and said he liked my stuff and asked if I'd be interested in taking a part-time DJ job at his nightclub. I was flattered, but I also was so busy I barely had time to breathe.

Add to all of that the fact that Chris didn't know I was underage and legally couldn't even be seen in a bar in Winnipeg, never mind work at one. But he was persistent, and he was big. If he didn't work in the hospitality business, he would have been a natural as a pro football player or maybe even the next Hulk Hogan. He wasn't someone you wanted to mess with, but he was also a huge teddy bear, and for both reasons, I couldn't say no. I really believe that when Chris offered me the job, he thought I was older because I had this cheesy moustache.

So, there I was, the Hot Rod of Transcona, working two DJ jobs, trying to keep my marks up in my last year of high school and still keeping my dream alive of somehow making it as an athlete. I don't know how I did it. Only a juggler at Cirque du Soleil could have so many balls in the air and keep smiling.

The nightclub gig was the craziest one. Being a DJ at a roller rink was one thing, but playing music for a bunch of dancing drunks was quite another. It was very different but also somewhat liberating; I didn't have to worry about playing inappropriate music, wearing my silly costumes, or tripping over a bunch of kids. No, this was adult entertainment at its best—and sometimes its worst.

The new job featured some new hazards I hadn't prepared for. At the rink, we would clear the floor if someone fell and got hurt. At the club, I'd have to turn up the lights and clear the floor if a fight broke out or somebody puked. Not surprisingly, that stuff happened quite a bit.

But, like the Saints rink, the Golden Oak was a great place to work. Great people, great vibe, and best of all, great money. I wasn't used to making that kind of cash at a young age, and if you happened to work a double shift, you could pull in five hundred to a thousand bucks a day—which was huge payola back then and something that most teenagers could only dream of.

The "Oak double," as we called it, might have been golden, but it also came with a unique challenge.

The first—and, as it turned out, last—time I was asked to work a double was by the club's full-time DJ, a funny, friendly dude named Ed Zdancewicz, who was known to all the "Oakers" as "Ed Zed."

Ed was a popular fixture at the club, and even though he was a decade older than I was, he really took me under his record-playing wing and helped me learn the ropes of becoming a club disc jockey. During my second week on the job, Zed asked me if I would mind working a double shift.

"It's a breeze," he told me. "It pays double time and a half. All you have to do is play music from noon to 5 p.m., take a break, and then come back for the night shift at eight."

Sounded easy enough, and since I was still a rookie at the Oak, I thought, *Why not? Long day. Big money. Let's do it.*

So, I showed up early on Friday morning, chest pumped out, ready for my first double. I remember walking into the club out of the Winnipeg sunshine and squinting into the inner darkness, where the only thing I saw was a few old-timers sitting at random tables, enjoying their first pints of the day.

As I walked onto the dance floor and into the booth, I was stunned by how different this place looked during the daytime. No big crowd. No pounding sound. No disco lights.

It felt like a funeral parlour—with a bar.

I had visited more exciting libraries.

What the hell am I supposed to do with this? I wondered. *And what the hell kind of music am I supposed to play?*

I stepped into the DJ booth, turned on the lights, powered up the turntables, and threw on a Foreigner album while a few people started to trickle in. I had walked down to the bar area to grab a Diet Coke when I bumped into my manager, Big Chris, who seemed genuinely surprised to see me.

"Ooooh," he said with a wink. "Your first Jamboree."

Jambo-what? I laughed as I took a sip and headed back to the booth.

Over the next half hour, more people, mostly men, started to filter into the area, some sitting at the tables, a few playing pool, and others just standing around, talking and drinking, seemingly enjoying a nice afternoon with their buddies.

So, *this* is the Jamboree. Must be a Friday afternoon boys' club.

Cool.

Zed was right on the money. Easy play. Easy pay. Just spin a few songs, do some homework, maybe take a little nap, and gear up for the night shift.

Or so I thought.

Just as I put my head down to the turntable to turn up the volume on a Loverboy track, I was startled by a sudden hard smack on my rear end.

Shocked, I quickly turned around to find . . .

A naked woman.

With a record in her hands.

I don't remember my exact reaction, but you can imagine what effect this sight might have on an impressionable seventeen-year-old kid who had not been around too many naked members of the opposite sex, especially naked ones that looked as exceptionally perfect as this one.

She was tiny but she was chiselled, and she smelled like a potently excessive mixture of Chanel and tequila.

"Oh, I'm so sorry," she shrieked, seeming as startled as I was. "I thought you were Ed. I'm so sorry. I'm Brandy."

I could feel the blood rushing to my face, not to mention other areas, as I mumbled and stuttered something out about filling in for Ed Zed and not being sure what I was supposed to be doing here.

"Oh, okay," I stammered. "Now I get it. *This* is the Jamboree." I realized that I was now the designated emcee for an afternoon Golden Oak *strip show*.

I tried as hard as I could to stare only at her eyes as she handed me the record and quickly blurted, "Can you please play side A—'Stars on 45'?"

My hands were shaking as I put the needle to the vinyl, turned up the lights, and announced to the now very attentive congregation:

"Gentlemen, please put your hands together for . . ."

And I completely went blank. I'd forgotten her name.

My eyes quickly shot her way, and I'll never forget how pissed off she looked.

And then, thankfully, I remembered . . .

"Brandy!!!"

The place went nuts.

My face still crimson, I glanced over towards the front door, where Big Chris gave me a quick nod and a wide, knowing smile. I wasn't sure what he was thinking at that point—probably something like *Welcome to the Jamboree, kid.*

I definitely knew what I was thinking: *Holy shit. This ain't no roller rink.*

Eventually, my heartbeat returned to normal, and Brandy—and others who looked and smelled almost exactly like Brandy—danced the afternoon away. Once the initial shock wore off, I had a chance to chat with most of the girls, who all seemed very friendly. They also seemed to share a common bond: They all loved to dance. They all liked the stage. But they all didn't really like what they were doing, and the only reason they were doing it was for the money.

Then again, so was I. I just didn't have to take off my clothes.

As profitable as this Jamboree thing seemed, I quickly realized that playing music for strippers wasn't exactly something I wanted to highlight on my resumé. I honestly felt a little embarrassed and was just happy that I survived the session with no major mishaps—and didn't see any of my buddies or my dad in the front row.

When the afternoon ended and the bar had emptied out, I was cleaning up the booth to prepare for the night shift when Big Chris walked up and asked me how things had gone.

I was really starting to like working for Chris—such a nice guy with a heart as large as his body. He was also a really good leader and manager, treating everyone with respect. His family owned a number of these hotel/bar establishments around Manitoba, and they took great pride in not only customer satisfaction but also employee appreciation.

I could tell he knew that I wasn't entirely onboard with the Jamboree deal, especially coming from something as wholesome as the roller rink. I told him that I really enjoyed playing music and entertaining during the nightclub shift—I just wasn't thrilled having to be the guy who played music for "peelers."

Big Chris looked at me quietly, nodded his head, and said, "I completely understand. I appreciate your honesty. Don't worry about it. We'll make sure you only do the night sessions."

I felt relieved when I shook his hand and thanked him for that. Then his face started turning red.

"I got one small favour to ask, though," Chris continued. "You're going to work tonight, right?"

Yes, of course, I told him, I had already committed to this double and was looking forward to the nightclub session.

"Well, tonight's a normal night except for the first hour," he said, his face getting redder. "We have another dancer to start the night. But it's only one dancer."

"Okay, if it's only one, I'm already booked." I shrugged, knowing that at least it would be my last one.

Chris then winced as he said the next sentence.

"And *he* starts at eight."

He?

He as in a *male* stripper?

And so, regretfully, the second part of my first and last double shift at the Golden Oak began with another naked dance show. It's more than a blur to me now, but I do remember how many women packed the joint and how many of them were going crazy when I introduced this nude dude whose name will forever escape me. If memory does serve me correctly, however, he also performed a naked puppet show on stage with Kermit the Frog while having a bath in an inflated swimming pool. You can't make that shit up.

If I was embarrassed earlier in the day, I was completely humiliated this time around. Anyone who saw me in the booth that night knew I would have preferred to be wearing one of my roller rink costumes so I couldn't be recognized. But I did live up to my promise to Chris, and I did finish the double shift, even though the male stripper was ready to punch me out when his act finished in his makeshift bathtub.

I wasn't trying to be snarky, just funny when I picked up the mic and bellowed:

"Ladies—let's give it up for a man who brings new meaning to the phrase . . . 'Tiny Bubbles.'"

Everyone in the room laughed—except the naked puppet master, who flashed me a slashing-the-throat sign, stormed off the stage, got dressed, and immediately started reaming out Big Chris for how unprofessional *his* DJ was.

I knew Big Chris wasn't going to be happy when he came up to talk to me later, and I had my apology list ready to recite. But I didn't need to. He just looked at me and laughed.

"Fuck him," he said. "He *did* have tiny bubbles."

We both roared.

The Jamboree day was certainly not the proudest moment in my journey, but it was definitely an eye-opener.

Thankfully, I never did announce another strip show, and Big Chris and I soon became not only great co-workers but friends for life. Like my buddy Graeme, Chris always had my back, and I always had his—even though it was a size XXXL.

Down the road, time and distance would get in the way of our relationship and we didn't see each other as often, but any time we got together, we seemed to be transported back in time so we could reminisce and laugh about our olden Golden Oak days, when life could be both simple and strange at the same time.

A time in my life that could not have been wilder, crazier, or busier. Full of school classes, sports events, roller rinks, dance floors, strip shows, growing pains, life lessons, and, as always—dreams. Dreams that were about to seriously take flight.

Besides, after surviving the "Brandy Incident," I was ready for anything.

4

BASKETBALL ROD AND THE HARLEM GLOBETROTTERS

I HAVE ANOTHER ADMISSION TO MAKE: I NEVER LIED TO MY PARENTS. NEVER. BUT, like most kids, I had some things I just never told them.

I didn't tell them I was working in the nightclub at the Golden Oak for about a month because I knew they would freak out since I was underage at the time. I also couldn't imagine what their reaction would have been had they known that I had also played music for strippers. Thankfully, no one let the naked cat out of the bag.

Some things were much better left unsaid.

Like the fact that I was also playing junior football at the time. Something that my mom, in particular, would not have been happy with.

That's because a few years earlier, my parents, Bonnie and Jack, had come out to watch me play football with the Transcona Nationals. I was a quarterback and a cornerback and was having a good game, running for a touchdown and returning an interception for a major score.

I remember feeling pretty good about myself. The sun was shining, my parents were on the sideline watching, and my team was kicking ass. Then things went sideways. As we continued to run up the score, our opponents decided to take out their frustration on the most logical target: the quarterback. I don't remember how many times I got hit, but they started whacking me around like a human piñata.

Keep in mind, in those days, equipment wasn't the safest, and concussion protocols hadn't been invented yet. Consequently, the pummelling seemed even more magnified. At one point, I was wondering if any of my teammates had heard about this technique called blocking. Proudly, or perhaps stupidly, I kept returning to the huddle and coming back for more.

We ended up winning the game, but I was so battered and bruised that I could barely walk to the car with my parents. Once I got in, my mom, in tears, just looked at me and said, "You're never playing that sport again."

My dad said nothing, but I could tell he was in total agreement. And so, I didn't play again. Until a few years later, when a couple of buddies talked me into trying out with the Winnipeg Hawkeyes, a junior team that had developed a number of very good college and pro players.

I certainly wasn't one of those prospects, and I had zero aspirations to play at another level. I did, however, get a chance to suit up as a tight end and then a backup quarterback. Sadly, but perhaps appropriately, I didn't get a chance to play very much.

It was probably a good thing my parents didn't know I was playing with the Hawkeyes, because if they did decide to come to a game, they likely would have seen their oldest son standing on the sidelines, wearing the cleanest uniform and holding a clipboard. When I did get the call to play, it was usually after an injury to the starter, or during garbage time, when we were either up big or down big.

Regardless, it was still fun. My pals were playing. I learned a lot about discipline, patience, momentum, and teamwork. Best of all, it was a perfect bridge for me between baseball and hockey seasons.

The interesting thing was that none of those sports were at the top of my list of favourites or seemed like they might be my ticket to a possible scholarship or potential pro opportunity.

No, the game that gave me the most juice in my teen years was basketball.

I honestly had no real interest in hoops up until I was about twelve years old. That's when I read a *Sports Illustrated* article on this superstar player named Julius Erving who went by the nickname "Dr. J." He was given that name because scouts and coaches said he played like a doctor—just "give him the ball and watch him operate."

I started following the Doc's career and began digesting more and more about the sport, which interestingly enough was invented by another doctor, a Canadian named James Naismith, who created basketball in 1891 at a YMCA in Springfield, Massachusetts. Those facts were ingrained in my brain forever, mostly because I had composed school essay after school essay on the subject, which just further cemented my love for this fascinating game.

When I first started playing hockey, I was a goalie, then I moved to forward. I was decent; then I started roller skating and my hockey skating got so much better. When I got to Midget AAA, I decided to concentrate on basketball and baseball while working at the roller rink. I can honestly say that I never practised anything more in my life than I practised basketball as a teenager. I fell in love with the sport, and I fell in love with watching it on TV.

I bought a book about Dr. J. and couldn't get enough of it. Years later, I ended up working with him. He was so cool—he had the big Afro, and he was this high-flying basketball superstar. When it came to basketball, I worked my butt off. I would play all day, and eventually I could do all the tricks with the ball. Years later, one of my biggest thrills took place when I got to play with the Harlem Globetrotters.

Next to Dr. J., my other basketball idol was Martin Riley. He was my Steve Nash. I am huge advocate of local sports and what they mean to a community. Martin was from Winnipeg, and I would watch him play for the University of Manitoba Bisons every Saturday afternoon on CKND-TV. Riley was everything I wanted to be in a basketball player. I never met him when I was young, but man, I watched him a lot and tried to copy his game.

I would watch NBA games on TV, although back in the 1970s, they were available only one day a week, and sometimes tape-delayed. I'd also watch university games on CKND. These college guys weren't pros, but to me they were larger than life, and I was inspired to be like them someday. That's why I picked up a basketball and started doing what I used to do as a kid on the hockey rink. I started calling my own games in my mind and pretending that I was Julius Erving or my local Dr. J., Martin Riley.

Only thing was, unlike today, there weren't nearly as many hoops courts to play on back then.

Today, the incredible growth of basketball in Canada has put a hoop in almost every driveway in almost every neighbourhood across the country. But back in the '70s, you would have to look long and wide to find a place to play. My baller buddies and I would often hop on our bikes and ride a mile or two to find an available court for a pickup game. When you did finally locate a spot to play, the rims rarely had nets, the backboards were old and rusty, and the concrete court was full of cracks, rocks, and weeds.

It wasn't very good; in fact, it wasn't close to being good, but it was the best we had.

I was lucky enough to live across from a Catholic school parking lot that was home to a lone basket affixed to a wooden backboard nailed to a decaying wooden pole. Not perfect by any stretch, but to me this was my own personal Madison Square Garden, Boston Garden, or Philadelphia Spectrum. It was my court of dreams.

It's where I was every day during the spring, summer, and fall from sunrise to sunset, pounding my half-deflated ball on the crumbling pavement as it echoed around the block so loudly that neighbours would often complain. I didn't care. I just kept dribbling, kept shooting, and kept developing my skills by playing one-on-one or HORSE with my brothers or the neighbourhood kids.

Most of the time, I was by myself, though, playing head games again, pretending I was Dr. J. or Martin Riley, emulating their moves and making sure I sank the game-winning shot.

Day after day. Shot after shot. Win after win. No one was talking about the ten-thousand-hour rule in those days, but if they were, I would certainly have believed in it because I was living it.

If you do the math, to reach ten thousand hours, a person would have to dedicate forty hours a week for five straight years to become an "expert" or "master" at their specific craft. Makes complete sense; the only thing is that putting in the hours doesn't necessarily guarantee success.

No one could have told me that back then, however.

Even though I had two part-time jobs, a busy school schedule, and so many other things going on, I honestly believed that I had a future as a pro basketball player.

Why wouldn't I?

I mean, I put in the hours, I was starting to get some local recognition as a high school player, and no one could tell me they loved the game more than I did.

I wasn't the best shooter or scorer, but I had good hands and could handle the rock. I loved to dish the ball off and create plays. I started to follow another rising American star who had another perfect nickname—"Magic"—and tried to incorporate some Magic Johnson wizardry into my own game.

Hour after hour, I practised so much that my fingers would blister and bleed. There were days when I could barely pick up the ball, but I continued to work on all the moves, trying to perfect every trick—especially the art of spinning the basketball, which I was eventually able to do on the tip of every finger and even the end of a stick.

Then, suddenly, and best of all—thanks to a growth spurt and constant jumping—I was able to dunk the basketball, which was really cool since I was only about five foot eleven at the time. Only issue, and it was a *big* issue, was that dunking was not allowed in high school basketball at the time.

That didn't bother me, though. Even though we played hard, our motley team at Transcona Collegiate didn't keep many scores close, so occasionally I would try to throw one down in the middle of the game to get a rise out of the crowd—and, inevitably, take the technical foul.

My teammates loved it, but my coach had a different response, and he would summarily dunk me back on the bench. Lesson learned.

The most awkward dunk attempt came when we paid a visit to a rival high school called Murdoch Mackay. Some of my co-workers from the roller rink were students there—everyone knew everyone at both schools—and let's just say any competition in any sport between these enemy institutions was nasty.

Unfortunately, we were getting throttled, and their boisterous student crowd was pecking away at our team like vultures on roadkill.

That's when I decided to get some payback. I was able to steal a ball and take it unimpeded to the basket for what should have been an easy layup. But instead, at the very last minute, I decided to change my flight plan and take it to the rim and throw down a thunderous dunk to shut up these yahoos.

That's what I *intended* to do.

Instead, as I flew towards the basket, I mistimed my takeoff and ended up clanking the ball off the front of the rim, from which it bounced to the ceiling while I plummeted to the hardwood on my tailbone. Not sure what hurt more, my ass or my pride—especially when a bunch of the Murdoch crazies started chanting at the top of their lungs:

"ROLL-ER RINK! ROLL-ER RINK! ROLL-ER RINK!"

Tough crowd, I thought, as I clambered to my feet.

I could just let it go, I thought, or I could put my head down and head straight to the bench—which I'm sure my coach had waiting for me. *Or*, I could come up with something more spontaneous.

So, I pointed my finger right at all of them, smiled, and took a bow.

The crowd loved it, rose to their feet, and gave me a standing ovation.

It wasn't exactly Showtime, but it was the only response I had.

Another tough lesson learned. But all those lessons and all that practice were starting to pay dividends. Input was starting to lead to output, and scouts and recruiters were taking notice. I was invited to summer camps, where I got to play with some of the best junior players in the country. I somehow held my own and even earned awards and accolades.

Martin Riley was a part of Team Canada at the 1976 Summer Olympics in Montreal. The coach of the national team was this guy named Jack Donohue. I went to my local library to read about him and study him. I found out he had coached Kareem Abdul-Jabbar at Power Memorial

Academy in New York City back when Abdul-Jabbar was still known as Lew Alcindor. Donohue was a basketball lifer and an outstanding college coach in the US before coming north to Canada in the early '70s to coach our national team, where he helped grow the game like no one before him except James Naismith. He walked taller than he was and carried a big voice—not loud, just big. When he talked, everyone listened. Donohue had a thick New York accent and an incredible resumé for developing talent. To any kid in Canada who loved and played basketball at that time, Jack Donohue was the man.

A few years later, I heard that Donohue was going to be the guest coach at a summer camp at the University of Winnipeg. I thought I was on the perfect path until I attended that camp. I remember my first impression of him as he walked into the gym. It was like a scene from the movie *The Matrix*—everything stopped and went into slow motion. Every head turned in his direction.

The Coach strolled to the middle of the floor and gathered everyone around, barked out a few instructions, and then stood on the sideline and just watched. And watched. And everyone on that floor knew he was watching, especially me.

It was one of the first times in my life in sport that I felt intimidated. My palms were leaking sweat like crazy, and I was having a tough time handling the ball. Eventually, I settled down and started making some good plays. When we got to the scrimmage portion, I was one of the assigned point guards, and with each positive possession, I was gaining more and more confidence, until my Hot Rod skills kicked in. I started dribbling through my legs, throwing passes behind my back, and generally showboating, which the small crowd of fans seemed to enjoy, but The Coach obviously didn't.

Near the end of the scrimmage, I burst baseline and, instead of making a pass to the open man in the key, decided to blow around a defender for an off-balance reverse layup that had a lot of mustard on it. Unlike my pitiful dunk attempt at Murdoch, this one was perfect: The ball went up, kissed the backboard, and dropped sweetly through the net just before the buzzer for a highlight-reel play—or at least that's what I thought as I high-fived my teammates.

I was excited. I was proud. And I'd pulled that off in front of a legend.

That's when The Coach quickly blew the whistle and shouted some words I've never forgotten.

"Hey, kid," he bellowed with that inimitable accent. "What do you think this is? The Harlem Globetrotters?"

Yikes. Another hard lesson. Words hurt.

He didn't even know my name, but he was right.

Luckily, I didn't let that criticism bother me. Those words stung for sure, but I sucked it up for the rest of the workout, realizing that he'd said what he said only to make me a better player.

When we gathered around in a circle to end the camp, I wasn't sure what to think. I knew I had performed reasonably well except for the Globetrotter moment, and bottom line, I had learned so much more than I had ever picked up from my high school coaches and my ragtag schoolyard games.

I also realized I had so much more to learn about the game, about teamwork, and about being the best player I could be. That's when The Coach stepped into the centre of the circle and started to hand out the camp awards.

I was staring blankly into space, not really listening, thinking about all the new stuff I had learned and how much more I had to grow, as Donohue continued to distribute the hardware.

"And the award for the best ball handler of the camp," he uttered as he scanned the campers and ultimately locked onto my eyes, "Mr. Rod Black."

I almost choked on my gum.

Are you kidding me?

Bashfully, yet proudly, I walked over to The Coach, who shook my hand and presented me with a brand-new pair of Converse Chuck Taylor basketball shoes.

"Congratulations," I recall him saying, and then adding a slice of sarcasm: "Good luck with the Globetrotters, Curly Neal."

Everyone burst into laughter.

Curly Neal, of course, was one of the stars of the 'Trotters and one of the greatest dribblers on the planet.

I smiled at the comment and looked up at my dad, who was standing by the railing above the court. I watched him as he proudly applauded with the rest of the group, and though he never admitted it, I remember him rubbing a little something from his eye.

I *was* a great ball handler—just couldn't shoot. This was before the three-point line was a part of basketball. I loved playing with flair. But there were other kids at that camp who could really shoot. Donohue told me, "Blacky, you have a big voice. Use it and get into broadcasting."

Donohue was a stickler for fundamentals and sharing the ball with your teammates. I hung on every word he said. He had three big lessons for us: ABC, ICE, and WIN. They were written on a stencil board when we walked into camp. The camp lasted four days, and he never told anybody what the letters meant. Then, at the end of camp, he went through all three: ABC stood for "Adversity Builds Character." ICE stood for "Intensity, Concentration, and Enthusiasm." And WIN stood for "What's Important Now." I wrote them down on my wristbands and my sneakers so I wouldn't forget. Jack loved his acronyms. Jack was also a guy who used humour to get his message across. Whatever methods he used, I ate it up. I use those lessons from Jack Donohue to this day in a lot of my speaking engagements.

I've never forgotten that camp or that moment, and crazily enough, years later, I would get a chance to work with Coach Donohue as a broadcaster and at a variety of speaking events. He always said he remembered me from that day, but I think he was just being nice because he truly was so nice. Not just a great basketball coach, but an even greater man, inspiring so many people in all walks of life until he passed away in 2003. Canadian basketball misses him every day but will be forever grateful for his enduring legacy.

Not to mention his quick wit and great lines. He had tons of them—some a little saucy, some a little sweet, but they would always provoke a reaction. Even when he jabbed you, you knew it came from his heart, just like those Globetrotter barbs.

The best line Donohue ever said, in my mind, was one he used often in life, including when we huddled up at the end of the U of W camp and were about to disperse. The Coach gathered everyone in, looked at all of our young, impressionable faces, and left us with the best message ever:

"Remember, boys, you can only be a good basketball player for a certain amount of time. You can be a good person for the rest of your life."

Valuable advice for every young athlete in every sport, and I took those words to heart. I also knew that if I wanted to take my game to the next level, if I wanted to be a better basketball player, timing was everything.

So, I went back home and went to work, with new shoes, new confidence, and most importantly, a new game. My obsession with basketball would soon yield some new opportunities.

The next couple months were hard-core. I grew a few more inches and put some muscle on my skinny frame. And the game was starting to slow down for me.

Even though I still had all the tricks, I put the fancy stuff on hold. I amped up the details and basics. I got my teammates involved more and became a better leader on the floor. Good things were happening, and coincidentally, more people were starting to pay attention.

Some local scouts were sniffing around, and college recruiters were sending letters to our house. There were no attractive offers yet, but it was clear that my hard work was being rewarded, and I had a good feeling something might hit in my senior year of high school.

Funnily enough, I wasn't getting a lot of steam from the schools in Manitoba, but that didn't bother me since Canadian universities didn't really offer scholarships in those days. I knew I was going to further my education, I just didn't know where; and honestly, I also didn't know what in the world I was going to study.

Basketball was consuming a lot of my time, but not all of it. I still had the roller rink and nightclub stuff going on—thankfully, minus any Jamborees—and while they were only part-time jobs, I clearly had a passion for the microphone and playing music.

Before I was finished high school, when I was about to turn seventeen, I interviewed legendary sports announcer Howard Cosell, who was in Winnipeg for a sports dinner. I went there, and they let me interview him with my portable tape recorder. I was a little nervous because Howard was a huge man. But he was so kind to me as I spoke to him. He said to me, "Make sure that everything that is live is rehearsed." He also said in that distinctive voice of his, "Young man, the best advice that I can give to you: Just be yourself." That was a thrilling moment along my life journey that helped carve the path for what I was going to do as a career.

I was also still messing around with voices and imitations, even dabbling in some high school theatre, thinking that a career as a radio announcer or morning DJ might be something I could pursue down the road.

And so, I was torn: Do I keep pounding the rock? Or do I want to play rock? Do I have a future on the court? Or in a studio?

Trying to carve out a future in a studio wasn't such a long shot, either. I had been doing some digging and discovered that there were several Canadian post-secondary schools offering courses in radio and television studies, and one that particularly interested me was Winnipeg's Red River Community College, which had a two-year course called Creative Communications. The curriculum was centred around journalism and advertising, with a sprinkling of broadcast studies, but it certainly checked a lot of boxes.

My high school English teacher Harry Pal, one of my favourites, initially told me about the course, thinking it might be in my wheelhouse. A soft-spoken man with a great sense of humour, Mr. Pal lived up to his name. He was more than just a teacher; he became a pal to many of his students. He came out to watch all our games, played a mean game of Ping Pong, and most of all was a positive influence, especially for me.

My grades in his class—and other classes—weren't great. In fact, they were brutal. But he was the one teacher who understood my crazy schedule, and he eased my homework load and gave me a lot of breaks on attendance. He was also the *only* teacher who believed in my potential, and he insisted that I apply for the RRCC program, which required references, a written essay, and an interview.

I was lukewarm to all of that, but Mr. Pal pushed me and told me that he'd take me out golfing if I applied and was accepted.

I told him I'd think about it.

I didn't know it back then, but I was very lucky. Unlike so many other kids my age, I had some mentors and some options, even a road map. But, like most teenagers, I still had no idea which direction I was headed.

Then I got a big hit.

My mom answered the phone one day and told me that someone from Minnesota had called and was interested in talking to me. She gave me the number, and I called the person back.

As I dialled the number, I thought one of my ball buddies was pranking me, but sure enough, the gentleman on the other end of the line said he was an area scout who had seen me play a few times and wondered if I wanted to come stateside to visit a couple of schools that might have some interest. One of them was Bemidji State, a Division II school about a four-hour drive southeast of Winnipeg and halfway to Minneapolis.

As you can guess, I was very excited, but also a little leery. Not because of the school or location, but because the scout had called me "Rob." I didn't correct him, but I was wondering if he had the right guy.

I shouldn't have been so suspicious. He did have my phone number, after all, and he did have a detailed scouting report on my game. He also mentioned my curly mop of hair and cheesy little moustache.

Yep, that was me.

So, after a long discussion, we made arrangements to meet in a few weeks in Bemidji to pay a visit to the school.

I was jacked. Finally, I'd got a bite.

Then again, I had no idea where this place was. Hell, I could barely pronounce it. There was no internet back then, either, so I couldn't do a lot of research on the school, the team, or the town. I got all my info from the local library, and after scouring maps, encyclopedias, and travel magazines, I knew the place was legit. In fact, it might be a perfect fit.

I told only a few people about the opportunity, and the reaction was surprisingly mixed. My friends in basketball kept telling me to chase my hoop dream. My friends at the roller rink and the nightclub, on the other hand, were playing shot blocker, insisting that I tune in to the broadcast world. The most important people in my life, my parents, left me alone to make my own decision, telling me to just believe in myself and good things would happen. I had a sneaky feeling, though, that my mom wanted me to stay close to home.

The day I left for the visit was a bit chaotic and emotional. My dad was travelling with work, my mom was at home with my brothers, so I had to find someone to drive me down south, since I still didn't have a licence.

I was scrambling to find a ride when my great friend Graeme came to my rescue, offering to take me. Even if it didn't work out, he said, at least we'd make it a road trip.

We left early, before sunrise, and I'm pretty sure it was only a few hours after I had finished a long night at the Golden Oak. We were both a little groggy, but as always, we chatted up a storm as the radio blared in Graeme's little Honda Civic. He asked me a lot of questions about the school, my chances of making the team, living in a different country, and being away from friends and family.

I don't exactly remember my answers, but I do recall that I was very apprehensive, and Graeme could sense that. That's what good friends do. He was also the one person who completely understood how much passion I had for both of my teenage loves—basketball and announcing.

About ninety minutes after we left Winnipeg, just as the sun was peeking over the horizon, we were approaching the Canada–US border. That's when Graeme said something that really made me think.

"You know, Rodney, I know the dream is to be a professional someday, but keep in mind, you are *already* a pro."

He was right. I was already getting paid to play.

"And hey," he added, "if it doesn't work out down there, you can always come home."

Those words hung in the air as we showed the customs officials our ID and crossed over into the United States.

About five minutes farther down the road, I was still pondering Graeme's comments when I tilted my head towards the passenger window and nodded off. When I woke up an hour later, the sun was beaming in. I looked over at Graeme and told him he was absolutely right.

"Fuck it, man," I said. "Let's go home."

It wasn't my first turning point—more like a turning-*back* point—but it was huge. Cutting short my road trip and heading back home was the biggest decision I had ever made. And, as it turned out, the best.

It was more than a game changer. It was a life changer. After abandoning a potential scholarship opportunity on some dusty highway in the state of Minnesota, I was now chasing a different dream.

I came home, applied for the Creative Communications course, somehow got accepted, and ended up getting a free golf game with my pal, Mr. Pal.

High school diploma in my pocket, I was now *officially* a college student. Big step forward. However, if I thought going to Red River was going to make my life less complicated, I was dead wrong.

With RRCC located at the exact opposite end of Transcona, it was a much bigger challenge to get to school every day. I was still living at home, still working two jobs at night, and relying on my dad, who worked in that area, to drive me to the sprawling campus every morning. My pops would drop me off, I would go to my classes—normally until about 4 p.m.—and then hop on a bus for a forty-minute trip all the way back to my hood.

I can't tell you how many times, during that long bus ride home, that I would doze off as soon as I got to my seat and end up sleeping through my final stop. I'd wake up four or five stops away from home, forcing me to add another thirty minutes to my journey.

I was a sleep-deprived mess.

On one particularly uncomfortable trip, I woke up on the shoulder of an elderly woman who was knitting and didn't seem too fazed by my intrusion. I wiped some drool off my lower lip, shamefully shifted back into my seat, and apologized profusely.

"No worries," she said, knitting away without missing a beat. "You looked so comfy, I didn't want to disturb you."

I laughed and fell back asleep.

That was pretty much the script for my first year in college.

This was the era of Ground-Rod Day. Get up. Go to class. Fall asleep on the bus. Go to work till after midnight. Go home. Go to bed. Get up five hours later.

Oh, and to top it all off, I also played basketball. Red River had a team, a pretty good one. I suited up for half a season, keeping the hoop dream alive, but after a less-than-successful mid-winter tournament in Quebec, I came back home and realized that something had to give. If I continued to play, one of two things would happen: I would fail most of my classes or I would end up as a zombie.

I had no choice. I had to step away from the sport I loved. That's because college was a grind. More than I ever imagined. But I was also learning a ton. *Way* more than I ever imagined. Creative Communications was living up to its name.

It was also starting to build a reputation.

Today, the CreComm program at Red River is one of the biggest and most respected media courses in Canada, developing award-winning talent in the public relations, journalism, advertising, and broadcast worlds. But back in my day, the course was still in its infancy, a bit of an unknown sleeper, and for many students who decided to apply, it was a bit of a flier.

For me, it was a launching pad. The only problem was that I was still very young. I had just turned eighteen and was the youngest person in a class full of students who ranged from their mid-twenties to mid-forties, from all over the province. Some were aspiring journalists. Others were heavy into advertising, marketing, or public relations. I was really the only person in the class who had designs on broadcasting.

We could not have been a more eclectic group, but one common trait we shared was that we all were storytellers.

Despite our age and cultural differences, we also found a way to bond as a team. My classmates were very supportive. Being "the kid" in the group, I constantly leaned on their guidance and experience to help push me through the intense workload.

Truthfully, I sucked up to them. Especially when I was having trouble understanding a concept or reaching a deadline, or was in need of a ride somewhere. I couldn't believe I stupidly still didn't have a driver's licence, an obstacle that just kept adding to the daily jigsaw puzzle I was trying to piece together.

To me, the best part of CreComm was the program's ability to place students in the workplace. My one and only internship was with a local radio station, CFRW, and I couldn't have been more excited. 'RW was one of the most popular music stations in Winnipeg, home to some great broadcasters like Ron Able, Dick Reeves, and Steve Jackson. Those names might not ring a bell to most people, but back in the '70s in the 'Peg, these announcers, like Don Percy, were superheroes to me. I listened to them all, hung on their every word, and was inspired by their larger-than-life personalities.

Unfortunately, my internship at CFRW wasn't with the announce team. Instead, I was assigned to the copywriting department, where I sat in front of a manual typewriter every day, learning how to churn out commercial scripts and promos. It took me a few days to get the hang of it, especially structuring the copy to a specific time limit, but with all the years of listening to local radio burned into my head, it started to come easily to me, and the stuff I wrote was actually getting produced. I was really pleased with my work, but as much as I liked the advertising side of the business, I also knew this wasn't my ultimate mojo. I wanted to be one of the cool guys on the mic.

Making that ambition even more enticing were the daily drop-ins from a few of the station announcers, who would stop by to chat about some of their assigned copy or just pay a friendly visit. At first, I was naturally intimidated by these radio heads, who I really knew only by their voices. I found it quite amusing to discover that most of them really didn't look like they sounded. It wasn't as if they were unattractive or anything like that, but I soon understood what the famous phrase "having a face for radio" was all about.

I really took a liking to two announcers in particular, Steve Jackson and Lee Marshall, both of whom were local stars but also very humble and gracious with their time. Every chance I had, I would pick their brains, informing them that I worked as a part-time DJ and aspired to be like them someday. Surprisingly, they didn't blow me off. They would plop down at the end of my tiny intern desk and just start chatting. For one of the few times in my life, my mouth was closed and my ears were wide open. I listened intently, taking copious notes while they shared some invaluable advice—priceless pointers and suggestions about timing, pacing, knowing the audience, and the best tip of all: to always be yourself.

They were such nice guys that when I casually asked them if they'd like to come down for a visit to the roller rink, they not only showed up but also took a turn on the microphone to entertain the crowd. My friend Graeme McGinnis, who was now one of the managers at the rink, couldn't stop beaming—especially the next day, when the rink was getting some serious love over the airwaves with both men sharing roller-skating stories from the night before. We couldn't buy that kind of publicity.

Lee Marshall actually became a semi-regular at Saints Regent, and whenever I invited him to a special event at the rink, he never said no. He told me that making community appearances was more than part of his job—it was a responsibility. Decades later, when I'd occasionally bump into Lee at CTV, where he had become the "Voice of God" for all the promos on the network, I reminded him of his generosity and how he had inspired me to "never say no."

Lee seemed surprised when I told him that. He sincerely appreciated the kind words, perhaps never realizing that he had made that sort of impact.

Trust me, Lee, you did.

Steve Jackson was also a big influence. While I was slogging away writing copy during my CFRW stint, Steve stopped by one afternoon and asked me if I'd like to record some voice-over bits for a few skits on his show. I naturally jumped at the chance, and while the recordings—appropriately, of my imitations—weren't anything significant, those bits were huge to a kid trying to break into the business.

That opportunity turbo-boosted my confidence. For the first time since my prepubescent Mr. Johnson days on Don Percy's radio show, I could actually say I was on the air. I wasn't getting my own show or anything like that—I didn't even get paid—but that didn't matter a speck. This was another one of those awakenings that jolted me to my career reality. I didn't want to be the person writing ads or promos anymore. I wanted to be the person announcing them.

It was one of those "aha" moments. I wanted to fly among the radio stars.

But then reality plummeted me quickly back to earth.

My 'RW radio internship came to an end, which meant the kid had to head back to classes at Red River, return to the monotonous grind, get back on the groundhog wheel, still working towards some sort of breakthrough.

Somehow, I was making it through college, but barely. My marks were below average or worse, with the exception of radio and theatre—not surprising, since they were the two subjects that most interested me. Ironically, I received an F from the television instructor, a former TV writer and producer named Serena Stone who seemed to criticize everything I did. She didn't like my voice, didn't like my style, and mostly didn't like the fact that I wasn't completing many of her written assignments.

The feeling was mutual. I didn't like her, either. She once told me that if I continued doing what I was doing, I would likely have a longer career *behind* the camera than in front of it. I'm sure there were other people over the years who shared the same sentiment, but at that time, her opinion of me, like the failing grade, seemed so grossly unfair.

In her defence, I have to admit I was still very green and did make a number of mistakes, but not nearly as many, I felt, as a lot of my classmates, who all told me she was wrong and that TV would be my calling. She wasn't just criticizing me; she was teaching me valuable lessons that I would use for years to come.

Serena was tough on me and marked me hard. But I deserved it. I was burning the candle at three ends. I was playing sports, working at the bar and at the roller rink, and trying to have something of a social life. I hardly got any sleep. She was hard on me, but she was right. At the time, I was doing an impression of a radio announcer. That was from all the mimicry that I'd done when I was younger. I thought I was good, but she didn't. Getting a bad mark from her bugged me; it made me so angry. The Creative Communications program featured a lot of writing and journalism, and I didn't like it. It was way too structured for me. Hardly anybody else in my class was interested in broadcasting, so I spent all my time in the radio booth. Veteran writer and journalist Holly Doan was also in my class. I was only focused on broadcasting. It was the school of hard knocks, and Serena taught me some valuable lessons.

As angry as I was with the F, I took it in stride. Serena was like most of the instructors in the course, I thought, living off her past credentials and using Red River as a bridge to another career in the media. To me, she just didn't seem fully invested. Rather than teaching the subject matter, she liked to talk more about her past accomplishments and the number of famous people she had worked with.

And I hate name-droppers. I once mentioned that to Michael Jordan.

I was so pissed that I'd have to retake the television class that I confronted her about my mark. I desperately needed to know what I could do to fix the situation. That's when she peered at me over her glasses and gave me a look that I had seen only from my mother.

"First of all," she said, "I know you're not lazy. I know you work hard. But, Rod, if you don't *hand in* the work, I can't give you a grade."

I apologized for the incomplete assignments, explaining that I thought all of the production work we were doing in the campus studio was way more important than anything we were learning in the classroom. I also told her about my frenetic schedule, which was inhibiting my ability to submit my written projects.

She shook her head.

"I don't care about your schedule. No one cares. Do you think your producer or director at your station is going to care?" she railed at me. "All anyone cares about is making sure you get it right, and you get it done by the deadline."

It was the first time she had said anything to me that actually made sense, and she wasn't finished. "Do you know why I'm hard on you? Do you know why I push you?" she asked, her tone changing. "It's because you have something that no one else in this class has. I'm not quite sure what it is. You may not even know what it is. But it's *something*. And the only way to take that something to the next level is for you to stop trying to be someone else. The best thing for you, Rod, is to be you."

Strong words, but she was right on the money. Precisely the same advice the radio guys had given me during my apprenticeship.

Just be yourself.

Serena's impromptu lecture had clicked on a light bulb.

Maybe all the years of having those voices swirling in my head, doing all those imitations, trying to be somebody else, was affecting the discovery of my own identity. Instead of trying to copy so many different people, I needed to do the best impression of . . . me.

I didn't say it then, but I appreciated her honesty. My opinion of her changed completely that day, especially when I handed in the overdue assignments and she bumped my mark up to a D. She was still being a hard-ass, but at least I knew that she, like all my supportive friends, had my back.

More than anything, she saw something in me that I wasn't seeing in myself: that I needed to be myself, and no matter how hard I worked at broadcasting, I wasn't going anywhere if I didn't find my own voice.

So, tail between my legs, I went into full beast mode. I spent hours and hours in our campus studio, refining my voice, producing bits, and most of all making sure I met deadlines. I even became a regular noon-hour host on the Red River college radio station, where I played music and made announcements.

Things were clicking. It was fun being me.

What wasn't fun was the fact that I was still very uncertain that any of this hard "work" was going to pan out. The job market wasn't the greatest, and although I'd sent demo reels out to a number of stations in Western Canada, the only thing I heard was radio silence.

5

SHOWTIME

ONE DAY IN THE EARLY SPRING, ONE OF MY FELLOW CRECOMMERS, RAY GAUTHIER, stopped by my locker between classes. Ray, one of the older guys in my class, was a terrific person and a huge sports fan with a great knack for writing.

"Hey, Rod, I'm not sure if you heard the news," he said quietly.

"What news?" I said, thinking this was something to do with the Winnipeg Jets, or perhaps a beer bash later in the week.

"I just got word that a local TV station is posting a job opening for a sports reporter," he said. "And they are looking to fill it with someone from here at Red River."

Wow, I thought, *what a great opportunity for someone like Ray*. I wished him luck and told him he should go for it, or something like that.

"Not for me," I remember him saying. "*You*," he said, pointing his finger at me. "This would be the perfect job for *you*."

Even as he said that, his words weren't registering with me. I was so committed to my radio ambitions that TV just seemed like such a reach. The fact that I was also still a teenager made it an even bigger outlier. It just seemed inconceivable.

I didn't really think about Ray's comments until later that afternoon on my bus ride home. For once, I didn't fall asleep because my mind was racing. I had learned that the news was absolutely true. CKY-TV, the local CTV affiliate, was searching for a sports reporter/late-night anchorman, and they were going to fill the position with someone from Creative Communications. The station's sports director, Peter Young, one of the biggest on-air stars on the CTV network, was going to pay a visit to Red River the following week to interview the interested applicants.

Another thing I found out was that almost *everyone* in the course was applying.

I didn't like my chances, but maybe Ray was right, I thought. Maybe this was the perfect job. Maybe this was what I'd been waiting for.

By the time I got home, however, I had already talked myself out of the possibility. I just couldn't see CKY hiring someone so young and inexperienced. All the sports people I watched on TV certainly didn't look or sound like me. It seemed like such a long shot.

When I mentioned the job opening to my parents, they both agreed with Ray and said I'd be crazy not to give it a shot. "What's the worst thing that can happen?" they told me. "You don't get the job? So what? Better to try and fail than to never try at all."

The more I got to thinking about it, the more it seemed to make sense. All of the crazy stuff that was happening in my life might have been happening for a reason. I mean, I'd already been a play-by-play announcer—in my own mind, calling my own games since I was a kid. Maybe this wasn't such a crazy idea. Sports, after all, wasn't just a part of my life. It *was* my life.

It might not have been the job that I had ever dreamed possible, but it was a dream job. I was still undecided until I reminded myself of a line I had come up with a few years earlier and tried to live by every single day:

"Why say 'why'? Why not say 'why not'?"

So, I cut down my huge head of hair, bought myself some new clothes, and put my name in the hat.

Why not this job? Why not take a shot? Why not me?

Interview day is still frozen in my memory.

I remember getting to the school earlier than I ever had, just so I could be first in line.

As I was sitting patiently, waiting, going through all of the things I was going to say, the journalism teacher, Alice Poyser, told me that Peter Young was just arriving and asked if I wouldn't mind going down to the entrance and escorting him into the building.

I didn't run, but I walked very fast to the parking lot, where I met the man I had watched so many times in my living room. Unlike the radio folks, Peter Young looked exactly like I expected. There was no mistaking him.

He was the same every day on TV: well tanned, nice suit, ready to go live on air—only here he was, at Red River Community College, trying to find a sports reporter.

As he got out of his car, I introduced myself, looked him in the eye, and gave him a nice, firm handshake just as the rain was starting to fall.

I popped an umbrella, motioned him underneath, and we walked and casually talked sports all the way through the front doors.

When I accompanied him down the hallway towards the CreComm

area, I noticed people staring at him as we walked by. He was a lot shorter than I thought he would be, but he carried himself like a seven-footer, oozing self-confidence with every step, almost as if the TV lights were still on.

I was only his chaperone, but even I felt the attention and puffed out my puny chest as we walked through the sports fans, continuing to chat away. I think Young sensed that I wasn't awestruck or anything. I was chill. He was cool and we connected.

Just be yourself, I had to remind myself. Just be yourself.

I guess you already know how the interview went, although I have no recollection of what he asked me or what I said. I just remember feeling really comfortable and, yes, trusting my inner voice.

Maybe that's why I got a phone call a few weeks later and nodded as I listened to what Peter had to say.

When I got off the phone, my mom looked at me and I told her I had bad news.

Then I threw my hands in the air and screamed, "I got it! I got it!"

Every sport I played, every game I won—nothing could have compared to that incredible feeling.

My mom had tears in her eyes; my dad came over and did something he never did—he gave me a hug.

Looking back, I'm not sure Peter or even I realized what he had done that day.

I'd like to think he made a great choice. Perfect man for the perfect job.

He would joke later that he had unknowingly unleashed a monster. However you looked at it, one thing was undeniable: Peter Young had changed my life forever. I had just won the lottery.

At least it felt like it.

It was 1982, and I was only nineteen years old. All of sudden, I was now working at a big-time network-affiliated TV station.

Call it the CKY turning point. Or the "no turning back" point.

When I got the job, it felt like the sun had blasted through a colossal cloud. I immediately cleaned out my locker at college and decided to never go back.

Never say never, but I was done with that chapter in my life. It felt like I had escaped from Red River purgatory, unlocking the CreComm chains, even though the program had been so instrumental in punching the ticket to my new career.

Deep down, however, I also regretted not finishing the course. That's because I had never quit anything—and yet, here I was, dropping out of college, rolling away from the rink, and signing off from the nightclub. A triple whammy.

No more juggling acts. No more bus rides. I even got my driver's licence.

I had to get it then because they wanted me to drive the CKY news cruiser all over Winnipeg. Even though I had been making good money, I'd been trying to save up for college. My mom and dad didn't have a lot of money, so I needed to work and save. Up until then, owning a car was never a priority; that's why I took the bus everywhere. I did spend some of what I earned. I played a lot of golf in the summer. I bought a lot of team jackets and jerseys when I was young. I went from nothing to making big money. On some Fridays, I would work as a DJ in the bar in the afternoon, then work as a DJ at the roller rink. On those days, I would make anywhere from a thousand to twelve hundred dollars in a single day. That was a lot of money in the late 1970s. That allowed me to pay my way through Red River College.

But now I finally had a full-time job. The dream job, but that didn't mean there weren't a few nightmares.

Like the time I anchored my first-ever sportscast on the *CKY Late News*.

I had been at the station for just over month, writing scripts, cutting highlights, reporting on local stories, and doing whatever I could do to learn the ropes before my sports director, Peter Young, finally gave me the word.

"All right, rookie," he said. "Time to get you on the desk."

Big gulp. Game time.

One of the people overseeing my training was Leslie Brown, a talented, personable sports reporter who was on the verge of leaving the station. Her departure had actually opened the door for my arrival, and as much as I owed Peter for hiring me, I suppose I owed Leslie more, because if she hadn't quit, I wouldn't have started, and I might have been stuck reading weather reports at some 1,000-watt radio station in northern Manitoba.

Leslie was actually a door opener for a lot of people. As one of the first female sports announcers in Canada, she broke down ignorant chauvinistic barriers and paved the way for so many young women, inspiring them to pursue careers in what was essentially at that time a little boys' club.

Leslie was one of a kind, literally and figuratively. I admired her obvious talent, her zest for life, and her unwavering passion for amateur sports. She went out of her way to make sure we gave our local athletes as much recognition as the professionals. She was patient, she was encouraging, and she didn't put up with any shit—especially from anyone who didn't pay her the respect she was due. I would have loved to work with her more, but she was transitioning to another venture.

On the day of my opening night on the *CKY Late News*, I was pumped but stressed. Loose, yet tight. The pressure switch was firmly pushed too high. I knew all my friends and family would be watching, not to mention the thousands who tuned in to the show nightly. It wasn't like I was appearing on a public-access cable station operating out of a basement or anything like that—CKY had the number-one newscast in the city, and now here I was, the rookie about to make my debut, hoping to keep it on the rails and not shit my pants.

As I would quickly find out, going on the air was the easy part; putting the sportscast together was the biggest challenge. For the twenty minutes that I would appear on the desk, it took eight hours or more to write the scripts, edit the highlights, and do the voice-overs.

We'd assemble the material from our isolated office in the dungeon of CKY, where we pounded away on manual typewriters, fixing any mistakes with the countless essential bottles of Wite-Out. We had to follow all the games, update the scores, and plunk them into a graphic machine called a Chyron. Late games and scores were always a challenge, and I can't tell you how many times, while scrambling to insert a last-second result, things went sideways and all I wanted to do was take a flamethrower to that convoluted contraption.

We would painstakingly select photo slides that corresponded with each different story, to be displayed onscreen in a graphic box next to the anchorperson's head. Sometimes—more often than we'd like—the slides would get mixed up or completely stuck, meaning whatever was being said by the announcer was not matching up with what was on the screen, which led to some very uncomfortable moments.

The director, in the control room, was like a pilot trying to avoid any turbulence. He or she would navigate the camera operators and the switcher, simultaneously barking instructions through a static-filled intercom to an adjacent "tape" area, where operators would roll videotape on primitive one- and two-inch machines, or the three-quarter-inch cassettes that were just springing up in the industry.

Hell, one of my first reports was shot on *film,* spliced together by hand using an X-acto knife and Scotch tape.

The studio, which had a permanent stench of fast food and cigarette smoke, was big and busy and stuffed full of sets for shows that aired every single minute of every day, from a kids' show featuring Uncle Bob and his puppet friend, Archie, to talk shows, church productions, musicals, pageants, a weekly live game of bingo—and, of course, three times a day, the news, weather, and sports.

Craziest thing was that back in 1982, all of this was considered modern and cutting edge. Nowadays, the studios are designed like something you'd see at a NASA space launch. The lighting, monitors, and graphics look like they come from a Marvel movie, and videotape is yester-decades news. Everything today is high-def—4K, 5K, whatever K—and digital. Everything is computer-generated, with satellites and livestreams beaming content into a central location, allowing easy access to downloads so that viewers can consume every highlight or any sound bite imaginable.

Today's announcers, with their expensive clothing allowances, never have to memorize a script or fear missing a word because everything is right in front of their eyes on a teleprompter. They don't have to worry about running out of Wite-Out, crashing Chyrons, or people in the studio smoking darts during a broadcast.

All you have to do today is read, recite, and smile.

Don't get me wrong. I'm not saying that's easy, and I don't want you to think that I'm one of those bitter old guys. But this is now and that was then. Two completely different worlds, and I was lucky enough to live and play in both of them. One thing that has never changed, however, is change itself—it's inevitable.

Embrace. Adapt. Evolve. Embrace again. That's really what life is all about.

That doesn't mean I can't bitch about our prehistoric technology and the way it was back in 1982.

Just be yourself.

At least that's what I thought when I was throwing some pancake makeup on my face in the men's bathroom at CKY in the last moments before my first live sportscast.

I looked in the mirror and told myself, *This isn't going to be easy—but let's go for it.* I remember walking into the smoke-filled studio, nervously saying hello to the hard-working crew. Everyone made me feel at home, from Alfie and Nelson, the highly skilled cameramen, to Louie, the veteran floor director whom everyone absolutely loved. Louie was a large middle-aged man with a loud but comforting voice who I'm sure had been there as many newbies like me made their debuts and tried not to puke their guts out.

Making things even more intimidating was the person I was working with that night—a local celebrity named Sylvia Kuzyk, who was making the transition from "weather girl" to news anchor. Everyone in Winnipeg loved Sylvia, even if her forecasts were sometimes inaccurate. She was a beautiful lady, somewhere in her mid-thirties, and there may not have been a bigger personality in the history of CKY-TV than Sylvia. What made her even more beloved in Manitoba was her compassion. She never said no to charity or community work, and people adored her for that.

Her detractors, and they were a minority, thought she was the inspiration for a lyric from the Don Henley song "Dirty Laundry," where the "bubble-headed bleached blonde comes on at five," but those critics could not have been more wrong. She was a pro. She was intelligent and savvy, and she didn't suffer fools. Anyone who got to know her well could tell she hated being objectified, and that's why she worked so hard to make people listen to what she said. She realized that she couldn't control what people thought about her; she could only control herself.

I sat down at the news desk right beside her.

Just be yourself.

She gave me a comforting smile.

Smile.

Some small talk on the set, and I put my microphone on my tie. Sylvia could see that my hands were trembling.

Breathe.

My mind was racing.

Slow down.

All those people watching right now . . .

Stop thinking.

Is there a booger in my nose?

Just be yourself.

Louie was starting the countdown . . .

Let's do it.

5 . . . 4 . . . 3 . . . 2 . . .

Showtime.

And away we went. As nervous as I was beforehand, my heartbeat eventually slowed down to about a hundred beats a minute and I was able to make it through the sportscast without incident. My first show wasn't an award-winner by any stretch, but I avoided any major fuck-ups or stains in my underwear.

When we signed off at midnight, I cracked a wide smile, heaved a heavy sigh, and thanked Sylvia and the crew for their much-needed support. I don't know what that night would have been like without their calming presence.

Leslie, who was watching in the studio, walked over and gave me a big hug. "See? Not so hard," she said with a lump in her throat. "Congrats. One down."

Then she looked at me and said something that I never expected and never forgot.

"You *do* realize that you're going to be a star," she said.

Wow. That was the first time anyone had said anything like that to me before, and frankly I didn't know what to say.

Trust me, I never got into television for any type of fame or recognition, but Leslie's comments, bullshit or not, meant the world to me.

I was emotionally drained when I got home just after 1 a.m., but my memorable night wasn't finished.

When I pulled into the driveway, my family, some friends, and a bunch of neighbours surprised me with a "First 'Cast" celebration party. Earlier in the day, I learned that my dad had set up a TV in the backyard so everyone could gather around to watch my CKY debut, kind of like a tailgate party. Instead of a sports event, however, these tailgaters were all watching a *sportscast.*

That was *so* Transcona. But also, *so* my family.

I was flattered. I was honoured. I was especially humbled when my mom told me she loved everything except my tie. She was joking, of course. Everyone was bursting with pride.

We all laughed and chatted until the wee hours. Then, for the first time in a long time, I was actually the first person who stood up to say good night.

"Thank you, everybody," I said, yawning. "Sorry, I gotta go to bed. I've gotta work again later tonight."

And so it began. My life as a sportscaster was off to a roaring start. I had no idea that it would be the beginning of a journey for a lifetime.

I also loved the people I worked with.

Peter, in particular, was the perfect boss. When he hired me, he was the face of CKY Sports and, like Sylvia, one of the most recognizable people in the city. He also had a busy travel schedule, fulfilling his CTV network obligations and broadcasting events around the world like tennis, auto racing, CFL football, and even the Olympics.

Peter was a master of his craft, possessing a unique skill set with an uncanny ability to ad-lib on the fly. He was really good at what he did. I definitely wanted to follow in his footsteps; I just wanted to do it my way.

Helping me along with that was the third person in our department, Barry Moroz, nicknamed "Bozo Morozo" from his days working local radio. While Peter was the wild child, Barry was the grumpy, quiet guy, often needing coffee or a cigarette to get the engine running.

I really enjoyed working with him. He was a good reporter, meticulous writer, and like Pete, a tremendous mentor. He sported a wispy, devilish moustache that worked well with his nasal, Howard Cosell–inspired cadence. Just like Cosell, Moroz had a wicked, cutting sense of humour that taunted many targets, particularly Pete, whom Barry would never back down from.

The two of them had worked together for so long, they were like a married couple who never stopped bickering but, deep down, always respected each other. Sometimes, however, things went way too far.

On one occasion, as the two of them screamed at each other in our tiny, ramshackle office, Barry blasted Pete with one of his vicious one-liners and walked away. I sat stone-faced, not saying anything, remaining neutral, but thinking Barry had won that one. That verdict changed quickly when Peter nonchalantly walked over to Barry's desk, pulled down his pants, and pissed in Barry's drawer. Like a little boy who didn't like to lose, Peter then pulled his pants up, picked up his scripts, and, howling with laughter, went upstairs to the studio to do his sportscast.

I couldn't believe it. I picked up my jaw off the floor, quickly cleaned up the mess, sprayed some air freshener, and never said anything to Barry.

And then I did what anybody else would logically do: I locked the drawer on my desk.

I definitely didn't want to piss off Peter, and I certainly didn't want to get pissed on.

For the most part, though, the three of us got along famously, and our CKY Sports team started killing it. Our competitors might have disagreed, but anyone who loved sports in Winnipeg was watching us. It wasn't even close.

From our pro coverage of the NHL's Jets to the CFL's Blue Bombers to anything and everything in the world of sports, we were the "must-watch" channel. We had more resources, more highlights, more time allotted to our sportscasts. We honoured an amateur athlete with a weekly CKY Sportstar Award. But mostly, we had way more fun. Peter had convinced the big bosses upstairs to let us do our own thing . . . and we did.

Soon, we weren't just reporting sports news, we were suddenly transporting sports news into daily and nightly entertainment packages. We enhanced our highlight segments to include more big plays—even misplays. We pumped up the background with modern pop music. We even started doing live interviews on the set with members of the Jets or Bombers or any star athletes who happened to be in town.

I even came up with the idea for the Plays of the Week, the first package of its kind in Manitoba. These weren't your normal sports highlights; these were the best plays mixed with the best bloopers in a well-edited montage, connected with movie clips and wacky sound effects. They were also introduced each week by a roster of well-known celebrities, from Wayne Gretzky to Hulk Hogan. You name the star, and there's a good chance he or she introduced the Rod Black Plays of the Week.

The segment became my signature, and ultimately the most popular feature on CKY News.

We were all living the good life. Kicking ass and taking names.

Keep in mind, we didn't throw away the traditional sportscast. We just stripped it down, polished it up, and created a product that looked more like something you'd see on network television.

Thanks to Peter's persistence, we were given a ton of rope, and we kept stretching it. It worked. We became more. More sizzle. More eyeballs. More ratings. More revenue, and more mojo.

The station capitalized on our popularity by erecting billboards promoting our award-winning sports coverage. They also connected us with a new movie coming out by splashing our faces throughout the city under the heading "Three Amigos."

The first time I saw one of those billboards, I almost rear-ended someone on Portage Avenue as I looked up to see the three of us, staring back down at me, in sombreros and Mexican costumes, just like Steve Martin, Chevy Chase, and Martin Short.

It was so stupid and so silly, but it was also so accurate. That's exactly who we were—the Three Amigos.

But I was also lucky to work with some other amigos: my *Late News* co-anchors, who made my job so much easier and life so much sweeter.

I developed some great bonds, first with Kathy Daley, who was like a sister to me, and then with Clay Young, who became my brother. Both were former radio reporters and consummate professionals, excellent news readers, and unconditionally amazing partners.

Kathy and I hit it off the first time we ever teamed up. We had a really strong connection that some people said radiated through the TV set. Others asked me if we were romantically involved, and although I probably did secretly crush on her, I would have to reveal that, contrary to their curiosity, we were only connected on the air.

Still, our chemistry was palpable, and our conversations were never scripted. We were something that most shows in those days weren't—we were real. If you tuned in to watch the *CKY Late News*, you might have also been watching an episode of *Friends*. She was the news version of Rachel or Monica, and I guess I was probably the geekier version of Chandler or Ross.

Unlike the TV series, however, we never had any drama. Going to the station was a joy. It never seemed like work. That's when you know things are clicking.

But all good things come to an end. With our ratings soaring past even the dinner-hour numbers, Kathy received an offer from our competitors at CBC that was too good not to take. Her dream was to increase her journalistic skills, and this move was not only logical but profitable. She was also probably getting tired of putting up with my silliness.

When she told me the news, I was genuinely happy for her, but honestly, I was also gutted. We had such a good thing going. Now what?

The answer was Clay Young.

Clay was a few years older than me, but surprisingly had less television experience. He was a stylish, good-looking dude with a booming baritone voice honed by his many hours forging a very successful career on radio. When he came over to CKY and first started anchoring part time, he reminded me so much of Ted Baxter, the neurotic, uptight newsman from *The Mary Tyler Moore Show*.

When I was told that Clay was going to be Kathy's replacement and my new partner, I didn't know what to think. I had previously worked with him on a couple of weekend shows, and while he seemed like a nice guy who sounded great, he acted like somebody had stuck a stick up his ass. He just didn't look comfortable.

Now, keep in mind, I was not the golden boy of broadcasting myself. I was still only a few years into my career, but the reps and success alongside Kathy had given me so much confidence, I really didn't want to take a step backwards and wondered where this new partnership was going to take me.

I wasn't the only one questioning the decision. When the "Daley news" broke about Kathy's departure, some of my colleagues in the newsroom were also very much in doubt, predicting that we were going to lose a large portion of our late-night audience.

Despite the negative whispers, Clay was still thrown right into the fire.

It wasn't pretty. The shows were good, but they weren't great.

I knew nothing was going to happen overnight, but the natural chemistry I had with my previous partner seemed so forced with the new guy. I was trying my best to make it work, but it just wasn't close to being the same. I was having some serious Kathy withdrawal.

That's when I decided it was my turn to step up. I knew if we were going to have any success as a team, it would be my job to loosen this dude up. About a week into our new union, we were just signing off at midnight when I looked at Clay and said, "Hey, man, we're going out."

I'm not sure what exactly happened that night, but all I know is we ended up at a popular Winnipeg night spot called the Rorie Street Marble Club, where we chatted, bonded, and got absolutely hammered.

Our relationship was never the same after that night. Our shows were never the same, either. Clay became one of my best buddies, and *CKY Late News* took off like a rocket ship. Our connection changed completely both on and off the air.

If Peter, Barry, and I were the Three Amigos, Clay and I became the Blues Brothers.

Just when I thought I'd never find another late-night sidekick, I was now sitting beside the best one I could have ever wished for. We became inseparable, and it showed in our on-air interactions. We were serious when we had to be serious, but we never took ourselves seriously. People liked the fact we were like two guys sitting on the couch, telling stories and sharing a few laughs. Exactly the way we wanted it.

We were funny and borderline goofy, and every night was a blast.

Just being ourselves.

It was also wildly unpredictable. Night after night, you never knew what might happen or who would show up. From local sports stars to celebrities like Jay Leno and Howie Mandel, we were more than a news show—we became the *Tonight Show* of Winnipeg.

Ratings shot through the roof, billboards shot up around the city, and we were on a serious heater. Everything that I had worked so hard for was starting to come into sight.

Looking back on my time at CKY, it breaks my heart. Currently, in Canada, the big broadcast companies have killed local radio and television. When you drive around the United States, every small town has a local TV and radio station. Local media helped make *Friday Night Lights* what it is. It helps the community get to know the local star athletes. In Canada, we don't hear about young, up-and-coming athletes anymore. Until they are in the Olympics or playing professionally, we don't hear about them at all. Back then, we were all about local. Winnipeg was a thriving media market with some very talented people working in it, in radio, television, and the local newspapers.

I didn't know it then, but I was working at CKY at the perfect time. Not only was I loving doing the late sports, but I was also getting a taste of the big leagues, hosting the Jets' weekly NHL games, which was taking my career to a completely different level.

Life in the toy department couldn't have been any better. Until it took another extraordinary turn when I started becoming more involved with the Jets and Blue Bombers. Not that I wasn't looking to expand my horizons, but I really wasn't expecting another turning point.

After ending a more than two-decade drought of futility, the Bombers had become a dynastic force in the CFL West, winning two Grey Cups over the last few years, and they were so much fun to cover.

They were the first championship team I had ever been close to. Unless you count my Pirates Mighty Mite hockey team, which captured the Transcona Under-7s title back in 1969. Sadly, it was true: The last time I had ever been around a champion in Winnipeg was the winter of '69, which I guess could also have been a sequel to a famous Bryan Adams song.

But being around the Bombers in the mid- to late 1980s was like being around a bunch of rock stars. Suddenly, the capital of Manitoba was known as "Winner-peg," and the football team was leading the way. Everywhere you went, people were wearing blue and gold, and even in the off-season, the Bombers would spread the love by travelling all over the vast province with a charity hockey team made up of many of their players, mixed in with a motley bunch of media types like yours truly.

That's right, football guys playing *hockey*. Something you would never see today, especially with so much money tied up in athlete contracts. Can you imagine the controversy or the lawsuits if a star quarterback tore his ACL playing another sport for fun?

But back then, that possibility obviously wasn't a concern, because every weekend in the winter, we would jump on a bus and barnstorm small towns and communities from Pilot Mound to Portage la Prairie, selling out arenas, playing local old-timer teams, and mostly raising money for great causes.

As hazardous as it could be to put football players on ice skates, the annual tour was a brilliant idea. Not only were the Bombers promoting their team, but they were also selling season tickets and merchandise, keeping their long-time fans happy, and picking up new ones at every single stop. It was like travelling with the Rolling Stones.

I loved being part of it.

As one of the better skaters on the team—which wasn't a stretch, by the way, with a bunch of football heads—I was mostly responsible for helping keep the games somewhat competitive, as well as teaching the newer players some of the techniques of a sport that was, quite frankly, foreign to some of them.

Willard Reaves, a CFL superstar and future Hall of Famer, was one of those guys.

I was fairly certain that the only ice Willard ever saw growing up in Flagstaff, Arizona, was in a margarita. He had never skated before he came north to Winnipeg, and I doubt it was something on his bucket list. But there he was, the CFL's Most Outstanding Player of 1984, out on the ice, wearing his familiar number 38, his knees shaking and his ankles bending, and just doing whatever he could do to stay on his feet. I'm sure his coach, Cal Murphy, knowing that Willard was starting to skate, was making daily visits to his neighbourhood church.

But one of the main things I learned through the years is that elite athletes are absolute perfectionists. Don't ever tell any of them that they can't do something. Willard was no different. He constantly bugged me to take him out to a local outdoor rink, where we would skate lap after lap and freeze our nuts off. The extra sessions paid off. Willard not only stood up, he stood out. He wasn't the next coming of Bobby Orr, but he found a way to get up and down the ice and, most importantly, not get injured.

One cold winter night at one of our stops in Dauphin, Manitoba, I was asked to centre a line with Willard and all-star linebacker Frank Robinson. Like my buddy Willard, Frank was an African American athlete who was also brand-new to hockey.

It might have been off-colour, but we were hilariously dubbed "the Black Line."

I'm glad Willard was the guy who came up with that.

Together, the Black Line rarely got over the blue line, but on one unforgettable shift, I was able to pass the puck over to Frank, who was parked right in front the goalie. Frank fanned on it, fell, and the puck trickled over to Willard, who was inexplicably standing *behind* the goalie when he took a wild swing and knocked the puck into the net.

The place went nuts. Willard Reaves had just scored the first goal of his life! We retrieved the puck and jokingly gave it to him as a souvenir. I'm sure he never put it in his massive trophy case, but I honestly had not seen Willard that happy since he lifted up the Grey Cup in 1984.

It was priceless.

Willard would be the first to admit he wasn't a great hockey player, but there was no doubt, he was one of the greatest running backs in CFL history. He shredded the Bombers record book like he tore through defences. Along the way, he also became a folk hero.

Everyone loved Willard. Not just because of his electrifying talent but also because of his enormous heart. Whenever he scored a touchdown, and he scored many, Will didn't do what most players do when they get to an end zone, especially in today's game. He didn't dance, yuk it up, or come up with some wacky celebration. Instead, he'd high-five his teammates, tuck the football under his arm, and then run into the corner of the end zone to a section of fans with disabilities, where he would hand the ball over to an adoring Bomber fan sitting in a wheelchair. He did that on every touchdown at every home game. Not because he had to, but because he wanted to.

Great player. Greater person.

Willard would end up getting a shot in the NFL, but he eventually returned to Winnipeg and made the city his lifelong home.

Football legend, community hero, and future politician, Willard also became the father of two pro athletes: Jordan—who, like his dad, played in the CFL—and Ryan, who made it to the National Hockey League, where, like Willard with a football, he was a hard guy to bring down. Unlike his pops, however, Ryan has scored way more than one goal in his life.

Whenever I see Willard today, we always reminisce about those wild days with the Bomber/media hockey team. We didn't win many games, but because we were sponsored by Labatt's brewery, we definitely won the post-games. If Netflix did a documentary on our team, the best title would likely be *Blue Bombered.*

After every game, every town would host a "social" in the community hall. These parties would start innocently enough, and by the end of the night, which would usually become early morning, shit would invariably happen.

From the innumerable hook-ups to the absolute debauchery, the Bombers were doing a lot of scoring off the field as well. Nothing illegal happened, but let's just say the team kept setting records for divorce proceedings.

The football players also loved to prank people. No one was safe, especially the media guys on the team, who were usually the victims of a good-hearted punking.

One late night in a small town called Minnedosa, I got back to my hotel around 2 a.m., only to see a bunch of furniture outside in the parking lot. It was about minus-twenty outside and the snow was coming down hard, yet there was a bed, a lamp, a desk, and an ice bucket all perfectly arranged underneath the hotel sign. I remember bursting into laughter, thinking what a great prank it was, until I looked closer and realized that all of this stuff had come from *my* room.

It took me over an hour to lug that bedroom furniture back into the hotel, past a baffled front desk attendant, and down the long hallway. I carefully opened the door to my room, not knowing what to expect on the other side. When I turned on the lights, the room was empty except for two items in the middle of the floor: a case of Labatt's beer and an autographed picture of Bombers offensive lineman Chris Walby.

Normally, payback would be a bitch. But Walby, aptly nicknamed

"Bluto," was nearly seven feet tall and over 350 pounds. He was a big teddy bear, but it was probably a wise decision not to poke that bear.

I had been working at CKY for a few years when the Blue Bombers won the Grey Cup in 1984. By 1988, I had a lot more reps and a lot more experience, both as a sportscaster and at covering the CFL.

The Bombers' coach that year was Mike Riley, one of the greatest people I have ever met in my life. He was such a good man. The 1984 team was great, but the players on the 1988 team were total underdogs. Not just underdogs but a very eclectic group of players. Bombers quarterback Sean Salisbury was doing some reporting and anchoring for us at CKY in 1988. A number of athletes who played in Winnipeg ended up doing some on-air work with us.

The BC Lions were heavy favourites to win the Grey Cup, and it came down to an interception of a Matt Dunigan pass near the end of the game to seal the win. The Bombers' Michael Gray made a game-saving play off of a tipped ball. Against all odds, the Bombers hung on to win a game they were not expected to win. I was standing right there near the end zone, getting ready to give the post-game report.

After they won, there was quite a scene in the Bomber locker room. Champagne was being sprayed everywhere, and we all ended up staying up very late. I ended up staying up all night, and we had an early-morning flight from Ottawa, where the game was played, back to Winnipeg. At the airport the next morning, I was absolutely exhausted. Broadcast legend Dave Hodge was in the security line with me, and I said to him, "I am going to sit down here and take a rest. I will wait for the line to die down." I fell asleep and missed my flight! Fortunately, I made the next flight—I had to work the same day. That was one of the few times I had to work with a serious hangover. But the Bombers had won the Grey Cup, and it was all good.

That was the last chance I had to cover the team in a Grey Cup game before I left CKY to work at CTV. I didn't start calling play-by-play of CFL games until 2000, when I started working at TSN. Until then, I was more of a host/reporter/correspondent.

The pranks, the stories, the laughs, the moments. That's what made being around athletes in the '80s so rewarding, so memorable. Also, it was such a different time.

Back then, many of the pros didn't consider the media to be the enemy, as they do today. Don't get me wrong: It didn't mean that we, as reporters, protected the athletes, or avoided being critical. It's just that things rarely got adversarial, especially when it came to covering hometown sports.

What you saw was generally what you got. There was no internet, no Instagram, no TikTok or Facebook, which meant fans could only voice their disapproval by booing or heckling someone at a game. The only tweeting in those days came from a referee's whistle.

There were also no smartphones, which was probably a good thing, especially around our travelling charity hockey team.

I have always lived by the philosophy that you should never miss an opportunity to meet somebody. Winnipeg had a thriving boxing scene, and the city had produced a few champions. Early in my career, I got to know a number of the local boxers, and one of them was Donny Lalonde. One of my first assignments was to cover one of his first fights in Winnipeg. This was in the mid-1980s and Donny was climbing the ranks in his sport, so I was covering more of his fights. Everyone in Winnipeg would watch when Donny Lalonde was fighting. He came to be known as the Golden Boy, and he fought as a light heavyweight.

We hit it off right away, became buddies, and would hang out together, a lot. Like most of us in Winnipeg, Donny also played hockey. He would come out and play late-night shinny with us, although he never dropped his gloves. After getting to know him, I got to know his story and how he had been abused as a kid by his stepfather. After he became established as a boxer, he became an advocate for kids who were being abused.

Donny's agent, David Wolf, was based out of New York City, so Donny ended up moving to New York to be closer to Wolf and the legendary boxing trainers in the area. I spent a month with Donny in New York, and at the same time, I worked on a number of stories, including one on his upcoming WBC light heavyweight championship fight with Eddie Davis. I was there every day at the iconic Gleason's Gym. I would watch Donny and Héctor "Macho" Camacho and all the other top-ranked fighters as they trained. Donny's trainer came up to me and said I should go over and interview this young boxer at the other end of the gym. I was told he was a Golden Gloves champion, and he was only seventeen years old. "His name is Michael." I walked over and interviewed this muscular, sweet, soft-spoken young man. He hardly said a word to me. I was actually startled at how polite and respectful this young fighter was. I might have been one of the first guys to ever interview Mike Tyson, who was being trained by the legendary Cus D'Amato. Tyson was such a nice guy, and he was so polite. Little did I know what he would become. I never knew that the right hand I shook would turn out to be so lethal.

As time went on, Donny won the light heavyweight championship and fought nearly everyone, including Sugar Ray Leonard. Donny knocked Sugar Ray down early, but in the end, Sugar Ray won the bout. Lalonde made a lot of money in that fight, which was held at Caesar's Palace in Las Vegas. This was a rare fight where two titles from different boxing divisions were on the line in the same bout.

There were times when I would go running with Donny. I thought I was in good shape until I ran with a professional boxer. We would be four miles into the run, and he would leave me in the dust. I had to tap out. I would tell him that I had to make a phone call! I was not making any phone calls; I just couldn't keep up with him anymore.

Donny was always gracious and kind and accommodating, but also a little flighty. He was hit hard during his boxing career, but he never ended up with the some of the cognitive issues that other boxers face. But he *was* absent-minded. One time, Donny borrowed my car. I was headed to Barbados, and I told him to use my car while I was gone. It was brand-new. About four days later, I phoned my mom just to say hi. She said, "Rod, the RCMP have been calling the house. It is about your car—the RCMP had to impound your car."

I couldn't believe it. It turns out that Donny had to go to New York quickly, and he drove my car up to the front of the airport terminal, got out, and boarded his flight. Oh, and he left the motor running. The RCMP kept putting tickets on the windshield, and when I got back home, I had a bill for twelve hundred dollars. Donny just said, "Sorry, Rodney." He never called me Rod, always Rodney.

When I was working in Winnipeg, I worked late at night, and then we would play hockey at noon. It was a good skate, and a few ex-pros would come out. One year, we were headed to Hawaii to play in a tournament, and we took Donny along with us to play on our team. It was for the Hawaiian Cup, and we were playing against members of the military. The tournament was in a roller rink that had an ice surface on top of it—the ice was terrible. On the bright side, I played two games and then went to the beach every day.

Donny showed up at the Winnipeg airport with no passport and no driver's licence—classic Donny Lalonde. But everyone at the airport knew who he was, and he was one of those people who would always find a way to make things happen. So, he managed to get his wallet shipped over to him at the gate, where he was able to rummage through it and find the necessary ID to board the flight.

When we landed in Hawaii, I told Donny the time of his first game. He went for a run on the beach, met a girl, and we never saw him again until the day we left! He spent the whole week with that girl.

Donny Lalonde was a close friend, and every time we connect, we always reminisce about the glory days. Donny loved to sing, and that was his theme song: "Glory Days" by Bruce Springsteen. In fact, Donny got me into Springsteen, whom he got to know in New York. He also got to know Bob Dylan. Donny was famous in New York, and Springsteen and Dylan were both into boxing. The old saying that musicians always want to be athletes and athletes want to be musicians was never truer. And most late nights after a few drinks, Donny and I would end up singing "Glory Days" together into a lamp that we used as a makeshift microphone. I also learned a lot about life through Donny, especially how input equals output. If you keep working and keep pounding away, good things will happen. Just keep working and keep getting after it. Donny was always a positive thinker, and anything he touched turned to gold. What I learned most is that even when he got knocked down, Donny always got back up. To this day, I am proud to say that Donny is still standing and smiling. And yes, I would still lend him my car if he needed it.

Life was good as a sportscaster at CKY. The only time I got some beef from an athlete was when I was hosting the Jets games and I heard that Philadelphia Flyer goaltender Ron Hextall wanted to talk with me. Hextall was a Manitoba native, and I had been covering him since he broke into the NHL as one of the most unique goalies the league had ever seen.

"Hexie," as he was called, could not only stop the puck but also handle it. He became the first goalie in NHL history to score a goal by shooting the puck down the ice.

He was a freak. No one could use the goal stick like Ron Hextall. Unfortunately, he didn't just use his stick on the puck. A notorious hothead with a fiery temper similar to Islanders bad boy Billy Smith, Hexie was suspended a number of times for brandishing that goal stick like a weapon.

Like most commentators, I regularly admonished him on my late-night highlight reels—okay, I tore him a new asshole, but frankly, I didn't care. Just because he was from Brandon didn't mean we would cut him any slack. Yes, he was a tremendous goalie, but he was acting like a nutbar. He was dangerous, and he could kill someone out there.

Despite the fact he was from Manitoba, I knew Ron only from the few interviews I'd done with him during the Flyers' rare visits to Winnipeg. Being a homeboy, he was the main pre-game story on these occasions and always obliged every request. He always seemed cool. Never had an issue with him.

But I knew something was up when I saw Hexie walk into the arena a couple of hours before our CKY broadcast that night. His face was glistening red, and smoke was coming out of his ears as he stomped up to look me eye to eye. I was just happy he didn't have a goal stick in his hands.

"Hey, what's up?" I said, extending my hand. Nothing. He creeped right up to me, and we were almost nose to nose.

Uh-oh. This wasn't going to be good.

"You know, I got family all around Manitoba," he fumed. "And they've been telling me that you've been making fun of me and calling me 'Axe-tall.'"

I stammered and stuttered a little bit, trying to tell him I was just trying to be funny, adding that I was sure I wasn't the first person to criticize his intense style of play.

Then I corrected him.

"Actually, it's '*Hacks*-tall,'" I told him. "I called you 'Hacks-tall.'" I wasn't being a smartass or anything, I just wanted to make sure he knew exactly what I'd said.

Our play-by-play announcer, Curt Keilback, and producer/director, John Cuccaro, were both standing behind me, watching all this unfold and probably wondering what was going to happen next.

Hexie then did something I didn't expect. He stared at me for a second, sighed, and then extended his hand. I shook it.

"Not funny," he snorted. Then he turned around and walked into his dressing room, which was right across from our studio.

Keilback raised his eyebrows and gave me a reassuring *Don't worry about it, kid* look.

Cuccaro was less comforting.

"Way to go, Blackie." John chuckled. "There goes our pre-game interview."

I didn't know what to think. Obviously, I had hit a nerve with one of the best goalies in the NHL, and at that moment, I felt like I was lucky to have my head still attached to my body. Thirty minutes later, I was still a little frazzled. I was telling our floor director the story when suddenly the studio door opened and in walked Hacks-tall—I mean, Hextall.

Smiling, he nonchalantly sat down on the stool next to me and courteously did the pre-game interview. When we finished, he smiled, shook hands with everyone, and then, as if nothing had happened at all, returned to his dressing room to put his gear on.

We all looked at each other as if to say, *Did that just happen?*

When the game began, Hextall was at his Jekyll-and-Hyde best. He lost his cool twice, took a pair of penalties, but as always, played a spectacular game, backstopping the Flyers to a 4–3 win.

After a quick post-game interview, I congratulated and thanked him. He nodded and shot me a wink.

We never had another conversation after that. We didn't need to. He knew he'd made his point, and I knew that no matter the situation, I would keep calling it the way I saw it. If you did something great, you would be praised. If you fucked up, you would take some heat. That's the way sports works. Just like life. All anyone can control is how they act and how they react.

By the way, I also never called him Hacks-tall again.

Despite the bizarre Hextall episode, being part of the NHL broadcasts was an awesome experience. Working on these broadcasts allowed me to get to know everyone in the NHL, past and present.

In the 1980s, while I worked at CKY, I also ended up hosting sports banquets in towns all over the province. All those events helped me get comfortable speaking in public. I learned so much from keynote speakers like Don Cherry, Bob Uecker, and Dennis Hull. I never got paid for most of these events; I honestly thought they were part of my job. Maybe that is why I got so many gigs: because they didn't pay me!

One day, I couldn't believe it when one of the big bosses, Rod Webb, called me upstairs and asked if I would be interested in becoming the host of *The Jets on CKY*. I was in my early twenties at the time, with only a couple of years of TV experience, but who wouldn't jump at this phenomenal opportunity? CKY had won the rights for the Jets' local telecast from CKND, and this was a big deal for the channel.

I peeled myself off his ceiling and skipped out of his office understanding full well that another dream job had just landed in my lap. I would still have my *Late News* duties, but for sixteen weeks in the winter, I would be busy with the most popular sports property in the province. As popular as the Bombers were, the Jets' following was humongous—hockey, after all, is king in Canada.

Our games were produced by Molstar Communications, a company partially owned by Molson Breweries that was responsible for televising *Hockey Night in Canada* on CBC, plus all the weekly games for the local Canadian teams. The people we worked with were some of the most powerful in Canadian sports television. Needless to say, the rookie was once again being thrown into the pressure cooker.

I was learning so much working the *Late News* shift, but I was about to step up to a completely different level with Molstar, which was led by legendary Canadian TV sports executive Ralph Mellanby, who was in charge of the best stable of sports producers in the country.

If I'd thought I might soil my pants during my first *Late News* sportscast, I should have been looking to buy a diaper before my first live hockey broadcast, which was in Edmonton, home of the Stanley Cup champions.

As host of the telecast, I was responsible for opening the show, setting the stage before sending it over to the game announcers. I would also do voice-overs of features, highlights, and promos, and of course do the obligatory between-period interviews, where, in those days, a star player would join us live for a sit-down conversation in front of a *Jets on CKY* backdrop. The protocol was set in stone: first intermission was an interview with a player from the home team; second period, the visitors.

Since the Jets were on the road for our CKY debut, our first guest was scheduled to be an Oiler, but not just any Oiler. Imagine how excited and nervous I was when producer John Shannon pulled me aside near the production truck in Northlands Coliseum and told me who he had requested.

"Hey, big boy," John said, smiling. All the Molstar guys said "big boy," it seemed, but Shannon always delivered the biggest "big boys."

"Welcome to the big leagues, big boy," he pronounced. "Gotcha the Great One for first intermission."

That would be *the* Great One, Wayne Gretzky, hockey's greatest player, now scheduled to join me between periods.

I had interviewed Wayne once before, as a reporter, prior to a game in Winnipeg, but it was very quick and informal and, being the shy, guarded superstar he was at the time, very forgettable.

Being one of the most popular athletes on the planet, Gretzky was constantly bombarded with requests. Everyone wanted a piece of him, and the Oilers were very protective of his time and his brand. He rarely did between-periods stuff, and the previous interviews I had watched were hardly earth-shattering.

This was different, however.

Shannon was beaming like a proud papa for pulling off the Gretzky coup when I headed back to the studio to voice over the tease and open up our first-ever *Jets on CKY* show.

In spite of that Gretzky bombshell and the swarm of butterflies doing calisthenics in my stomach, everything was going remarkably. Great opening, smooth start, no stumbles, and once again I didn't have a gastric explosion.

As our announcers, Curt Keilback and former referee Bruce Hood, were calling the first period, I sat quietly in the studio, focused on the action of the game and mentally preparing for my first-intermission interview with the Great One.

When the horn sounded at the end of the first period, the Oilers were leading. We were just throwing to a commercial break when I heard producer Shannon's voice in my earpiece. "Bad news, big boy," he said with disappointment. "Gretz has to see the team doctor and can't do the interview. Stand by."

My heart sank.

The Oilers' PR director, Bill Tuele, scrambled to get a quick replacement, but the only person close enough to fill in for Gretzky was . . . his agent, Gus Badali.

Really? I thought. *A friggin' agent?*

But then again, this wasn't just any sports agent—this was biggest agent in hockey at that time. He represented not only Gretzky, a player he'd helped discover, but fifteen of the top twenty players in the NHL, including two stars with the Jets: superstar centre Dale Hawerchuk and all-star defenceman Dave Babych.

We were just coming out of the commercial break when Badali, a handsome middle-aged man with a slick moustache, quickly shuffled into the studio and plunked himself on the stool beside me.

I had never met him before, but I had heard everything about him. He had a reputation for being both firm and fair in negotiations. A few NHL general managers didn't like to deal with Gus, but the players he repped absolutely loved him. He was Jerry Maguire before Tom Cruise made *Jerry Maguire* famous, but he also was a doppelgänger for actor Peter Sellers. If you didn't look too closely, Badali could have easily passed for Inspector Clouseau from the *Pink Panther* movies. The resemblance was uncanny.

The interview, despite being a last-minute switcheroo, went surprisingly well, even though I had no idea what to ask Gus. Our broadcast also went off without a glitch. The only bad news for our viewers back home was that the Jets lost the game.

Afterwards, I walked out of the building with the crew into the cool Edmonton night and remember having another one of those turning-point epiphanies.

I knew it was only one game—hell, it was my very first game—but I just knew right then and there that as much as I enjoyed doing the nightly sportscasts, *this* is what I really wanted to do.

Amazing what happens when you get a little taste of something really sweet. You just want to keep tasting. Keep dreaming.

Yep, I loved this taste, I thought. *Now it's time to dream even bigger, big boy.*

We were about to hop into a taxi to take us back to our hotel when I bumped into Gus again. I thanked him for the interview, wished him good luck, and told him I hoped that we would see each other again down the road.

He gave me his card, I gave him my phone number, and we kept in touch—a lot.

Gus lived in Toronto but made quite a few trips to Winnipeg to see his clients. When he came to town, I would see him at the rink and often go out for lunch with him and Hawerchuk or Babych. Every time I ran into Gus, he would keep bugging me and say, "You know you should really go to Toronto and work there."

We developed a great friendship, one that would last a lifetime, and I couldn't help but think that I never would have met this guy if it weren't for Wayne Gretzky *not* doing an interview. Life really is all about timing. Being in the right place with the right people at the right time can be game changing. You never know what can happen.

But sometimes you also need a little push. And Gus Badali was the pusher I needed. Yes, he was an outstanding agent, but he was acting more as a friend when he kept giving me advice about my broadcast career. He told me not to get too comfortable being a big fish in a small pond, and said that I should really think about coming out to work in Toronto.

"Yeah, yeah," I said. "Whatever."

For some reason, I wasn't buying what he was selling. As much confidence as I had in my abilities, I was still apprehensive about leaving my dream jobs. I was quickly becoming "the guy" at CKY, starting to make some really good money, and the Jets telecasts were soaring at a completely new altitude.

John Cuccaro was a big reason for that. He and I would meet regularly to discuss the upcoming games, and we both decided that we wanted to shake things up a bit. Nothing wrong with what we were doing; it was just that we felt it was time to do things a little differently by putting our own creative stamp on the broadcasts.

So, thanks to John, whom everyone called "Kook," since his was name was pronounced KOOK-a-roh, things got really kooky. Like me, he had a wacky sense of humour, and we started to come up with some off-the-wall openings.

I started one show riding the Zamboni around the rink. Another time, I opened up on the arena roof during a snowstorm before pretending to be locked out.

The openings would get wilder and sometimes weirder. When the New York Rangers came to town, Kook had me ride up on a white horse, dressed as . . . yep, the Lone Ranger. Just before Christmas, I was one of Santa's elves, riding along on his sleigh with a reindeer before Santa kicked me off for being "naughty."

Nothing, it seemed, was too outlandish. People were tuning in for the game, of course, but they were also wondering what we would do next. We were having a ball, and I didn't mind being the goofball, even when some angry Bruins fan showed up at Winnipeg Arena carrying a sign that read "Rod Black is a GOOF." Dude looked creepy, like he'd just got out of jail, but we still ended up showing him and his sign on the broadcast.

The shit hit the fan—or maybe, the fan hit the shit—because my buddy Cuccaro, who was directing the show, took some serious heat for zooming in on the guy. I wasn't offended. I laughed. I never minded playing the goof. But I also took great pride in telling great stories, especially during a live broadcast when anything can and often will happen.

Like the time in the bowels of dingy Boston Garden when I was about to interview Ken Linseman, whose nickname was "The Rat" because of his tenacious style on the ice. Just as we came out of a break, right on cue, a huge rodent scurried between our legs, which made us both jump.

"Welcome back to Boston Garden," I quickly chimed. "Back in studio with two Rats and a Rod."

We chuckled, carried on nervously, and kept our eyes glued to the floor. Thankfully, our special guest didn't return.

The most unpredictable moment during our NHL broadcasts, however, came in Los Angeles in the spring of 1990, and it wasn't lighthearted.

The Jets were slumping at the time, and captain Dale Hawerchuk was struggling. The guy everyone called "Ducky" had seen his points and minutes plummet to career lows, and he was visibly frustrated when he came into the studio for his between-periods interview.

I knew Dale very well, especially from my relationship with Gus, and I could sense something was clearly not right. During our live conversation, I asked him if the Jets perhaps needed a change.

I didn't expect Ducky to duck the question, but I also didn't expect to hear what he said next.

"You know, Blackie, I'm not sure what's going on." He paused, wiping the sweat from his face. "I just think maybe . . . it's time for me to move somewhere else."

That interview rocked the hockey world.

There were a lot of whispers that Hawerchuk had been feuding with team coaches and management over his decreased playing time, and tensions had obviously boiled over to the point that he decided to force their hand—during a live interview.

Normally, when someone requests a trade through the media, the response is predictably unpleasant. I'm sure some fans were pissed with Dale, but you could tell by the tone of the interview that he was at the end of his rope. This was not premeditated. He was candid. He was honest. It was just Dale being Dale.

And he didn't back down from his words. He meant what he said, and like a true pro, he kept giving it his best until the Jets eventually moved him to Buffalo in a blockbuster draft-day trade. It was a sad day for Jets fans, but what was even sadder was that Hawerchuk never really wanted to leave—and he often said that he left his heart in Winnipeg.

As a testament to his enduring legacy, the Jets would honour Hawerchuk years later by retiring his number 10 and later erecting a statue of him outside the new arena in Winnipeg. Unfortunately, Dale never had a chance to see it, as he passed away far too young, losing a heroic fight with stomach cancer in August 2020.

Personally, I loved the guy and miss him dearly. He was not only one of the classiest athletes I've ever dealt with, but also one of the very best people. Duck had no ego, always had time for everyone, and always gave back to the communities he lived and played in.

Over the years, I was lucky enough to spend a lot of time with Dale at charity old-timer games or golf tournaments. We'd always talk about the good old Winnipeg days and often laughed about how that fateful night in LA changed the paths of both of our careers.

Dale, of course, continued his hockey brilliance for a few teams, and despite never winning a Stanley Cup, he ended up where he always belonged—in the Hockey Hall of Fame.

Much less significant was my story. But that little interview we did was soon beamed all over North America. Had there been social media back then, we would have broken NHL Twitter, but even back then, the clip got a massive amount of attention. So much so that I soon had a number of calls from some agents and TV people who wanted to congratulate me on the way I managed a tricky situation.

I appreciated the compliments, but really, I was just the guy who asked the question, thankful that the Greatest Jet Ever showed enough faith in a budding broadcaster to let him be the guy to break his story. It really was one of the most memorable nights of my young career.

What I didn't know at the time was that my career was only just beginning. A career that would take me places that I never dreamed of. And introduce me to some people who would change my life forever.

6

HELLO, TORONTO, AND WHATEVER YOU DO, DO NOT MAKE PAT BURNS ANGRY

THE JETS BOWED OUT OF THE PLAYOFFS, AND THE HOCKEY SEASON CAME TO AN END. Hawerchuk would soon shuffle off to Buffalo and I would return to the late shift at CKY. That's when I got a long-distance phone call I didn't expect.

From CTV.

Man, I'm a lucky *bastard.* That's all I could think when I hung up the phone.

Everything I had accomplished up to that point had a lot to do with dedication and determination, but it was borderline freaky how my biggest strength seemed to be that I was always in the right place at the right time.

Dreams are only dreams until you put the work in, but it was becoming obvious that the harder I worked, the luckier I got. And the luckier I got, the more restless I was becoming. Don't get me wrong: I loved my job, and I loved Winnipeg, but after getting a taste of NHL hockey, covering local sports just seemed like an appetizer to the main course that everyone in broadcasting coveted—a chance to work for a big network. I was hungry for the opportunity and thought I had done everything to earn a seat at the grown-ups dinner table, but for whatever reason, I kept getting overlooked.

Trust me, there was never any grand illusion that I deserved better. Hell, I was still living the good life. But I was starting to think that the national network dream was a hallucination.

Until that phone call in November 1990.

On the other end of the line was a gentleman I had worked with from time to time on our Jets broadcasts, Doug Beeforth. Doug, a quiet but well-respected producer, had been a part of the ultra-talented production rat pack with Molstar and *Hockey Night in Canada* and had recently been hired by the CTV network as one of its vice-presidents of sports.

Prior to the call, I had worked a couple of CTV events, including the National Gymnastics Championship in Winnipeg. At the time, they had a director and a producer who partied way too much. Both of them came into our morning meeting looking like they had been up all night, and they smelled even worse. *That is okay*, I thought. *This is national TV, and they must know what they are doing*. And I respected their network experience. But that thought somersaulted out of my mind quickly when they started making rude comments into my earpiece about the athletes. And also the sponsors. Thirty minutes before we were about to go live, I had to pre-tape an interview with an executive of this sponsoring company. The gentleman was nice, but he clearly had never done a TV interview. The producer was losing his patience when the sponsor wouldn't look into the camera. The producer told me number of times in my earpiece to get him to look into the camera. We did it again, but still no-go, he wouldn't look into the camera. I thought whatever, it was fine. That is when my hung-over, network-experienced director screamed into my earpiece, "Rod, you tell that fucking asshole to look into the camera!!!" It was so loud that the sponsor heard every word that was said. He looked at me, smiled, and said, "I guess I better look into the camera." That was just the beginning of a litany of rude, misogynistic, and chauvinistic comments from the director and the producer. The broadcast went well, but when we signed off the air, I said to myself, "I will never work for CTV again." It was such a bad experience. It was a different time back then. I was at the tail end of the era where people were drinking on the air, during the broadcast. I wasn't like that; I loved sports, and I wanted to work my butt off and get better.

But things changed quickly with a new regime at CTV. Doug Beeforth and long-time broadcasting executive Ralph Mellanby were putting plans in place to form a new team to take over. Which meant I wouldn't have to deal with those party animals anymore.

A few months earlier, Beeforth had brought me out to Oakville, Ontario, to host the Canadian Open golf championship. I was both excited and nervous during that week at Glen Abbey Golf Club, knowing I was only being loaned out for the assignment but also cognizant that CTV was expanding its sports department with the retirement of iconic veteran announcer Johnny Esaw after an illustrious career.

I remember Doug pulling me aside during the tournament to remind me that there were more than just golf fans watching the Open. He also told me that CTV Sports had acquired the rights to the next two Olympic Games—the 1992 Summer Games in Barcelona, Spain, and the 1994 Winter Olympics in Lillehammer, Norway—and executives with the network were looking for a new host or hosts to take them through those events. He didn't tell me I was one of the candidates in the running, but he didn't have to. I knew immediately that at Glen Abbey, I would not only be in the spotlight but also under the magnifying glass. This wasn't an official audition, but it was an audition nonetheless.

"Roddy, just do what you can do," the bespectacled Beeforth told me. "Just be yourself."

Jesus, that "just be yourself" thing again.

I took those words to heart, but I have to admit that I was a little intimidated coming into the environment. The Canadian Open was one of the most prestigious sports events on the national calendar, and CTV had put some serious resources into the production. Veteran British announcer Ben Wright would be in the booth alongside Canadian PGA Tour star Jim Nelford, with LPGA legend Sandra Post reporting live from the course. I was responsible for all the openings, highlights, features, and clubhouse interviews. It wasn't the biggest role in our coverage, but I didn't care. This was definitely *my* biggest deal to date.

I remember it also being my most nerve-racking deal to date.

Even though I was a golfer, loved the game, and had watched tournament after tournament on TV, I couldn't get it out of my head that this was like nothing I had ever done before, and I didn't sleep a wink before the first round.

Thank God we had some pre-Open rehearsal time because I was not feeling comfortable at all. It was a good thing I was wearing a dark CTV golf shirt, because my pits were spritzing like the fountain on the eighteenth hole.

But then I started to rewind back to my first days at CKY, and what I did to bring my heartbeat down. How I was able to breathe, calm my nerves, and make sure my ass didn't pucker up. Just stay focused, trust the process, and . . . be *me*.

It had worked before, I thought. Why wouldn't it work now?

And obviously, it did. I somehow got through the tournament (which was won dramatically by Wayne Levi), gained some invaluable experience, and got to interview some of the game's biggest stars. In golf parlance, I didn't shoot the lights out, but I definitely had more birdies than bogeys. Overall, I thought I was better than par for the course. Still, when I said goodbye to the production team at the Abbey, I wasn't sure I would be working with any of them ever again.

A couple weeks later, my mood changed again when another CTV Sports executive, Peter Sisam, contacted me to let me know I was seen as a contender for the network host job. Peter told me they were still a long way from making a decision about me, but he would like to meet with me face to face in Winnipeg.

When that day came, I picked Peter up at the airport and we went to a local restaurant to chat. Sharp-dressed and personable, the silver-haired Sisam was known as a slick dealmaker, and it didn't take long for him to set the tone. He got right down to business, talking about the opportunity for national exposure and the chance to become the next network star.

When he stopped talking, he gazed pensively down at the table before giving me a serious look.

"I'm also here to test your *real* sports knowledge," Sisam said.

Really? I thought. *What the hell? Dude flew all this way to test me?*

"So, here's the question. Very few know the answer," he continued. "Can you name the person who played for the New York Rangers, the New York Knicks, the New York Jets, and the New York Mets in the same season?"

Good one. Trick question. I didn't miss a beat. "The organ player," I answered quickly.

Peter smiled, nodded, and pointed a finger like he was shooting a gun right at my chest. "You're good, you're good," he said. "Bingo."

I'm sure I didn't change anyone's mind because I answered that stupid Trivial Pursuit riddle, but I was pretty confident after our meeting.

Wow, I've got a chance at this shit.

But then, nothing. TV silence. Days went by, and then weeks, and finally a couple of months. Nothing. No offer. No rumours. No answers.

In the meantime, thinking the CTV opportunity was dead, I decided to try fishing elsewhere. I solicited the advice of a high-powered sports agency in New York City to help me land something in a bigger market. Gary Green, the former NHL coach turned broadcaster, whom I had worked with on the Jets telecasts, turned me on to Art Kaminsky and his firm, Athletes and Artists.

Kaminsky and his agency had a remarkable success rate when it came to placing clients in high-profile positions around North America. With their connections, we were getting a couple of serious nibbles south of the border, increasing my confidence that something really good was going to hit really soon.

The sooner the better was the key.

Just as all this was going on, adding to my stress level, CKY-TV was in an acrimonious fight with its union, which I was apparently a member of. Negotiations had gone sideways, and there was a very good chance that all of the station's unionized employees were going to walk off the job in the next few weeks.

Holy snipe, this was not good.

And then that phone rang. Doug Beeforth offered me the job.

And of course, I said yes.

And like Peter Young eight years earlier, Doug probably didn't realize it, but that call was another life changer.

Lucky bastard . . .

Instead of an affiliate guy on a CTV station, I was now a network guy.

With a big job!

So big, it needed two people.

The network soon made the announcement that both Tracy Wilson and I had been named as co-hosts of CTV Sports, as the faces of all of the network's properties, from the Olympics to the Toronto Blue Jays and Montreal Expos to golf, tennis, curling, and figure skating—the sport Tracy, a Canadian champion and Olympic medallist, had recently retired from.

I was extremely excited, but I was also sad to leave my hometown. CKY had been so good to me, and I really felt I would never have been in this position if it weren't for all the people who'd had my back for so many years.

And while I shed a tear or two on my flight to the bright lights and the big city of Toronto, I did have a built-in bonus in the fact that I was contracted to remain the host of the *Jets on CKY* games as long as my CTV schedule permitted. So, in reality, I was leaving home—but with the door still open for a few more visits.

Moving to the big city, however, was not everything I expected it to be. Especially considering that I actually took a pay cut to move into the network job. Yep, you read that right. I took a *pay cut.*

As glamorous as the job was, CTV clearly had me by the balls. I should have done a better job with Sisam and the negotiations—in fact, the agency I was working with even tried to play hardball—but I really didn't have much leverage, and the network obviously knew that I would take anything to make the move. The fact that they hired two of us to do the job likely changed their budgetary strategy as well.

I'm not saying CTV cheaped out, but they definitely got a two-for-one Costco deal.

I wish I could disclose the discrepancy in numbers, but unfortunately, I can't. That just wouldn't be right . . .

Ah, screw it.

In Winnipeg, at the local station, doing two jobs and accruing overtime, I was pulling in over $85,000 per year. Great money back then for a young buck.

In Toronto, a network job, I was signed to a contract that paid me $65,000 per year. That same job in the US? Add a zero or two.

But the truth was, it wasn't about the money. Even though management at CTV were tight with their money, I didn't want to tell them that I would probably have done the job for nothing.

Then again, considering the cost of living in Toronto, it certainly felt like I was working for free.

I didn't have to tell Toto that this wasn't Kansas—er, Winnipeg anymore. The "Big Smoke," as Toronto is often called, is an expensive place to live—and really expensive when you don't have a place to live.

That's when my buddy Roy rode to the rescue.

"Roy" was the nickname of NHL defenceman Dave Ellett; he'd earned that moniker from the Roy Hobbs character in the baseball movie *The Natural.* Roy had become a good pal while I was covering the Jets. That was during the era when you could get close to the players. I was around Wayne Gretzky during his peak, and I was never intimidated by it. When you were in the media, and you were covering the team, you were a part of the team. Nobody carved anybody, and you mainly told positive stories about the team. If you told a negative story, it was generally because that person was not on the team anymore. There was a great trust there between the players and the media in Winnipeg. I didn't put myself in their shoes, but we developed a mutual respect for each other during those years.

In November 1990, I was at the arena, hosting a Jets game, when I found out Ellett had been traded to the Toronto Maple Leafs. Coincidentally, it was the same day I got promoted to work at CTV.

When I first arrived in Toronto, I was living at the Westin hotel while I looked for a permanent place to live. Ellett was staying at another hotel. Not long afterwards, he called me up: "Blackie, I got a place. It is so close to Maple Leaf Gardens, and it is close to CTV." At the time, CTV was based on Charles Street in downtown Toronto. "It is perfect," he added. "It is two blocks from CTV and three blocks from Maple Leaf Gardens. Real nice place, if you wanna be roomies."

Roomies?

A pro hockey player and a network broadcaster? Living together?

That's a new one, I thought. Something I'm certain that never happened before, especially considering the obvious conflict of interest. But then again, as I always told myself: Why say why?

Hell. Why not?

That is how we became roommates. Kind of like a sequel to the TV series *The Odd Couple*. Dave was naturally Felix, the neat, quiet guy. I was Oscar, the loud slob/sports reporter.

Despite our differences, we had an ideal living arrangement in a beautiful four-storey downtown condo. Our schedules meshed impeccably. For the most part, when Dave was home, I was on the road. When I was home, he was playing somewhere else. Perfect pairing.

When it got ugly was when we were both home, and suddenly our place became a "palace"—as in "party palace." Almost every night of the week, especially after Leaf home games, hockey guy and sports guy became the "shaker" guys, the hosts with the "most." The most beer, the most pizza, the most noise, the most guests staying over, and of course, the most hangovers. We might as well have put up a neon sign in our window that said "Blackie and Roy's—Open Late." You can just imagine how crazy things got. And the many stories that came out of all of those late nights and early mornings. We somehow survived and thrived. A couple of single guys who worked hard and played harder.

Dave Ellett and I didn't live together too long. We often joked that we were roommates for 540 days and three thousand nights! It was an insane time to be around the Leafs in Toronto.

One of our key running mates was Wendel Clark, the legendary Leaf captain and one of the best people I have ever met. Dave and I hung out with Clarkie a lot, and if we weren't ripping it up at our condo, we were at Wendel's house, which he had had decided to renovate, removing all his furniture and installing much more important fixtures—a pool table, a hot tub, and a beer fridge.

Again, good thing there were no camera phones back then.

It's also a good thing that the Maple Leafs head coach, Pat Burns, had a good sense of humour.

Like Ellett and Clark, I had become pretty close to "Burnsie," a former cop. Not just any cop: Burns had once worked in the biker gang division and on other demanding assignments. To some people, Burns seemed to give off the impression of being a grumpy grizzly bear. Not even close. As much as he was a man who demanded respect from his players and media, anyone who got to know Pat personally would soon find out that he was a big, mustachioed teddy bear with a compassionate, tender heart.

I was fortunate to hang around with the real Burnsie when I hosted the 1991 Canada Cup hockey tournament. He was part of the coaching staff under another guy who gave off those strict-disciplinarian vibes, "Iron" Mike Keenan. I got to know what Pat Burns was really all about, and I discovered that he was a great man. I also became friends with Brian Sutter. The whole experience was magical.

This was the tournament where Wayne Gretzky got hurt in Game 1 of the final after he was hit by Gary Suter of Team USA. But as much as I remember Gretzky being hit, I also remember Eric Lindros. That was Eric's coming-out party. I will never forget Lindros, on his very first shift, absolutely wallpapering Sweden's Ulf Samuelsson with a huge hit. I thought, *Oh, I like this kid!* He'd just been drafted by the Quebec Nordiques, but made it clear he wouldn't sign. Even though I hated the idea, one of our producers wanted to portray him as public enemy number one in Quebec City, where Team Canada played the Soviet Union. As intimidating as Eric could be, he is one of the most misunderstood athletes ever. The media tried to portray him as something other than what he was. Eric was a phenom. Nobody had ever seen a player that big *and* that talented before. He was really nice off the ice, and so quiet, so well spoken, and very smart.

Gus Badali was helpful for me during this time. Not only did he connect me with agent Elliott Kerr, who would help guide my career, he helped me get to know all the big stars of the game who were part of the tournament. Spending time with Pat Burns and developing a friendship with him meant a lot. You could never do that now; people might accuse you of being a "jock sniffer." I was never a jock sniffer; I was covering and interviewing people I considered friends. Because of that, they trusted me when I spoke to them. They respected me, and I respected them.

On one of the off nights in the tournament, a bunch of us were asked to make an appearance at the Canadian Country Music Awards, which were being held next door to Copps Coliseum, the Canada Cup host arena. CTV was the broadcasting the show live, and I was lucky enough to be asked to present one of the awards along with Burnsie and Iron Mike.

The three of us were backstage after the show, enjoying a couple of beers and commenting on how we felt out of place with all of these music stars. Burnsie called us "country award bumpkins" and said that it was a good thing we had day jobs. We were having a few laughs and talking some hockey when two of those music stars came up to introduce themselves. They were twin brothers, Bruce and Brian Good, part of the famous Good Brothers band, who had added to their large award collection earlier in the night.

The Good Brothers handed us some more beers, telling us how much they loved hockey, how they were big fans of all of us, and then asked us if we would join them onstage for a post–awards show presentation.

If we felt out of place before, we were really playing out of position when we walked out to the stage to find about fifty of Canada's best country musicians, all of the award winners that night, lined up in choir formation under the lights.

Burnsie gave me a look that said, "What the hell?" before Bruce and Brian asked us to stand beside them in the back row because we were all going to sing a new version of the Canadian national anthem, and it was going to be filmed in a "We Are the World" inspirational style and be shown every night when TV stations signed off for the day.

But after about one second of trepidation, there we were, the country award bumpkins, arm in arm with the Good Brothers, about six beers in, proudly singing our favourite song with some of the biggest stars in Canadian music. It was weird, but it was beautiful, and it was so Canadian.

When the video finally came out, everyone was pretty happy with the finished product, and of course the three of us wanted to see if we'd made the final cut, which we had—kind of. One of my eyebrows and the side of my face could be seen in one shot, the top of Keenan's head in another. But the guy who got the biggest cameo was the dude doing the full Burnsie, beaming proudly and belting out "O Canada" like he was Gordon Lightfoot.

All photographs courtesy of the author unless otherwise noted.

Hello, Canada. During a typical year, I will host over one hundred charity, sports, and corporate events all over the country.

Jack Armstrong and Leo Rautins are more than just work friends. They are like brothers to me.

Working with Special Olympic athletes is one of the highlights of my career. We can learn a lot from athletes like the amazing golfer Tess Trojan.

With my three amigos: Jack Armstrong, Sam Mitchell, and Leo Rautins.

You never know who will walk into the booth. How about Hank Aaron and Joe Carter?

I always have a great time hosting the NHL Legends events. It brings out the kid in all of us.

I loved covering Wayne Gretzky during his playing career. I have worked with the Great One at various events since he retired from the NHL.

Left: My wife, Nancy, and I with our son Tyler. Watching your child get a hit in a Major League Baseball game feels like winning the World Series.

Right: Nancy and I with our son Brody—one of our two favourite baseball players.

Growing up, I idolized Bobby Hull when he played for the Chicago Blackhawks and the Winnipeg Jets. Never did I think that years later I'd be hosting an event with the Golden Jet at the Hockey Hall of Fame.

Calling Blue Jays games with Pat Tabler was one of the highlights of my career.

I cherished every moment I spent with Guy Lafleur. Especially visiting members of the Canadian Armed Forces. He is a Hall of Famer in every sense of the word.

I had no idea what an incredible speaker Carey Price was until we worked together at a sports banquet. Price is one of the nicest human beings I have ever met.

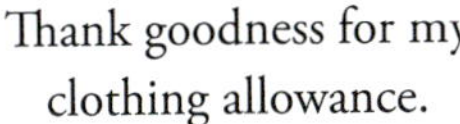

Thank goodness for my clothing allowance.

Basketball has always been one of my true loves. Here I am calling the play-by-play for the Scarborough Shooting Stars of the Canadian Elite Basketball League. *Courtesy of Jim Lang*

Left: Emceeing the Aurora Sports Hall of Fame induction ceremony in November 2025. Long-time friend Kris King was among those inducted. *Courtesy of Jim Lang*

Right: Hosting a banquet. I often appear at various functions to support the community. Check out the very bad tie and my Ron Burgundy moustache.

Interviewing NHL superstar Paul Kariya rinkside at the 1994 Winter Olympics in Lillehammer, Norway.

At the Special Olympics Sports Celebrities Festival. *From left:* Blue Jays Rob Butler, Tony Fernández, and Candy Maldonado; me, Duane Ward, and Cito Gaston.

With Magic Johnson (*left*) and Charles Barkley.

With two of the greatest: Gordie Howe (*centre*) and Wayne Gretzky.

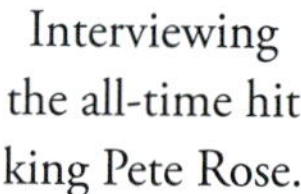

Interviewing the all-time hit king Pete Rose.

That night was another game changer for all of us. Mercifully, our microphones were all turned off, and we definitely didn't sign any record deals, but from that chance meeting at a country awards show, we all became great friends.

Bruce and I connected immediately, and to this day we have enjoyed an incredible life-long friendship. He is funny, talented, and classy. I always remind him that he's not just Good—he's great. Both Bruce and his beautiful wife, Margaret, are godparents to one of our kids.

Iron Mike continued with his quirky style of coaching and years later would become one of my broadcast partners for NHL games. Keenan wasn't anything like the intense guy you saw behind the bench. He was a brilliant hockey mind but also a really nice guy. We had some great times together, and of course many great beers.

And Burnsie, who thought he was an adopted Good Brother, made numerous guest appearances with the band across the country. He loved music almost as much as he loved hockey, and I often think back to those days when the guy with the moustache and whistle would show up onstage with a cowboy hat and a guitar.

I was so blessed that I got to know the other side of the coach, although I do remember one occasion when he wasn't exactly pleased with my living arrangement with one of his best defencemen.

It was early in the 1992–93 season, when the Leafs made an unforgettable run to the NHL's Final Four. The team looked so good, so confident, and everything seemed to be falling into place. Being the reporter that I was, and also the roommate that I was, I was naturally getting some good intel on the direction of the team. My roomie, Roy, was playing some of the best hockey in his career, Clarkie was the perfect captain, and all-star Doug Gilmour was living up to his nickname, "Killer."

There was just something special about this team, and I was getting a unique inside, close-up view.

Since I was hanging out with the guys, probably more than any media member should, I could always tell if something was askew, if someone had a beef with someone else, or if someone was unhappy with his ice time. But as hard as I looked, I couldn't find any trouble spots and couldn't help but notice that these players really seemed to like one another. They were like a band of brothers believing that the team that played together stayed together.

And these guys played hard—scoring on and off the ice.

Burnsie thought they might have been playing too hard. As much as he loved this team and his players, he knew that nothing good ever happens after midnight.

That's when I got another phone call. This time, a message was left on my answering machine.

"Hey, Blackie," huffed the recognizable voice on the machine. "Burnsie here. Listen, I don't give a fucking shit that you and fucking Ellett are fucking roommates. Just do me a fucking favour: Make sure my fucking defenceman gets some fucking sleep at fucking night."

BEEEEEEP.

Word for word. Spoken like a true hockey coach.

Message sent. Message delivered, and a message that I saved for years.

Later, I would tell Pat how much I appreciated his F-bomb intervention, how it helped me realize that maybe I was getting too close to some of the players, and how it was probably a career enhancer to tone down my late nights with the Leafs.

My "shaker" days with Roy did eventually come to an end, not because of Burns, but because my former roomie was traded to New Jersey. I was sad to see a great friend go, but honestly, my liver was very relieved. Ellett and I remain great friends to this day and often joke about how the "Odd Couple" had a great run in Toronto, full of cups—just not Stanley's.

Burnsie and I also kept in touch over the next few years, but certainly not as much as we did in our days hanging with the country band. After being fired from the Leafs, Pat moved to Boston, where he won his third Jack Adams Award as NHL Coach of the Year. When he was let go by the Bruins, he ended up in New Jersey, where he finally accomplished the dream that he had as a little boy growing up in Montreal: that dream of lifting up the hardest trophy to win in professional sports. I'm sure it was heavy, but it didn't look like it that night because Pat Burns, the honorary Good Brother, was finally a Stanley Cup champion.

The last time I heard from Burnsie was during the final days of his courageous battle with colon cancer in 2010. It was mid-September, and I remember listening to my car radio when it was reported that Pat Burns had passed away. I was not shocked, since I knew that he was in a tough fight, but I'm sure I was wiping a tear away when I got a call on my cellphone from a familiar area code.

"Blackie," the strained voice at the other end said, "what the fuck? The media is trying to kill me off."

It didn't sound like a ghost or a voice from the other side. Nope, there was no doubt. It *was* Burnsie!

Apparently, a few radio outlets had erroneously reported that Pat had died, but clearly, reports of his death were greatly exaggerated. We had a bit of a chuckle, but I could tell he was pissed. We didn't talk long, but he wanted to make sure that the public knew he was still very much alive. If there was one thing Burnsie absolutely hated, it was when the media got it wrong.

This time they got it dead wrong.

Sadly, Pat lasted only another two months before he passed away, but even in death, he managed to be that coach who always left the final message.

Not long after his death, a special memorial was staged at the famed Horseshoe Tavern, where hundreds of his Toronto friends showed up to pay their respects and celebrate his life. I was honoured to host the event, which was unlike any ceremony I had ever attended and probably unlike any I ever will.

This wasn't going to be about loss. This was going to be about life, laughter, and music. Exactly how Pat would have wanted it.

Former NHL goalie Glenn Healy started the proceedings by piping in family and close friends. A couple of bands were backstage, ready to play, and it felt like we were at a going-away party, but the freakiest thing of all was when I started the show by asking for a moment of silence, then directed everyone's attention to the video screen and announced, "Ladies and gentlemen, here's Pat Burns."

At that moment, the video rolled and there was the coach, sitting at a picnic table at his home in Magog, Quebec. He looked weak and tired and certainly not like the gregarious coach we last saw ripping into a referee or challenging Barry Melrose between the benches.

At this point, I'm sure some people were wondering if he had returned from the dead again. But no, Burnsie had recorded the piece a few months before he died, knowing that his fate was inevitable, and taking the opportunity to tell everyone that this was likely the last time they would ever see him and that he knew he was destined for a better place. He thanked everyone, told everybody that he loved them, and whispered goodbye.

It was one of the few times in my life that I was absolutely speechless.

I stood there transfixed as the applause started and didn't stop for about five minutes. I've never seen so many people smiling and crying at the same time, but that was the effect that Burnsie had on everyone he met.

As always, the coach got the last word.

Surprisingly, no F-bombs, but his message was so powerful, so impactful, it almost brought me to my knees.

I've never been a deeply religious guy, but this was definitely some kind of spiritual awakening. I had always thought that things happened for a reason. Right place, right time—life will work itself out. But seeing Burnsie facing death with such dignity made me appreciate how precious and unpredictable life really is. How important it is to chase your dreams, to make a difference in the world, and to live every day like it's your last. To stop worrying about the little things, even though they can become big things.

Just when I was believing that I was seriously just a lucky bastard, the truth was inescapable: All that luck meant nothing if I didn't do something with it. Pat Burns really had a lasting impact on me.

7

THE OLYMPICS

CITIUS. ALTIUS. FORTIUS. **LATIN FOR FASTER. HIGHER. STRONGER.**

No, not the way I was feeling after a night on the town. Those three powerful words actually make up the age-old motto of the Olympic Games.

I guess you can add *Richer* to the mantra, because back in the 1990s, the Olympics had become more than just games—they were now a gold mine.

And we're not talking about a gold medal mine.

Rights fees set by the International Olympic Committee were astronomical, television ratings were through the roof, and CTV Sports was making a serious investment by buying into the 1992 Summer Games and the 1994 Winter Olympics.

Four years earlier, CTV had been the host broadcaster of the 1988 Calgary Olympics while its rival network, the Canadian Broadcasting

Corporation, carried the '88 Summer Games from Seoul, South Korea, and the 1992 Winter Olympics in Albertville, France.

Even though the two networks shared some properties, CBC was the clear leader in sports television during that era. Being a public broadcaster with seemingly unlimited resources and funds, CBC owned most of the sports TV landscape in Canada and was a Goliath when it came to negotiating network rights. Those of us Davids who operated within the private television sector always looked enviously upon the government-funded juggernaut, knowing that we were operating on an unlevel playing field, especially when it came to bidding up for the biggie—the Olympic Games.

I was not a fan of the CBC, or as many call it, the Corp, for a number of reasons.

The biggest issue I had was that the network was being bankrolled by taxpayers. I had no problem with the CBC producing news, documentaries, music specials, or even comedy shows, especially if it meant more opportunities for Canadian broadcasters. Some of the greatest homegrown talent, after all, was born, nurtured, and developed because of the Corp. It was a network by Canada, about Canada, and for Canada. Or at least it should have been.

To me, there was always a place for the CBC—just not in pro sports or the Olympics, which were becoming more about the money by the day. But the CBC just kept bidding and acquiring properties like a drunken real estate broker. No one, except the private broadcasters, called them out on it or asked the Corp to account for all of the money being wasted at the taxpayers' expense.

Lamentably, the average viewer didn't really care. They just wanted to see their games. Had someone revealed the real cost of the broadcaster to the public, there might have been protests. But the CBC suits would always deny any impropriety, tell the world how important the network was to Canadian culture, and then just kept gorging at the public trough, gobbling up more and more properties, writing off rights fees and expenses, and then burping out ad revenue.

It was ridiculous—and wrong.

If this diatribe sounds like sour grapes, you're right.

My disdain for the network began back in Winnipeg, where we competed against the local CBC outlet, and their sports department would show up at a game or press conference with three reporters to our one, yet they still didn't tell the story any better than we did.

My anti-Corp contempt grew even more when I was getting itchy for a move and applied to CBC Vancouver for a vacant sports reporter position. I didn't hear back from them for a couple of months until the day my audition reel was returned to me at CKY, which of course meant I didn't get the job.

No worries. Not the first time that I had been rejected, and it wouldn't be the last. However, what really pissed me off was that when I opened up the returned envelope, I found a note that had been inadvertently stuck to the audition reel case by the news director, who clearly didn't know the tape was being sent back to me. On the tattered piece of paper were scribbled ten words:

Not a good fit. Too private for a public broadcaster.

Whatever the hell that meant. I pinned that note above my desk until I left CKY—more fuel for my fire.

As resentful as I was towards the CBC when I was in Winnipeg, that spite percolated to a boiling point when I got to CTV in Toronto.

Again, please don't get me wrong: The CBC was consistently doing quality work and had journalistic standards we all aspired to. The public broadcaster liked to set the bar very high, and didn't give a shit about how much it cost and who it rode over. That's because it really didn't have many challengers. Back then, streaming was something that only a river did, and the multi-channel universe was only about thirty channels strong. The Sports Network, TSN, was still in its infancy in Canada, available only on premium cable, and nowhere near the beast it would someday become. Sportsnet hadn't even been born yet, so there really wasn't any competition in the CBC's crosshairs, other than CTV.

But they were the champs, and they knew it.

They carried big broadcast chips on the shoulders of the gaudy, bright-orange CBC blazers they wore to all the big events, looking like they just came out of a pumpkin patch, with some of their announcers strolling around like they were bigger than the star athletes they were covering.

When the CBC orange coats came to town, they would roll in with two or three production trucks, an army of staffers, writers, makeup people, and a budget fit for a Super Bowl, even though they were producing something significantly less momentous.

It wasn't like that all the time, but it seemed it was like that most of the time. They walked the walk and talked the talk. They had a reputation. They had *swagger*. They were the Yankees and the rest of us were an expansion franchise. And just like the baseball Yankees, CBC spent a lot of money, and they didn't like to lose—especially when it came to Olympic coverage.

So, you can imagine how pissed they became when they found out that CTV was trying to invade their territory by building their own sports department, buying up broadcast rights, and going head to head with the Evil Empire.

The war had begun.

No weapons needed. Just words, dealmakers, and money. Public vs. private. CBC vs. CTV. Faster. Higher. Stronger. Richer.

There might have been some hyperbole to those last few sentences, but there was no doubt—the battle lines were being drawn. The two networks were already duking it out in the news world, with heavyweights Lloyd Robertson of CTV and CBC's Peter Mansbridge anchoring their respective nightly national newscasts. So why not expand the combat zone to include the toy—I mean, the sports department?

When Tracy Wilson and I signed on to be the co-hosts for the new CTV Sports, the network wasted little time sending us into the trenches. With the Summer Olympics over a year away, we were quickly thrown into the fire, even though one of our first assignments together was the plummiest of plums, sending us to Pasadena, California, on New Year's Day, to broadcast the Tournament of Roses Parade.

You read that right. The Tournament of Roses parade. We broadcast a *parade*.

But not just any parade—this was the GOAT of parades. I guess you could call it the GOAP—Greatest of All Parades.

Over a million people were jammed along a mile-long roadway, soaking in the warm California sun, enjoying scores of marching bands, entertainers, and of course the immaculately decorated flowered floats, all part of the annual pre-game procession to the Rose Bowl football game.

I had watched it many times before, but seeing it in person made me realize that television did not do it justice. This wasn't just a parade—this was Flora-palooza. It was amazing. It was also sensory overload. Anyone near the parade could not help but be overwhelmed by the powerful scent of millions of rose petals.

I'm sure Tracy, who was brand-new to the sports-TV world, was probably thinking the same thing I was at this point: Wow. Rose Parade. Man, I love this network gig.

If only.

Once we got back home and back to reality, both of us knew the parade—I mean, party—was over. No more time to smell the roses. Now we had to buckle down and start showing why they'd hired us in the first place.

We had a huge run of major national events, including the Canadian National Skating Championships, World Curling Championships, Blue Jays and Expos telecasts, and the Major League Baseball All-Star Game, which was coming to Canada for the first time.

It was so cool to be a part of all these big-time shows, but it certainly wasn't smooth sailing for either of us, particularly Tracy, who was pregnant at the time and still learning the ropes of a business that, to everyone on the outside, looked easier than it was.

Despite the fact she had previously done only some colour commentary on a few figure skating events, Tracy was already a next-level communicator and one of the nicest people I had ever met. She was great to work with and loved by everyone, and she approached every assignment with the same intensity she had as an Olympic athlete. She knew what it was like to be in the spotlight, to perform under pressure, and most importantly, she knew what it took to win.

Along with her skating partner, Rob McCall, Tracy was a seven-time Canadian ice dance champion, three-time world bronze medallist, the 1988 Olympic bronze medallist, and an esteemed member of the Order of Canada, the country's highest civilian honour. Together, Tracy and Rob were magical and would have danced together for many more years, but in 1990, just as Tracy was about to embark on a broadcast career, Rob was diagnosed with AIDS, which a year later would sadly take his life.

To this day, I don't know how Tracy was able to get through that challenging time. New job, new baby on the way, but also having to deal with the devastating loss of her skating partner and best friend. She was such a strong person, but she also had her rock—her husband, Brad Kinsella.

A former rugby player and successful construction developer, Brad was a bear of a man, as warm and friendly as his wife. He and I also became close pals, and he was a huge help in my transition to the big city by bringing me into his close circle of buddies, who got together almost every night of the week to play some sort of recreational sport, which of course was followed by the obligatory post-game beverages.

Inevitably, I'd see Tracy the next day at work and would always have to sheepishly apologize for keeping Brad out late the night before. She'd always give me a wink and a smile and say it was likely that Brad was keeping *me* out late.

That was Tracy—always finding the best in people.

I couldn't have asked for a better teammate, especially someone making the transition from Olympic athlete to Olympic broadcaster. She came with eyes and ears wide open, ready to embrace whatever was thrown her way, and while she was on a steep learning curve, she was managing everything like she did as a skater, hitting every step without missing a beat.

But like skating, broadcasting has its own judging panels, and as both of us were finding out, TV critics could be very harsh on both technical merit and artistic impression.

Some of the criticism was fair, some was not, but a lot of it seemed very petty and almost personal. It was almost as if our CBC rivals were stoking the fire by leaking inside information.

It was frustrating, but we both knew there was nothing we could do about what people printed or said, and an old theme was replaying in my head: We could only control what we could control.

• • •

What was getting more uncontrollable was the obvious—the sports war was full-on, and we were stuck right in the crossfire. We tried our best to be bulletproof, but as the scrutiny intensified and the 1992 Olympics drew nearer, PR machines at both networks were shifting into high gear, spewing production propaganda. With their orange blazers now hanging in the closet, it was becoming apparent that CBC was dissing whatever CTV was doing, constantly pecking at our inexperience, and telling anyone within earshot that we basically sucked at doing major events.

Our public relations people countered with an all-out blitz, getting our names and faces out to a number of media outlets to go along with guest appearances on a variety of TV and radio shows.

I had no problem with any of that promotional stuff, especially since I was brand-new to the network, but I wasn't happy when one of our publicity coordinators booked me on a national daytime talk show called *Shirley* for an episode about Canada's most eligible bachelors.

As soon as they told me it was a good idea, I knew it wasn't a good idea. I had been down this road before.

Back in Winnipeg, when I first started sporting my cheesy moustache and half mullet, the CKY programming department had me mimic actor Tom Selleck in a parody promo. They put me in a Detroit Tigers cap and a Hawaiian shirt and had me replicate the *Magnum, PI* pose, complete with the Selleck grin and eyebrow flash. At the time, the spoof was harmless fun, and everyone got a good chuckle.

But this "eligible bachelor" crap was different. Even though I was single at the time, the last thing I wanted was to perpetuate any perception of me as some sort of playboy sportscaster. I was already fighting the style-over-substance stigma, but being the new kid on the CTV block, I just nodded my head and went with the flow.

That was a mistake.

Why that PR person thought the *Shirley* appearance was beneficial to the CTV Sports brand was beyond me. It was clueless, it was embarrassing, but it didn't end there. *Flare* magazine, a Canadian fashion publication, also did a feature article on me. Not about sports or my broadcasting career but—you got it—once again listing me as one of Canada's most eligible bachelors.

Enough already.

Isn't this freaking great, I thought. I came all this way to Toronto, took a pay cut for my dream job, and now I wasn't even being taken seriously by my own network.

I needed another turning point.

So, I decided to take it to the top and pay a visit to the big boss, John Cassaday, the president of the CTV network, a man I really admired for his vision and leadership. Cassaday, who had come to the TV business after a successful run as an executive at Campbell Soup, was one of the best bosses I ever had. He was sensible, kind, and classy, and what I admired most was that he got to know all of his employees' names—something every CEO should put on their resumé.

I told John that I was enjoying my brief time at CTV, that I was starting to get comfortable in my role, but I was having a real issue with the way the network was showcasing me.

"With all due respect, Mr. Cassaday," I said with some hesitancy, "I came here to be your network sports host, not an eligible bachelor or a boy toy."

John laughed at my comment, but then, sensing my frustration, he promised me I didn't have to fulfill any interview requests I was uncomfortable with.

"Roderick," he said (he was one of the few people who called me that), "just say no. If somebody has a problem with that, you tell them to call me."

I appreciated his words, shook his hand, and got up to leave, only for him to tell me to sit back down for a minute. He clasped his hands near his chin, and then, with a more serious look, gave me some invaluable advice that switched on another light bulb.

John told me how much the network believed in my abilities and how much he appreciated my teamwork and commitment. He also said that he admired the way I could improvise on the fly—tap-dancing, as he called it—but he also cautioned that I should be careful with my approach.

Even though he was new to the TV world, Cassaday said that everything he had achieved in business was a result of good communication—what you say, how you say it, and the impact your words have. Every story a person tells needs to be crafted with meaning. It has to make you pay attention, and everything has to have a message or a punch line.

He told me that when you watch a great leader give a speech, it may look like he or she is ad-libbing, but every word, every sentence, every breath is scripted and well rehearsed. Comedians have told jokes hundreds of times, he added, but they make it look and sound like it's the first time they've ever told them.

"Words count," he said. "When you talk, make sure what you say makes people listen."

Cassaday lived up to his own words. He was a good talker and was good at making people listen, particularly me. I took his advice and ran with it. I knew I would always have the ad-lib ability in my pocket; however, it was obvious that if I was going to become a truly elite network announcer, I was going to have to tone down my tap-dancing and work on my structured storytelling.

• • •

John's constructive input came at the perfect time. The Olympics had crept up on us quickly, and suddenly, we were all cramming to get ready for Barcelona.

The lead-up to the Games was gruelling, with numerous production meetings, seminars, and rehearsals, not to mention the endless hours of study. With no internet or Wikipedia back then, we had to rely on encyclopedias, newspaper articles, library books, and our Olympic research manual, which made *War and Peace* look like a short story. That book was our bible, and we carried it with us like a passport.

As much as sports is about fun and games, it's also hard work. You had to prepare. You had to train. You had to visualize. You had to practise.

Hard practice, I learned early in my life, made the games easier.

It was the "6-P rule": Perfect preparation prevents piss-poor performance.

I knew we were only the messengers, but as the Games grew closer, it was almost as if we were the people competing. Then again, in light of the network war being waged, I guess we were.

The executive producer for the Barcelona Games was Scott Moore, who had earned the nickname "The Wonderkid" after winning an Emmy Award for producing the 1988 Calgary Games for a US network while he was still in his mid-twenties. Scott, who had started as an assignment editor at TSN a few years earlier, was a lovable guy with a great sense of humour and an insatiable desire to tell great Canadian stories. Most of all, he was a terrific leader who always seemed to motivate those around him.

CTV covered all the bases, assembling an all-star team consisting of network-affiliate announcers and many famous former athletes as analysts to call each individual sport. The network's mission was to put the best people in the best positions, making sure everyone would land in Spain ready to roll.

As much as I wanted to work alongside Tracy, CTV decided to team her with veteran sports host Dan Matheson. Together, they would work the live afternoon slot in Barcelona while I would work the late, late shift.

At first, I thought it was a ploy by CTV to make sure I didn't spend my nights on Las Ramblas—the iconic Barcelona boulevard that never sleeps. It was a wild place, kind of like a cross between Times Square and the Las Vegas Strip. But with the time difference in Canada, the late-night assignment meant I had the privilege of hosting the highest-rated show of the Games—*Olympic Prime Time*. It was both an incredible opportunity and a huge responsibility, more of an honour than a challenge, but with it came the inevitable comparisons to CBC's long-time host Brian Williams.

That was the last thing I wanted.

Nothing against Williams, who had lived up to his reputation as the "Dean of the Olympics," but his style wasn't mine, and whenever someone called me the next Brian Williams, I honestly wanted to stick my finger down my throat.

It's not that I disliked the guy. Hell, he was legendary. A lot of people would have been flattered by the association. My goal, however, was not to be the next something or somebody—I just wanted to be myself.

Tell that, of course, to the smartass critics who were on me like flies to cow shit. Wait, did I just compare myself to . . . uh, never mind.

Let's just say they loved to take their shots. Most of them cheap.

One national writer called me "Brian Williams Lite." Another said I was "a moustachioed manifestation of Fergie Olver," the gregarious game show host and baseball announcer who loved his Blue Jays.

A couple of *Toronto Sun* columnists were particularly nasty. TV and radio critic Rob Longley, who was always Mr. Congeniality whenever he bumped into me, loved to take swipes from his basement typewriter, ripping me a new one when he wrote: "Rod Black is a nice guy but should never host his own show." His *Sun* colleague Steve Simmons, both popular and controversial, was more veiled but equally scalding when he penned this beauty: "Comparing Rod Black to Brian Williams is like comparing Candy Maldonado to George Bell."

If you're too young to understand that line, let's just say there was a big difference in the talent level between the two former Blue Jays.

Thanks for the compliment, Steve. At least Candy won a World Series.

Sticks and stones. But none of those names were going to break me.

Even though the words stung, I decided not to take them personally. I wasn't going to be bitter. I was going to be better. My skin grew thicker. My will to succeed grew greater. I didn't come this far to come this far. Let the Games begin. The Olympic dream lives. A chance to represent your country at the greatest Games on earth.

Like most of us mere mortals, I could only imagine what it was like to be an Olympic athlete. Oh sure, I had fantasized about going for gold when I was a young kid, but I soon realized that I had very little chance unless miniature golf became an Olympic sport.

But being named prime-time host for CTV's Barcelona coverage was the next-best thing to jumping on a podium. It was the opportunity of a lifetime, another dream come true.

However, as the wise philosopher Ben Parker often said to his nephew, Peter Parker (yes, that would be Spider-Man), "With great power comes great responsibility." And with all that can also come great anxiety. If I said I wasn't nervous, I would be lying through my teeth. Yes, I already had some big events under my broadcast belt, but this was definitely the biggest.

I remember we were a few minutes from going live, and my heart was beating like a freaking jackhammer. I wasn't having a panic attack or anything, but it was almost as if someone had turned the heat up in the studio to full blast and Eminem was in a time machine, singing "Lose Yourself."

Just breathe, I thought.

Thankfully, we had an amazing prime-time team led masterfully by my old hockey producer, John "Big Boy" Shannon, who was in charge of putting our nightly shows together and keeping everything on the rails.

Early in his career, John had a reputation for being a bit of a hard-ass, even a borderline bully. He didn't put up with incompetence, especially from people who didn't work as hard as he did. He could be impatient, inflexible, and just plain stubborn, which unfortunately caused a few uneasy moments with colleagues from time to time. His blow-ups in the control room became the stuff of legend. He would be hired, fired, and rehired by almost every network in Canada, and while John's demeanour softened through the years, two things about him never changed: his infectious passion for producing sports and his incredible ability to frame great stories.

I loved the guy and loved working with him. He was no bullshit, and if things ever started to go sideways, I would invariably get this terse but comforting voice in my earpiece saying just one word:

"Roddy."

A slight pause. Then, just like an experienced air traffic controller, John would calmly explain what was happening, what we were doing next, and how he was going to reconfigure our flight plan. Big Boy just knew how to keep TV broadcasts in the air without crashing. He also knew how to keep his Olympic host from crashing.

A week before the Games began, our prime-time production team was busy wrapping up a rehearsal session around 4 a.m. when our makeup artist, Jacquie, suggested that instead of taking the shuttle, we could *rollerblade* back to our hotel.

Love it, I thought. It was only about a thirty-minute ride, but what a great way to unwind, get some early-morning exercise, and then head off to bed to get ready for the next show.

And so, we rolled. For three straight nights, just Jacquie and me, cruising under the Barcelona moonlight, wheeling through the empty streets, even recreating some of my old roller-skating moves. We didn't tell anybody; it was our little secret, and it was a great way to wrap up a hard day in the studio. It was a blast.

And then, two days before the Games, my "Blades of Glory" sessions ended abruptly when my skates went missing from my hotel room. I called down to the front desk to ask if someone had seen my rollerblades, insinuating that they might have been "misplaced" by the housekeeping staff, but the English-challenged operator could only mutter, "*No, señor, no entiendo.*"

I was pissed as I shuttled over to our broadcast compound wondering why in the world someone would have the audacity to steal my skates, and worst of all, knowing there was zero chance I could find a sporting goods store to buy a new pair in downtown Barcelona.

Later that evening, the mystery was solved when I walked into Shannon's office for a meeting and saw my skates sitting in the corner.

"Sorry, big boy," he snarled. "No late-night skating till the Games are over. I don't need my host in the hospital, or worse—a coffin."

I half-smiled and tried spitting out some sort of retort, but Shannon would have none of it. He just put up his hand, giving me the Heisman, and shushed me away.

That was John, always straightforward, always navigating around any possible bumps, and as usual, always right.

Just when I was thinking he was being a little unreasonable, I quickly gave my head a shake and realized that there was a good chance no other host in the history of the Olympics had even *thought* about rollerblading during the Games. And while the visual made me laugh, I couldn't imagine NBC's Bob Costas or CBC's Brian Williams racing through the city streets in slow motion, TV hair blowing in the wind as the Olympic flame blazed in the background.

Yes, it would have been pure television gold, the two broadcast B's, splendid in spandex, buzzing around Barcelona, but it would never have happened, except on an *SNL* or *SCTV* skit.

That's because they were trusted and respected pros. They both worked their asses off to be put in a position that very few on the planet had a chance to experience. As much fun as I'm sure they had away from the cameras, I'm certain they never contemplated doing something as idiotic or as potentially dangerous as I was doing, especially around the biggest show, the Olympic Games. I was either stupid or ignorant—or both.

Another lesson learned. Another potential disaster adverted. Time to grow up and finally put my "big boy" pants on.

"Roddy?"

Shannon's piercing voice brought me back to the moment.

"Thirty seconds to live. Buckle up, big boy. Let's have fun. It's only the Olympics." He chuckled.

A few minutes earlier, with my heart pounding and my armpits leaking, I honestly thought I needed a barf bag. My mind was spinning. I couldn't help but think of all the people watching, but mostly all my friends and family who were tuned in halfway around the world. I felt like an astronaut about to take off into orbit.

Oh no, not this shit again.

"Five . . . four . . . three . . . two . . ."

The opening tease started to roll—the announcer's voice boomed:

"This is a presentation of CTV Sports, where the world comes together for the Games of the Twenty-fifth Olympiad in Barcelona."

Just breathe, I whispered. *Please don't choke.*

And then, just like it had before, something happened: The apprehension, the nervousness, that familiar rush of adrenaline just stopped. It was like someone turned off a tap and turned on my brain.

"From CTV's International Broadcast Centre in Barcelona, Spain—here's Rod Black."

The red light blinked on. I opened my mouth, and the words came out.

Thankfully, I didn't choke. And I didn't vomit all over myself.

Even better, it was like a wave of calmness had descended over my body. Almost like someone had tasered me. Everything seemed to morph into slo-mo.

I don't know how to describe the feeling, but suddenly I knew what a high-performance athlete felt like when they were getting into the so-called zone. It was like an inner peace had penetrated my skin, allowing all those belly butterflies to float in a nice, neat formation.

The words kept tumbling out. I kept my focus. Shannon kept our plane in the air, and I realized right then and there that all of that trepidation and anxiety I had been feeling before the cameras turned on was actually like rocket fuel.

It wasn't nerves. It was actually excitement. And it was *good* to be excited.

Maybe because it was the biggest stage I had ever been on, or maybe because it was a moment of self-discovery, but knowing that I was able to actually keep my cool and hold it together in a seemingly stressful situation made me realize that if I can do the Olympics, I can do anything. I mean, what was the worst thing that could happen? Sweat? Stutter? Shit my pants?

"Roddy!" Shannon barked in my ear as we went to our first commercial break. "Great stuff, big boy. Let the Games begin."

And so, they did. For sixteen days and nights, we were locked in our studio, bringing the emotional sights and sounds of the Summer Olympics to our viewers back in Canada.

The Games opened with a bang. Actually, a bull's eye.

Rather than lighting the Olympic flame in the traditional manner, the Spaniards came up with an ingenious way to ignite the event by using a Paralympic archer to sling a flaming arrow into the cauldron, which burst into a brilliant flame and illuminated the Barcelona sky for the duration of the '92 Games.

They didn't know what they'd started. From that day forward, every Olympic organizing committee would go overboard trying to find a unique, creative way to open their Games. From a ski jumper to a *Mission: Impossible* boat race to the unforgettable appearance of the great Muhammad Ali lighting the cauldron in 1996, every host city had its own claim to a show-starting flame, but in my mind, Antonio Rebollo's arrow is still the best of the best.

But that shot seen around the world wasn't the only highlight of the opening ceremonies, as Barcelona became a serious "Games changer."

When the athletes marched into the stadium, you couldn't help but feel that you were witnessing an enormous Olympic transformation. South Africa, with apartheid finally abolished, was back competing as a nation for the first time since 1980; East and West Germany, with the Berlin Wall broken down, were unified as one; and the flag of the USSR was nowhere to be seen, the Soviet communist regime having splintered into fifteen separate countries.

The changes weren't limited to politics. The International Olympic Committee, after allowing professional tennis players to compete in

1988, threw its arms and bank account wide open by welcoming in the stars of the NBA.

If you needed proof these weren't your dad's Olympics, all you had to do was look down at the stadium floor and see the USA Dream Team, with Michael Jordan, Magic Johnson, and Charles Barkley, signing autographs and taking pictures with athletes who were absolutely star-struck.

Welcome to the new and improved Summer Games. We definitely didn't run out of stories to tell from our prime-time studio. We had it all: Drama. Excitement. Glory. Heartbreak. Redemption. The range of storytelling was staggering, and it was non-stop. Every day. Every event. Every emotion possible.

And every night, we were lucky enough to reframe those stories by bringing special guests and athletes into the studio to talk about what had happened that day.

I'll never forget interviewing swimmer Mark Tewksbury after he won Canada's first gold medal of the Games, in the 100-metre backstroke, coming back down the stretch to nip his American rival, Jeff Rouse, by six one-hundredths of a second. One of the greatest athletes and classiest people I had ever been around, "Tewks" was still on cloud nine when he strolled into our studio with his proud parents, Roger and Donna, who were absolutely beaming. I shook Mark's hand firmly, gave his parents a quick hug, and sat him down to rewatch his race live for the first time.

It was one of Canada's greatest Olympic moments, and the call by announcer Rob Faulds and long-time commentator Byron MacDonald brought chills.

"It's going to go to the wall," Faulds frantically announced. "And at the wall . . . it's . . . it's . . ."

"Tewksbury!" Faulds and MacDonald both screamed.

"He's done it! Olympic record?" Rob roared. "The dream lives!"

I watched Tewksbury as he watched the monitor from the edge of his seat, moving his arms and body as if he were racing all over again. When it was over, he burst into his mile-wide smile and a tear rolled down his cheek as he sat back in his chair.

His life had just changed forever—and he knew it.

That moment is still seared in my mind. I had never been around an Olympic champion, never mind someone who had just realized the ultimate golden dream, but it was so cool to sit across from a new Canadian sports hero who looked like a little kid on Christmas Day, grinning ear to ear and shaking his head like he couldn't believe the gift he'd just got.

But there was much more to the interview than the triumph. Mark revealed that he had been a bundle of nerves all day leading up to the race, bringing himself to tears several times, knowing that in the heat of all of this pressure, he was on the verge of something special.

He shouted out to all of his friends and family who were watching back in Calgary, and of course, he thanked his biggest fans, his parents, for all of the sacrifices they made, the endless drives to competitions and early-morning training sessions, not to mention their guidance and unwavering support.

It was magic TV. Shannon even surprised Tewks by rolling a video of all the calls of his race from Olympic announcers around the world. We weren't sure what any of them said, but it didn't matter; they all sounded as excited as our guys—except for the American announcers, who were lamenting the Rouse loss.

When the interview ended and we went to commercial, Tewks slouched back in his chair and let go a deep sigh. The smile left his face for a moment when I asked him how he was going to celebrate.

"Sleep," he said. "Sleep."

I laughed, but only for a moment because I realized he wasn't joking.

Tewksbury had no time for celebration because he had to race the next day, where he followed up his gold with a bronze medal in the men's 4x100 medley relay.

Four years earlier, at the Summer Olympics in Seoul, South Korea, Tewksbury had won a silver medal in the same relay, but those Games didn't have quite the same vibe for Mark and Team Canada. That's because almost all of the best stories in Seoul were overshadowed by an event that took as long as it took me to type this sentence.

9.79 seconds.

That was the world-record time of Canadian sprinter Ben Johnson as he blew away the field to win the gold medal in the 100-metre final, only to have the medal and the record ripped away a short time later when he tested positive for anabolic steroids.

The news reverberated around the world. A jubilant nation shifted to absolute outrage and then embarrassment. No one fell further than Big Ben, who went from being the world's fastest man to being the most disgraced athlete on the planet. Only a couple days after Canadian Prime Minister Brian Mulroney had called Johnson's gold medal win "a marvellous evening for Canada," the mood had shifted considerably.

Back in the athletes' village, Mark Tewksbury, the future Olympic backstroke champion, was hanging a bedsheet from his balcony, scrawled with the words "Hero to Zero in 9.79 Seconds."

Now, in 1992, after serving a three-year suspension, Johnson was also in Barcelona, trying to make a comeback as a so-called clean sprinter.

I saw Ben more than a few times during the Games, mostly hanging around our CTV broadcast centre, where he stayed out of the spotlight and chatted amiably with some of our staff. For the most part, he looked like a lost puppy. At one point, he was sitting on a couch in our lounge, just watching TV all by himself. *Man*, I thought, *how the mighty have fallen*.

I felt sorry for the guy. Not because of his plummet from grace. He cheated, and he got caught. Plain and simple. He knew what he had done, and like everyone else who would be nailed for doping, Ben had to suffer the consequences.

The disqualification, the stripped medal, and the suspension came as a result of his actions, but as we were all starting to learn, he wasn't the only one who was juicing.

In 1989, less than a year after the Ben ban, the Canadian government stepped up and commissioned the Dubin Inquiry to investigate the "Use of Banned Drugs in Sport." The inquiry, led by the former chief justice of Ontario, Charles Dubin, lasted three months, cost millions of dollars, and was broadcast daily on Canadian network television. High-profile athletes, coaches, doctors, physicians, and pharmacists were all called to testify. The stories were mind-blowing. Sport was on trial, and it was must-see TV.

And as we would soon discover, the Ben Johnson doping scandal ran deeper than anyone had thought. The biggest revelation was how systemic and rampant doping had become within the Canadian track world, with nearly fifty athletes admitting to using illegal performance-enhancing substances.

Ben was the last to take the stand, and although he had long denied any allegations of "knowingly taking illegal drugs," he now gave a full confession, acknowledging that he had originally lied and disclosing that he had indeed been using PEDs in a steroid regimen designed by his coach, Charlie Francis, who had taken a few athletes under his wing.

Johnson and Francis also both testified that Ben had been given an "all clear" before the '88 Games, and it would have been impossible for him to be caught unless his test had been tampered with or someone had sabotaged or spiked his water bottle. The words sounded implausible, but what really got everyone's attention was their accusation that

Ben wasn't the only one who was cheating that day. Both sprinter and coach firmly maintained that everyone on that starting line, including American legend Carl Lewis, was "dirty."

That story would take on several new layers decades later, but at the time, Ben, who could have been the GOAT (Greatest of All Time), was actually feeling like the scapegoat, becoming the demonized poster child for all of those who were using illegal substances.

I was invested in the Ben Johnson saga more than your average reporter. Only a few months before the 1988 Games, while at CKY in Winnipeg, I'd written and produced a multi-part exposé on drugs in sports in which we unveiled the deep, dark side of PEDs and the alarming effects they had on competition and the unknown dangers that anabolic steroids had on athletes' health.

The investigative report was both an eye-opener and a jaw-dropper. We poured hours of research into the series, interviewing a number of athletes, pro and amateur, protecting their identities by masking their faces and disguising their voices, which only further reinforced how secretive the steroid underworld had become.

They came from all corners of the sports world—football, hockey, cycling, track and field, and bodybuilding, which unsurprisingly seemed to be the biggest incubator for PED abusers. All of those interviewed were honest and candid and didn't pull any punches.

I was obsessed with the story. The more I found out, the more I wanted to find out. And the more appalled I became with the depths some athletes had stooped to in order to gain an unfair advantage.

What I found most revealing was the fact that nearly every one of the athletes I talked to regretted taking these substances. What I found most disturbing was that, despite the obvious risks, almost all of them were also willing to do whatever it took get any extra edge. The shit worked. Even if it could kill you.

We were really proud of the piece, which shone some much-needed light on a subject that few people were talking about. Still, there were a few critics who felt that we were overdramatizing the story, even embellishing some of the information, and that we were trying to bring noise to a topic only being whispered about in the shadows.

In other words, they felt it was a non-story.

That criticism was silenced a few months later, when the whispers turned to a roar and the steroid volcano erupted after Johnson's positive test and subsequent suspension.

But everyone loves a comeback story, especially Canadians, and as vilified and scorned as Ben had become in the eyes of the public, his return to track and field in 1992 was captivating.

CTV went full throttle on the comeback, and I was assigned to cover the journey every step of the way, including broadcasting Ben's first event back, a fifty-metre race in Hamilton and the national indoor championship in Saskatoon, which he won.

The narrative around the Johnson camp was one of atonement—that he had paid his penance, served his suspension, and was now ready to show everyone he could become the fastest "clean" man in the world. Ben said and did all the right things in all of our interviews leading up to the Olympics. He was contrite; he was humble. He said he had learned a very hard lesson and wanted to make people believe in him again.

It all sounded positive—and I'm not talking about a test.

I wanted to believe him, but after all I had learned from my investigative series and the revelations from the Dubin Inquiry, my PED radar in Spain was not only permanently turned on, but also beeping loudly.

Deep down, I was saddened by my skepticism, since I was such a believer in the power of sport and those who played clean. I also hated the fact that Ben's comeback was overshadowing some great performances from other athletes who, like Mark Tewksbury, were having golden moments in Barcelona.

Another Mark was one of those athletes, but like Johnson, Mark McKoy was one of the many track stars who had given testimony at the Dubin Inquiry and admitted to using PEDs. McKoy, a mercurial personality, was suspended and actually retired from the sport. But only for a short time—he, too, was on the comeback trail in Barcelona.

His vindication was victory and a gold medal in the 110-metre hurdles. But with the PED meter in my head still buzzing, this Mark's gold didn't seem to have quite the same glow as Tewksbury's.

It should have been another great sports moment for Canada, but the lingering stench of the Seoul scandal seemed to mute McKoy's incredible accomplishment. Understandably, that was the unfortunate consequence for anyone embroiled in any type of controversy. People can forgive, but they rarely forget. There would always be speculation. There would always be suspicion.

Still, I was impressed by McKoy when he showed up on our Olympic set and answered all the tough questions with both contrition and class. Mark McKoy was a natural, he was honest and engaging, and he was so good on TV.

He was the real McKoy, and he didn't give a shit what anyone thought.

I didn't realize it at the time, but he also helped me start to understand the complexities and pressures that sometimes force athletes to make some bad decisions in life. He also made me believe that, depending on the situation, everyone deserves a second chance.

That was the first time I had actually met Mark, but through the years, we stayed close, and decades later, after McKoy embarked on a career as a world-class trainer and motivational speaker, I would count him as one of my closest friends.

That's what the Olympics can do: create bonds that last forever and memories that last a lifetime.

That was what the Canadian rowing team was doing in Barcelona. They were kicking ass, winning four gold medals and one bronze that felt like gold. That bronze, in my mind, was the *true* comeback story of the Games.

World champion Silken Laumann was a favourite coming into the '92 Olympics, but a couple of months before the Games, her boat was accidentally rammed by another boat in a training session, causing serious injuries to her leg that required five operations to repair the damage. At one point, Silken was worried that she might lose her leg. She was told she would never row again.

But somehow, some way, Silken persevered. She trained through the pain, and ten weeks later, she found herself in the women's single sculls final at the Olympics. I was brought in early that day to handle the post-race interviews live from the venue, making the trip to beautiful Lake of Banyoles, about an hour's drive north of Barcelona.

I remember being dead tired since we had signed off from the studio only a few hours earlier, but nothing was going to make me miss what potentially could be a history-making day.

Even though it was early, the sun was already blazing, and I knew that the scorching heat would be a huge factor. It didn't affect the Canadian men's and women's eights teams, however, as they both captured gold medals to go along with the double gold won the day before by Canada's women's coxless four and world champions Marnie McBean and Kathleen Heddle in the coxless pair. The Canadian anthem was becoming the most popular song at Lake of Banyoles.

But now, all eyes on that golden pond were on Silken. Most people had doubted that she would even be able to compete, never mind make the final. But there she was, a shattered leg but an unbroken spirit, looking to do the unthinkable.

The crowd on the banks of the lake that day was coloured completely red and white, hundreds of Canadians waving flags and boisterously cheering every stroke Silken took. In the end, that support would help push Laumann all the way to the finish line, where she finished third.

With my cameraman in tow, I scrambled down to the landing dock, where I was about to do a live interview with Canada's newest bronze medallist. In retrospect, I really wish we had waited a few more minutes, because when I got there, Silken looked like she was ready to collapse. Her body was shaking; her damaged leg was quivering; and she could hardly breathe, never mind talk. She honestly looked like a living skeleton.

But with amazing grace, she did the interview, proud of what she had accomplished against all odds. She didn't win the race, but it didn't matter; this was one of the gutsiest performances in Olympic history, and I was so glad that I was there to see it live. I think I was more choked up than she was.

Silken's bronze medal victory—yes, you can *win* a bronze—was destined to be a made-for-TV movie a couple of years down the road, but the climax of her odyssey at the '92 Games was her selection as the Canadian flag bearer at the closing ceremonies.

She wasn't the only one who could have carried the Maple Leaf.

No one had to endure more heartache in Barcelona than synchronized swimmer Sylvie Fréchette, whose fiancé took his own life only a week before the Games. Devastated, Fréchette decided to carry on and still compete while grieving this sudden loss.

One of the favourites going into the Olympics, Sylvie was somehow able to compartmentalize her emotions and swim beautifully, only to be the victim of a judge's error—they accidentally input a lower score, which ultimately cost Fréchette the gold medal. She finished second to American Kristen Babb-Sprague. The Canadian public and media were outraged by the controversy, and you could feel it from all the way across the Atlantic.

When Fréchette joined us in studio after the medal ceremony, it was obvious she was still struggling with her entire ordeal. Graciously, she managed a slight smile as she fought through her tears, but you could tell she was gutted. If you didn't feel her pain, you didn't have a heartbeat, and I know how hard it was for all of us to hold it together. This was one of those stories that just didn't seem to have a happy ending. The silver medal was hardly a silver lining.

The Canadian Olympic Committee kept fighting on her behalf, and over a year later, after a number of appeals, the International Olympic Committee admitted that an error had been made, reversed its decision, and decided to award both Fréchette and Babb-Sprague gold medals.

Sylvie would receive her gold medal at a special ceremony in the famed Montreal Forum in front of thousands of adoring Canadian fans. There were some more tears in the building that day, but there were also many more smiles than we saw in Barcelona.

Sometimes it takes time for a happy ending. That's something you learn at the Olympics the hard way. No matter what you think, what you plan, the only thing you can expect is the unexpected. That was certainly the theme in Barcelona, especially for a rookie Olympic host who was getting his fill of unforgettable moments.

Like midway through the Games, when my producer, John Shannon, and I were killing some time, walking around the International Broadcast Centre before bumping into world heavyweight boxing champion Evander Holyfield, who was making a special visit to the IBC and was in line at the ice cream stand.

"Let's get him to come in to our studio for an interview," I told John, who laughed but didn't seem too convinced it was going to happen.

So, I did what any hard-working, respected journalist would do—I walked right up to him, introduced myself, and bribed him by buying him an ice cream cone.

The Holyfield interview in our studio was one of the highlights of our broadcast.

Yep, anything can and generally will happen at the Olympics.

And of course, the number-one rule: You can't write endings before the competition begins. Otherwise, Ben Johnson's comeback story would have been considerably different.

All the hysteria about Ben's return percolated to a boiling point when he got into his crouch in the men's 100-metre semifinal. Only Ben knew what he was thinking, but I'm sure it wasn't what was going to happen next. Maybe it was four years of rust. Maybe it was the self-doubt. Maybe it was the Olympic gods. But Johnson stumbled out of the blocks, never regained his speed, and finished last. Gone was the hype. Gone was the bravado. Gone was the comeback story.

No happy ending: The Olympic dream was dead.

Two years later, the Olympic dream was rekindled in the unlikeliest of places. The 1994 Winter Games in Lillehammer, Norway, was the most charming Olympics I have ever been to. Having a chance to host in Lillehammer was a magical experience. It was a tiny little town of just over twenty thousand people, located in the Norwegian mountains. The hockey rink was built into a cave in the mountains; it was like something out of a James Bond movie. I also a had a front-row seat for the Tonya Harding–Nancy Kerrigan saga as it played out. I spent a great amount of time covering figure skating. (That year, figure skating drew a lot of viewers, and a lot of male viewers.)

At that time, Canada didn't win a lot of medals at the Olympics, but in 1994, Myriam Bédard won two gold medals in biathlon and Jean-Luc Brassard won a gold medal in freestyle skiing. Despite all of that, all eyes were on the figure skating rink. Going into the 1994 Winter Games, everyone thought Canada's Kurt Browning was going to win gold, and there was a chance we could win a medal in pairs.

I was also a host for CTV at those Games, and producer John Shannon came up with the great idea for me to host from the venues of each day's big events. I would co-host with Valerie Pringle in the morning in our studio, then we would drive to the event I was hosting live. My wingman for the rides was Dave Toms, one of our writers and also our driver at the time. My future wife, Nancy, was there with me. Often, it was Nancy, Lloyd Robertson, and I who would end up being driven home after the day events. A big man with a big personality, Dave was always playing the Eagles and singing along to "New Kid in Town" or "Take It to the Limit." We would giggle in the back seat, listening to him sing. We were on a Norwegian mountain, driving back from an event, and Lloyd was sitting in the front seat with Dave. Lloyd, the dean of Canadian newscasters, in his deep baritone voice, would be singing along to "Peaceful Easy Feeling"!

One night, we had to pull over so I could take a pee by the side of a snowy mountain road. I was standing there alongside Lloyd and Dave. Dave was smoking a joint, and we all looked up, and the Northern Lights were dancing over top of us as we relieved ourselves. We took it to the limit that night.

Because of this concept of hosting from the event venue, I was rinkside the day of the women's figure skating final. Debbi Wilkes and Brian Orser were calling figure skating, and I was hosting and would do the interviews. So, I was standing right beside the boards. When Harding came out to skate, she was in the warm-up before the main competition. She broke her skate lace, and then she started crying. She skated over to where I was standing by the boards, sobbing, and looked at me as if I were an official. Tonya asked, "What do I do? What do I do?" Over and over again. She put her broken skate up on the boards to show me the problem. The delay that was needed to fix Harding's skate went on so long that it really affected Canada's Josée Chouinard, who had to skate next.

Kerrigan skated beautifully, but Ukraine's Oksana Baiul ended up winning the gold medal. I was standing in the kiss and cry area, waiting for the medal ceremony. Kerrigan walked over to me and, in her thick Boston accent, said, "What is going on?" Nancy Kerrigan was tougher than Tonya Harding. She had an inner fire about her, and a potty mouth to boot. I told her we were waiting for Oksana to put her makeup on. Nancy looked at me. "Oh, who cares? She is going to come out here and cry anyway!" My mic was hot, and it picked up everything she said. I got home two days later, and I was watching *Entertainment Tonight*. The headline was "The Bloom Is Off the Ice Princess." They were talking about Nancy Kerrigan and what she had said to me at the Olympics!

One of Canada's great hopes going into the Games was figure skater Kurt Browning. He had won the gold medal at the world championships in 1993 and was one of the most popular athletes in Canada at the time. However, Kurt was not at his best in Lillehammer, and he ended up in fifth place. People were upset with me because of my interview with him. He was very emotional after his routine, and viewers were irate because they said that I made him cry.

Figure skating fans get upset when someone cries. And Browning started crying. Everyone thought this took place right after his skate, but if you looked behind us, you'd see the arena was empty. The interview took place thirty minutes after his skate ended. Yet people say I am the guy who made Kurt Browning cry. All I said was, "What happened?"

Kurt later told me: "You didn't make me cry. I was crying already." That was a good lesson in broadcasting. Looking back, would I have done anything differently in that moment? No. I asked him the question that everyone wanted to know about. Athletes are not robots, and sports can be emotional. Sometimes you have it, sometimes you don't. And when you don't, you have to find a way to explain what went wrong. To this day, I consider Kurt and me to be good friends. I don't see him as much as I once did. We only share tears now when they are tears of laughter.

Kurt Browning was a showman, and Elvis Stojko was more intense—he was a gladiator. Back then, the two didn't like each other, and neither did their respective camps. I liked Elvis because he brought rock and roll to figure skating. During the lead-up to the 1994 Winter Games, I covered one of the most electric skating events ever in Edmonton: the National Championships. This was basically Kurt's backyard, and the Northlands Coliseum was jammed to the rafters. It was Elvis against Kurt, and the atmosphere in the building honestly had a WrestleMania feel to it. Everyone in Canada was transfixed, watching that event. That men's final had better ratings than *Hockey Night in Canada*. It marked a changing of the guard in Canadian figure skating. Kurt, shockingly, missed a critical element and was fourth after the short program. And even though he had a phenomenal free skate, to music from the movie *Casablanca*, he would relinquish his Canadian title to the new king, Elvis Stojko.

This was all a precursor to what would happen in Lillehammer, where, once again, Elvis outskated Kurt and went on to win a silver medal. However, I, along with many others, was convinced that Stojko had beaten the gold medallist, Alexei Urmanov of Russia. My suspicions were confirmed when I later heard rumblings from Skate Canada that someone had come up to Elvis the night before the final skate and said to him, "I'm so sorry, Elvis." Because a deal had been made with the judges.

Can you believe that? I was so upset—it felt like pro wrestling. The judges didn't make any money, but they loved being around the sport, and they knew that their future travel plans all depended on them staying on as a judge.

In 1996, I reported for CTV News at the Atlanta Summer Games. The night of the bombing in the Centennial Olympic Park, I was at the Madison Pub in Toronto when I got a call. They asked me, "Can you get down to Atlanta?" I said yes, and the next day I was reporting on the bombing. I stayed there and did reports for the network. Because CTV didn't have rights to the Games, I went on the rooftop of our hotel and brought on medal winners and interviewed them. One of them was Donovan Bailey after his historic gold medal win in the men's 100 metres. With my first words to Donovan, I reminded him about the time a few years earlier when he'd told me that one day, he would be the fastest man in the world. And he wasn't finished. Days later, he won his second gold medal in the men's 4 x 100 metre relay. In a span of a week, Donovan erased the stain of the Seoul steroid scandal and became a new Canadian hero.

The 2010 Winter Olympics were held in Vancouver, and I was part of the TSN/Sportsnet Olympic consortium. I ended up calling figure skating and short-track speed skating. I went from the art and grace of figure skating to short-track speed skating. The stories from the 2010 Games were incredible. Canadian skater Joannie Rochette's mother died just after arriving at the Winter Games, and Joannie still competed. I loved the way she was as a skater, and as an athlete. Her whole story was heartbreaking. I worked with a variety of colour analysts for the figure skating coverage. Jennifer Robinson and Elizabeth Manley were my on-air partners for women's figure skating. Liz told amazing stories about her time at the 1988 Olympics, while Jennifer was broadcasting for the very first time. Jennifer did a terrific job. It is even more impressive when you consider that, months earlier, she became a mother for the first time. She was worried about her kid, whom her family took care of back home while she was working. I will never forget the one night when we were about to go on air and Jennifer said to me, "Oh my God, I am lactating." Because motherhood, like live TV, waits for no one. I just loved working with her.

When Joannie Rochette skated, she looked sad at her first practice. All eyes were on her in Vancouver. She caught our attention in her warm-up and nodded to me, as if to say she was okay. She went out there and was remarkable. When she finished her free skate, the crowd rose as one and showered the ice with more stuffed animals than you would find at a carnival midway. Everyone in the broadcast booth was crying as we watched her win a bronze medal. After a long pause, with a huge lump in my throat, the only words I could find were these: "One of the bravest young ladies you will ever meet. And under the circumstances, one of the greatest skates you will ever see." It still brings tears to my eyes. Patrick Chan was Canada's star in the men's event but finished off the podium. Then, in ice dance, we had Tessa Virtue and Scott Moir. I had covered Tessa and Scott since they were seven and nine years old, respectively. The first time I saw them skate, I had a feeling they would be stars someday. As a matter of fact, on the air, I said, "These two got it; they could be World Champions someday." I got to know them well over the course of their career. They went everywhere to get better every year. Their skate in 2010 was magic. When they won the gold medal, it was incredible. No Canadians had ever won the Olympic gold medal in ice dance. After the Sidney Crosby golden goal, this was the highlight of the 2010 Winter Olympics in Vancouver. The gold became shinier after the Olympics as Tessa and Scott appeared on a number of TV shows and were special guests on *The Ellen DeGeneres Show*. To see Tessa and Scott win that gold felt close to watching the Blue Jays win in 1992 and 1993.

The 2010 Winter Olympics was one of the first times people were really proud to be Canadian. We all pumped out our chests with pride. Everything about the experience was special. It was also special for me personally because Tyler and Brody, our two oldest boys, were ten and eight and they were there with me. My wife, Nancy, was also there. Balancing work and a growing family can be tough, especially since I travelled so much for work. That is why it meant everything to me to have them there with me. Tyler and Brody ended up seeing so many events while I was working. Sports is the one thing that is unscripted. But if you had to script a Winter Olympics, you could not have done it any better than Vancouver. That experience was a major inspiration for both boys to excel at sports. One of my favourite photos from the 2010 Vancouver Olympics is of me and my two boys on the ice after the gold medal ceremony. The funny thing is, neither one of them understood how special that was. They thought every kid got to do that!

At the 2012 Summer Olympics in London, England, I called artistic and rhythmic gymnastics with gold medallist Kyle Shewfelt. Canada is not a superpower in gymnastics, and I gained a whole new appreciation for the sport. I ended up calling Rosie MacLennan's gold medal win in trampoline gymnastics. The pride of King City, Ontario, Rosie won Canada's only gold medal in London. And, thanks to Rosie, a lot of young Canadians got into trampoline.

All of which leads me back to my problem with network television in Canada: their lack of coverage of amateur sports. Canadians should have known all about Rosie MacLennan before the start of the Olympics. However, during the year leading up to the Olympics, the CBC and CTV covered hardly any of the events. That really bothers me. The

CBC has all this time on Saturday afternoons to air amateur sports in Canada. However, they often end up airing American programming or professional sports. TSN and Sportsnet are equally guilty of it. Canadian broadcasters don't do a good enough job of covering and reporting on amateur sports. Say what you want about the United States, but their amateur athletes are covered locally and nationally. As Canadian broadcasters, we don't do that. In Canada, we often only hear about great athletes for the first time when they do something special at a major event. That should never happen; we have the talent and the resources to do so much better. I hope someday we will.

8

LIFE AT CTV SPORTS

AFTER I GOT TO CTV, I WAS ON THE FAST TRACK, GOING FROM SPORT TO SPORT. I soon found out that life at CTV Sports in the 1990s was a source of many stories you just couldn't make up. It was crazy the lengths that they would go to so we could shoot openings to taped events. Events that we would voice back in the Toronto studio.

I flew to the Austrian Alps to shoot a twenty-second on-camera report for a ski-jumping event. I flew to Aspen, Colorado, for a downhill on camera. I flew to Moscow to interview a coach. The most mind-boggling trip of all was when an international broadcaster sent me to Egypt for twenty-four hours to shoot an opening for a squash exhibition in front of the Pyramids. Tracy Wilson and I would go to figure skating events to do the on-camera so that we had the background, then we would fly back to Toronto and announce the event from the studio. They spent so much money on us to do all of these things—it was unreal. Some of the events, like the squash tournament in Cairo, were not that big. I did what I was told, no questions asked, and I went wherever they asked me to go. Even though they were not big events, they were backed by generous sponsors.

The new CTV Sports era was exciting. But also very challenging. Johnny Esaw had bought the Canadian rights to *Wide World of Sports* from ABC. In the early 1990s the network decided to rename it *CTV Sports Presents*. They tried to make it like *CBC Sportsweekend*, but we didn't have many live properties. I would cover tennis, golf, and the Blue Jays, but these live events didn't take place every week, whereas every Saturday we had a show. So, I would throw to everything from ringette to Formula Atlantic motorsports. I once threw to a lawn bowling event that was two years old! We had to pretend it was live, and we would give updated scores—during an event that took place two years earlier. During breaks, we would update live events that were taking place at the time. Then it was back to the Canadian national lawn bowling championship, or cricket, or whatever we had. It was all pre-recorded, and it was all on two-inch tape. It was a crazy time.

I once hosted a golf event, the Du Maurier Classic in Edmonton. If it rained, we would have to find some way to fill the two-hour block of time. What we did that year was what everyone in that era who covered golf would do during a rain delay—we decided to replay the tournament from the year before. Lo and behold, I threw to the fourth-round coverage of the previous year's event. As I watched the tape roll, I noticed that it also started to rain the year before! The whole thing was like a circus. One of the TV sports columnists called us out for throwing to a rain delay during a rain delay. We deserved to take heat for that one.

TENNIS

I loved doing tennis, spending time in the booth with legends like Virginia Wade and Tracy Austin, and occasionally having a chance to work with John McEnroe and his brother Patrick. I also worked with Peter Burwash, who was not only a tennis analyst but a motivational speaker as well.

Calling tennis was a lot like figure skating: We would let the play breathe. They were long days. We would start broadcasting in the morning at nine and wouldn't finish until around midnight. I was lucky enough to call matches featuring Pete Sampras, Andre Agassi, and a rookie named Roger Federer. I was also able to call Monica Seles's triumphant return to tennis after she recovered from her on-court stabbing attack. When I was at CTV, we would only call the finals. When I was with TSN, we would call the matches during the week, as the finals were on Sportsnet.

In August 2003, a huge blackout hit southern Ontario in the middle of the women's Canadian Open in Toronto. We had a two-hour break during the broadcast, and my wife was up north. I lived a twenty-minute drive from the tennis stadium, so I figured I had time to go home and let the dog out. As I drove, there was a massive traffic jam, and it took me almost an hour to get home. As I discovered, the power was out everywhere, and I naturally thought the event was cancelled for the rest of the day. Still, I made my way back to the tennis centre at six o'clock, and the traffic was getting worse. We were scheduled to be back on the air at seven, and I honestly felt that with the city in darkness, there was no chance of anyone playing that evening. But as I was on the way there, my producer called me and said we were on. It was the only place with a generator. Everything else in the city was cancelled, but the tennis was still on. I arrived five minutes before the start of the broadcast. We went back on the air, and it was haunting. Hardly any people were in the stands, and we were the only place with lights on. You would look out from the stadium and there was nothing but blackness everywhere. It was a freaky experience—like a scene out of a zombie movie. All I could think, while sitting beside my analyst Mary Carillo, was that people are playing, we are broadcasting, and nobody is watching. Ratings are not going to be very good tonight.

One of the things that I liked best about covering tennis is that I would arrive early and hit balls with someone like Virginia Wade. Here I was, a kid from a working-class family in Winnipeg, hitting balls with a tennis legend like it is no big deal. I have never been around such an elite sport as tennis. Everyone wore expensive clothes and watches, and the food was great. I would be sitting there and eating lunch with Pete Sampras or Boris Becker. *Man*, I thought, *this might be the best gig yet*.

There were only a few reporters who covered tennis on a regular basis, and I got to know them. I wasn't a big fan of some of the press who covered sports. I find it funny; it has been my experience that most TV people can write. However, not all writers can be broadcasters—that is the difference. Even so, writers often looked down on us broadcasters and slagged us. There were some writers I really enjoyed, especially the veteran ones. I got to become close with Michael Farber, Jim Hunt, Rick Fraser, Bob Elliott, and Dave Perkins, who I adore. I loved to talk with Rosie DiManno because she had an edge. I would run into her at skating events. Long-time sports writer Steve Milton also covered figure skating. Rosie and Steve treated figure skating as a sport, and they loved it. Until, of course, the inevitable scandal. When they were not afraid to bring out the knives. Truth be told, most writers and broadcasters rarely share late-night beers together. Different deadlines, and different worlds. But on the rare night we did get together, we all realized that we were chasing the same thing. Telling stories, covering games, and getting paid. We just did it under brighter lights and with a little more makeup.

MOTORSPORTS

I love life in the fast lane, and I gained an appreciation for auto racing when I covered the Formula Atlantic series. CTV sent me to different races, where I would do cut-ins during commercial breaks and then post-race coverage. I hosted the Indianapolis 500 in 1994 when Canadian Scott Goodyear finished second to Al Unser Jr. by 0.043 seconds. I got to know Jacques Villeneuve really well. I was there in 1995 when he won the famous Indy 500. I followed Jacques's career and watched him inspire a new generation of Canadian drivers, including Greg Moore and Paul Tracy, two very different people. And Greg Moore, rest his soul, one of the great people I met in sports. Greg tragically lost his life in a crash in 1999. Paul Tracy was so aggressive behind the wheel; he treated auto racing like a hockey game. I even got a chance to drive a Formula race car at the Mont Tremblant track one day. That is when I learned how talented drivers are. Driving a race car is dangerous work. I thought I was flying. But after watching the video, someone on a bicycle could have beaten me! That experience, like my job at CTV Sports, was still an unforgettable ride.

This was all because of CTV having the *Wide World of Sports* franchise in Canada. I'd taken over Johnny Esaw's job as the host every Saturday. Esaw was a legendary broadcaster, and one of the most notorious dealmakers in the history of Canadian television. Johnny would cut deals that were written on a napkin. Remember that years-old lawn bowling event we covered? We had all sorts of sponsorship deals Johnny had cut, so we were obligated to run those taped events. I would shake my head sometimes to think of it. You name the sport, we aired it—even obscure sports like Irish hurling. It was a steep learning curve for all of us.

ROD BALL

It's a question that I get asked often: What is your favourite sport?

Good question, and not an easy one to answer, especially considering I've called almost every sport known to man, with the exception of dodgeball and darts. (Then again, if CTV had secured sponsorship, I'm sure we would have broadcast anything, including rock paper scissors.)

But seriously, my answer to that question is usually that my favourite sport is whatever the next day brings. That response always elicits a laugh or a raised eyebrow, but trust me, it's not a cop-out. The truth is that I honestly love covering any sport, any game, any event on any given day.

So, I guess that means that of all of the sports I cover—they are all tied for first.

Now, if someone were to ask me what sport I'm most *passionate* about? Then my answer would unequivocally be baseball. It's a game I've had a love affair with since my boyhood days in Winnipeg, watching my heroes like Pete Rose, Johnny Bench, Reggie Jackson, and Rod Carew (who earned my affection through our shared first name).

I also grew up watching and loving Canada's team at the time, the Montreal Expos, whose minor-league franchise actually played in Winnipeg, as the Whips, in the early 1970s. I went to many of those games, and like most kids, I was more interested in chasing down foul balls than watching any of the action. Still, getting a chance to see the Whips up close further deepened my budding romance with baseball.

The Expos weren't contenders at the time, but they were fun to watch despite the fact that you could watch them only once a week, every Saturday on CBC. That's when players like Rusty Staub, Steve Rogers, Andre Dawson, and "The Kid," Gary Carter, were making names for themselves and becoming all-stars. Little did the Expos know the impact they were having on impressionable kids across Canada who had big-league dreams.

I was one of those kids.

During the summers, I played from sun-up until sundown, competing on the local community teams, the city all-star teams, and even a senior semi-pro league while working at CKY. If there was a game scheduled on a night I was working, I would prepare my scripts and highlights in short order, quickly hustle to the local diamond, play as many innings as I could, and then race back to the studio to deliver the late-night sports.

It was often quite comical, especially if I was running late. I pushed into scramble mode, forcing me to throw my jacket, dress shirt, and tie over my dirty, muddy baseball uniform. Even funnier, I sometimes kept my metal cleats on, which would make a lot of noise on my way into the studio. It was never a problem until one memorable night when I scurried onto the set, hit a wet patch, and took a flying tumble only seconds before going live to air. I jumped back up as though nothing had happened, delivered my segment without a flaw, and then sheepishly returned to my desk with a huge bruise on my ass.

That was the second-worst baseball injury I ever had.

Number one on the hit list was the time I got too close to a centrefield wall in Grosse Isle, Manitoba, which is about thirty minutes north of Winnipeg. I was playing for my senior team, the Blue Jays, when I experienced my worst sports moment.

We were playing in the opener of a tournament early on a Saturday morning in July. I had the weekend off from my TV duties, which meant I could devote my entire time to playing a bunch of games without having to worry about sprinting back to the studio. I was so excited for a full two days of high-level tournament ball with my buddies, many of whom were former pro hockey players.

I remember jogging out to my position, thinking how perfect the day was—a spectacular summer morning on this Field of Dreams carved immaculately into some Manitoba farmland. I got a quick stretch in, adjusted my glove and cap, and focused in as the opening pitch was delivered and immediately smashed towards me in centre field.

The ball was scorched, sailing over my head as I sprinted back towards the chain-link fence.

"You got room! You got room!" shouted my left fielder, a newbie to the team. I shouldn't have listened to that moron. In full stride, I lunged into the air as the ball hit my glove—and I crashed through the fence!

I don't remember much after that, except the hole in the chain-link and the look of concern on the face of my right fielder, former NHL tough guy Daryl Stanley, who hovered over my prone body.

"Oh boy, Rod," Daryl said, his voice shaking. "You better stay down."

I loved Daryl—great guy who, after hockey season, always came home to play baseball with the local team. He was as cool a dude as they come, but at that moment, Daryl wasn't exactly the epitome of comforting.

He was right, though. I needed to stay down. My face was all cut up, blood gushing all over the place, my jaw felt like it was broken, and I wasn't quite sure what day it was.

Worst of all, I looked down at my glove and the ball wasn't there. Shit. I didn't make the catch.

So, just one pitch into my much-anticipated all-baseball weekend,

I was headed for the hospital. I spent the day there, getting stitched up, licking my wounds, and most of all, being jolted by a serious reality check.

The biggest thing that popped in my head—besides metal chain-link—was the undeniable fact that I was making a living, working on television, where people actually see your face: a face that shouldn't look like it was to appear in the next *Halloween* movie.

The only thing hurting me worse than my jaw was the inescapable truth that my competitive days of semi-elite baseball were, unfortunately, over.

But that didn't mean I was done with a team called the Blue Jays.

When I left Winnipeg for Toronto, one of the big assignments that CTV threw at me was an opportunity to host the national broadcasts of Toronto Blue Jays games. Wow, another dream job. I was so excited, I would have run through a wall—oh, wait, never mind.

The Blue Jays, sharing the national stage with the Expos, had quickly become a contending team and had developed a huge nationwide audience. Their games were broadcast across the country on the CTV network twice a week, Wednesdays and Saturdays, and I was responsible for opening the show, setting the stage, and then appearing in the middle of the fifth and seventh innings with a sports update sponsored by Coca-Cola, showing highlights and scores of other games. It was a great gig with huge visibility, and while I was on air for only a few minutes every game, it was not an assignment I took lightly.

What was even better, the Blue Jays weren't just a good team—they were becoming a great team, especially after making the biggest trade in franchise history on December 5, 1990. I had just started my new job in Toronto when I reported the news that the Jays had traded perennial all-star Tony Fernández and future Hall of Famer Fred McGriff to San Diego in exchange for young, slick second baseman Roberto Alomar and slugging outfielder Joe Carter. It was a blockbuster trade that would reshape the Blue Jays' fortunes for years to come.

I got a chance to meet the newest Jays when I went to my first spring training camp a few months later in Dunedin, Florida, which was another eye-opening experience. Just when I thought this job couldn't get any better, covering spring training was like nothing I could imagine.

The days were gruelling: Wake up in a beachside hotel, head to the stadium to do some interviews, take in the afternoon ball game, do a couple of post-game interviews, and then, in mid-afternoon, hit the golf course for a quick nine before wrapping up a hard-working day with happy hour and a nice dinner. The most difficult decision I had all day was whether to use a 25 or 50 SPF for my sunscreen. If any reporter complained to me about the grind of reporting from spring training, I immediately wanted to kick them in the shins.

How could you not love this job? How could you not love this game? And how could you not love covering this team?

The Jays were loaded. A team full of studs.

Both new acquisitions were great to deal with. Alomar was more soft-spoken but always available, while Carter was friendly, loud, and ultraconfident. Even in spring training, you got a sense that these two guys were going to make a big difference—and they did. Joe and Robbie made an immediate impact, and both represented the Jays at the 1991 All-Star Game, which was coincidentally played in Toronto, giving the city a chance to show off its spectacular SkyDome, the world's first stadium with a fully retractable roof.

I hosted the Canadian broadcast of the All-Star Game, which was carried on the CTV network, and I was as stoked as a kid making his first visit to Disney World or, maybe even better, Cooperstown.

I thought I had died and gone to baseball heaven.

All of the stars of the game, present and past, seemed to be in

Toronto, including legends Joe DiMaggio and Ted Williams, whom I had chance to chat with before they took to the field to be honoured for the fiftieth anniversary of their magical 1941 seasons. I had goosebumps as I shook their hands, knowing what those hands had accomplished five decades earlier—the Yankee Clipper with an incredible fifty-six-game hit streak and the Splendid Splinter being the last player to hit over .400 in a season. To me, these weren't baseball players, they were gods.

As thrilled as I was, I was even more excited for my parents, who had come into town for the festivities and were having a blast. I was already on the air, but I glanced down from my host location and smiled as I saw something I had never seen before from my mom and dad. For all of the games that they had taken me to, for all the times they let me and my brothers enjoy special sports moments, this was the first time I saw them cheer for someone they had worshipped. And so, there they were, Bonnie and Jack, on their feet, wildly applauding two stars from their generation. It was beautiful. My parents looked like kids again.

The ovation for DiMaggio and Williams was thunderous, but it wasn't as loud or as long as it was for the hometown contingent, those Blue Jays who were selected as all-stars. Manager Cito Gaston was named as one of the coaches and waved his cap to the adoring crowd. Alomar, the starting second basemen, received a deafening introduction as he ran out of the dugout, but the comedic moment came when Carter was announced while the camera was on Jays pitcher Jimmy Key, who was in the wrong spot on the third-base line. The crowd roared anyway while Carter stood bemused with his arms crossed. It was a little uncomfortable, but it was funny, and both Jimmy and Joe eventually broke into big smiles, soaking in the slightly embarrassing spotlight.

The craziest thing was that, had any of us been able to peek into the future, no one—and I mean no one—would have upstaged or forgotten about Joe Carter.

Despite that botched introduction, Toronto's All-Star Game was spectacular, emotional, and historic. It was a broadcaster's delight.

The mid-season classic played out like a midsummer night's dream, and all the stars and stories were colliding.

Baseball's all-time home-run leader, Hank Aaron, was introduced as an honorary captain alongside Rod Carew, who was only few weeks away from being inducted into the Hall of Fame with Chatham, Ontario's Ferguson Jenkins, who was about to become Canada's first inductee into Cooperstown. Fergie, a former Cy Young Award winner, got a hero's welcome when, appropriately, he threw out the first pitch.

Watching with pride, Williams and DiMaggio also became part of the game's plot line, linking past and present as baseball always seems to do masterfully.

Robbie and Sandy Alomar Jr. became the first brothers to play in an All-Star Game together since Joe and his brother Dom DiMaggio back in 1949. The Alomars also became the first brothers ever to be voted into an All-Star Game by the fans.

Meanwhile, Carlton Fisk, at forty-three years old, became the oldest player to record a hit in the game, taking the torch from—you guessed it—Ted Williams, who was forty-one when he got an All-Star Game hit in 1960.

From first pitch to last out, the night was electric, and taking in all the action were Canadian Prime Minister Brian Mulroney and US President George H. W. Bush, who we interviewed during the broadcast. President Bush, a former baseball star at Yale and a huge fan, wasn't the only Bush in attendance. So was his son, George W.—the owner of the Texas Rangers—who I had a chance to interview during the All-Star Game workouts.

Maybe I caught him at the wrong moment, but W, who was on the path to follow in his dad's presidential footsteps, didn't seem that well versed on the city of Toronto or the country of Canada. He mangled some names and almost forgot where he was. Fortunately, the interview was on tape, and we decided not to use it, which was a good thing for everyone. I thanked the Rangers' owner for his time, and as I walked away, I remember telling my cameraman, "That guy might own a baseball team, but he's as dumb as a bag of hammers."

That opinion changed the next day, when I bumped into him in the bowels of SkyDome and he apologized for his poor responses, saying he was distracted and had a difficult time hearing all of my questions through the noise of the crowd.

I told him no worries and added that we didn't use the interview anyway. "That's why we love you Canadians, son," the future president said with a wry smile and walked away.

The game didn't disappoint. Blue Jay Jimmy Key got the win; Joe Carter got a hit and scored a run as the American League defeated the National League, 4–2. The biggest story, beyond Toronto's celebration, however, was Baltimore Orioles superstar Cal Ripken Jr. Cal had won the home-run derby the day before and followed it up by hitting another homer in the actual game to earn MVP honours.

I hustled down to interview Cal post-game and was struck by his calmness and humility. Most players would have been emotional in the spotlight, but not Ripken. This just seemed like another day in his life, another game, another highlight in the terrific season he was having. He was a true gentleman and, as it would play out, a future Hall of Famer. I didn't know it at the time, but here I was, standing in the locker room with a guy who, five years later, would break a record no one thought would be touched: Lou Gehrig's "iron man" streak for most consecutive games played.

For a young TV guy from Winnipeg who had dreamed about being in the big leagues, that whole night could not have been any cooler. How lucky was I to be hanging around with all of my baseball heroes?

From Mr. 56 to Mr. .400 to this ordinary dude who someday would become Mr. 2,632, I really needed to pinch myself.

But I was able to keep it together. I didn't freeze, didn't ask for any autographs, and didn't drool on anyone. That '91 All-Star Game was the best icebreaker a rookie baseball broadcaster could ever experience. It was an intimidating eye-opener, but I knew that this was a place I belonged, and if I wanted to have success in the boys-of-summer club, I would need to take a page out of Cal Ripken's book: Don't get too high, don't get too low, and show up every day ready to play.

And so, that became my approach, and for the most part it worked—except for one game that season that I almost didn't make.

It was in late July, and the Jays had an afternoon game in Chicago. We had a telecast scheduled to start at 1:30 p.m., which was not an issue except that I had to make a network appearance early in the morning at Lionhead Golf Club in Brampton for an upcoming televised skins game that would feature Canadian Dave Barr, Fuzzy Zoeller, Peter Jacobson, and the "King," Arnold Palmer.

I knew it was going to be a busy day with a lot of moving parts, but I was more than confident that our golf crew could get all of our feature and preparatory work done before I had to leave the course, which was around a forty-five-minute drive to the downtown CTV studio.

Things were going as smooth as Arnie's swing until we lost complete track of time. That's when my colleague, Canadian women's golf legend Sandra Post, looked at her watch and remarked that I should really think about hitting the road, since it was already 11:30 a.m.

She was right. But no problem, I thought, as I hurried to my car, realizing that I still had plenty of time and conservatively should get into the studio by 12:30, an hour before the first pitch. Another built-in bonus was that I was not part of the opening of the broadcast that day, so I really wasn't required until the middle of the fifth inning. Lots of time.

Except traffic, as it normally is in Toronto, was brutal.

I was cruising along nicely until I hit Lake Shore Boulevard, which was at a complete standstill. I looked at my watch. It was slightly before noon, but no worries, I thought. I was only another twenty minutes or so from the studio and still really wasn't needed for a couple of hours.

Thirty minutes later, after moving approximately five feet, my mindset was changing considerably. Making matters worse was that mobile phones weren't quite what they are now. I had one of those big, clunky in-car cell boxes, and after my calls to our control room had dropped a number of times, I was finally able to touch base with my producer and explain the situation.

"I'm stuck in traffic," I yelled into the phone. "But don't worry—I will be there. Looks like it's clearing up."

I couldn't have been more wrong. Glaciers moved faster.

I was pounding my steering wheel as I turned on the radio to listen to the Jays pre-game show with the voices of the dynamic duo, Tom Cheek and Jerry Howarth. Not only was I not moving, but I was running out of gas.

The radio broadcast started with Jerry's familiar "Hello, friends," and my bulky phone rang.

"Are you close?" pleaded my producer.

"Yep, getting through. I'm real close," I lied through gritted teeth.

Now I was really starting to panic. The only thing fading faster than my fuel gauge was my confidence. Even more troubling, the game was clipping along at a bullet pace, with both pitchers wasting no time as they threw clean innings.

It was the top of the second inning when I decided I had to make a move. Desperate times call for desperate measures. I pulled over to the shoulder of the road, got out of the car still wearing my golf clothes, grabbed my suit, which was on a hanger, and then dashed through the maze of cars. People were probably wondering where this nutbar had come from and where he was going.

I clumsily hurdled the concrete barrier and then, like a scene out of Tom Cruise's *Mission: Impossible*, I had to dodge the traffic going full speed the other way to make it across the road. I vaulted over another cement wall, continuing my sprint uphill for another kilometre until I hit a major intersection, where I was fortunate enough to be able to hail a taxi.

Breathlessly, I asked the cab driver to get me to CTV at 42 Charles Street East as fast as he could, and could he also please turn on the radio. Unfortunately, in my haste to escape, I'd left my phone in the car, so I had no chance to communicate with the control room—which, I was certain at this point, was sending out an APB.

The driver tuned in the radio and turned up the volume, and my mood worsened. It was now the bottom of the third inning.

I'm toast, I thought. *I'm not going to make it.*

But my cabbie, realizing my urgency—not to mention the sweat pouring onto his back seat—set a land speed record and got me to the front of the building just as the radio broadcast was breaking away before the start of the bottom of the fourth. I wanted to hug the guy, but he was probably happier with the hundred-dollar bill I gave him, since I had no time to get change.

I flew into the building, ripped past the security guard, took the elevator up to the fifth floor, towelled myself off, hurriedly threw on my shirt, tie, and jacket, got a quick powder from the makeup artist, and then brashly walked into the studio in the top of the fifth inning—still wearing my shorts and golf spikes. I sat down, put my earpiece in, and heard exactly what I expected to hear.

"Holy fuck, man," my bellicose producer bellowed. "You know how to give a guy a heart attack."

I don't think he realized I was closer to a cardiac arrest than he was, but I nonchalantly put my hands in the air, looked into the camera, smiled, and mouthed one word: "What?"

When we finished our updates and post-game show, which surprisingly went off without a hitch, I knew I had some explaining to do. I apologized to the producer and crew for putting everyone in a precarious position, but after I'd relayed the details of the entire escapade, they all understood it was an extraordinary situation, and they couldn't believe I'd actually pulled it off.

Craziest thing of all is that around 6 p.m., when I returned to the Lake Shore, fully expecting my car to have been towed away, there she was, still on the shoulder, middle of rush hour—no tickets, no damage, just waiting for me to take her home.

Thankfully, I didn't have any more traffic jams or panic attacks that season. The broadcasts went well, and the Blue Jays were humming along like a major championship contender, finishing with ninety-one wins in the '91 season. They made it to the playoffs—which, unlike today's era, didn't feature wild card or divisional series. The math was pretty simple: You had to finish first in your division to make it to the post-season. Two winners in each league. The best in the East vs. the best of the West. Winners meet in the World Series.

I hosted the playoff games on CTV and, just as I did with the All-Star Game spectacle, felt so lucky to be part of something so meaningful, not only to Toronto but to an entire country.

Carrying the weight of huge expectations, the Jays split the first two games of the American League Championship Series with the West

Division winners, the Minnesota Twins, and returned home to Sky-Dome, where they had set an all-time attendance record, becoming the first team ever to draw four million fans in a season.

Game 3 was the turning point in the series, but it also became another turning point in my career. The Jays and Twins were tied, 2–2, late in the game when CTV somehow lost the audio of the CBS feed, which the network was simulcasting. I was in our host position in the press box when our producer jumped on the intercom, telling me I would need to apologize for the technical difficulty and then would have to call the game until the CBS audio was restored.

I didn't know what to think, and I had no time to ask questions.

The only other time I had done play-by-play for baseball was when I was a kid calling my pretend backyard games, but now there was no pretending. This was suddenly and unexpectedly *very* real. I was thrown right into the fire—and as it turned out, I loved the heat.

We were live for only half an inning or so, and I called it like I saw it. The game stayed tied. The Twins' Dan Gladden got a hit, and fortunately, nothing consequential or controversial happened before CBS restored its feed.

Whew. Another speed bump overcome. Huge sigh of relief.

I got some love from our executives and the TV critics for being able to seamlessly leap into action, but to me it was just another step on the learning curve. Like everything else in this business I was consuming, I was loving the taste and craving more. I knew right then and there that someday I wanted to call baseball.

Unfortunately for the Jays, they not only lost that game in extra innings but also dropped the next two to the Twins, who would go on to win their second World Series in four years.

• • •

That loss, for the Jays, was bitter. It stung just like it had in 1985 and 1989, when they also had their hearts broken in the ALCS.

But in the grand plan, the 1991 loss might have been the best thing that could have happened in Toronto. The team realized it still had work to do, that it wasn't quite there yet but was getting closer, and needed to load up even more in the off-season in order to climb to the top of the mountain the following season.

The Jays' management, led by team president Paul Beeston and general manager Pat Gillick, had the mentality that if you can't beat them, go get the guys who beat you. And so, they didn't just add players, they added superstars, signing two future Hall of Fame free agents in Jack Morris, who had just pitched the Twins to the World Series championship, and veteran megastar Dave Winfield, a long-time enemy of Blue Jay fans.

Most of the hate for Winfield came naturally, since he had played for the evil empire, the New York Yankees, but some of the vitriol also stemmed from a bizarre incident that had occurred at the Jays' old ballpark, Exhibition Stadium. The Ex was an eyesore on the best of days. A sprawling football field that was converted to a bad facsimile of a baseball stadium. The old Cleveland Municipal Stadium was often called the "mistake on the lake." Well, Exhibition Stadium in Toronto did the job, but just barely, and many despairingly referred to *it* as the mistake on the lake. Beeston once told me in an interview that "it was not only the worst stadium in baseball—it was the worst stadium in sports."

Beyond the shoddy facilities, the rock-hard artificial turf, and the fierce winds that whipped off Lake Ontario, it was also a breeding ground for hungry and intuitive seagulls that liked to swarm the stadium on game days.

It was during a game against the Yankees in 1983 that Winfield, while warming up between innings, threw a ball and struck one of those pesky gulls, killing it dead on the spot. Whether the fowl ball was premeditated or an accident (which Winfield later claimed it was), the story took a crazier turn when Winfield was actually arrested and charged by Toronto police for causing the bird "insufferable harm."

Either the police officer was a Yankee fan or this was a Monty Python skit, but the whole seagull saga was blown completely out of proportion and charges were quickly dropped. Still, every time Winfield came back to Toronto, the fans were merciless. The boo-birds never let him forget about the dead white bird. But now, all was forgiven because Dave Winfield was a *blue bird.*

The Jays weren't done. GM Gillick, who in the past had been called Stand Pat by some media members, was suddenly known as Trader Pat as he continued to wheel and deal, including trading for Mets ace David Cone in late August, adding a final piece to the puzzle.

The team responded to management's moves, winning ninety-six games, finishing first again, and setting another attendance record.

We were off to another American League Championship Series, broadcast again on CTV, and this time the opponents were the West Division champion Oakland Athletics. The pre-*Moneyball* A's were a powerful team with great pitching, but the Jays took two of the first three games, and then in Game 4 in Oakland produced a series-changing defining moment.

Trailing by two runs in the ninth inning, with lights-out closer Dennis Eckersley on the mound for the A's, Roberto Alomar shocked the Oakland–Alameda County Coliseum crowd with a game-tying home run to right field. Even Alomar looked stunned, his mouth wide open and his outstretched arms reaching for the sky.

The Jays would miss a chance to clinch in Game 5 in Oakland, but they were still in the driver's seat, up 3–2 in the series. History, however, was still not on their side as they returned home to see if they could shake King Kong off their backs and finally advance to the biggest show in baseball.

If they were nervous, they didn't show it in batting practice. Joe Carter gave me a smile and a wink as he launched bomb after bomb into the empty SkyDome seats.

"We got this, Rodney," Joe boldly told me in a pre-game interview.

He was more confident than I was, but when he stepped to the plate in the bottom of the first and belted a two-run home run off A's starter Mike Moore, I was becoming more convinced.

I became a complete believer in the bottom of the third inning, when Candy Maldonado hit a three-run bomb, and right then, everyone in the stadium had a feeling that something special was in the air besides the smoke from all the fireworks going off.

The A's would never threaten, and the Jays wouldn't stop hitting and scoring, building an insurmountable 9–2 lead heading into the ninth inning.

I was getting wired up for the post-game show from our hosting perch high above the field, and I remember looking down to see *every* person in the building standing on their feet, hands clapping, watching with intoxicating anticipation, like a countdown to midnight on New Year's Eve. This was something I had previously seen only on television, and I had always wondered what it would be like in real life.

In one word: indescribable. Fifty thousand times better than TV.

When the "Candy Man," Maldonado, made the catch in left field for the final out, I honestly thought the SkyDome roof was going to blow off. No New Year's Eve bash could ever top this, I thought. It was pure pandemonium in the stands and absolute bedlam on the field. The players dove into a dogpile at home plate and our cameras caught all of the emotion.

I'll never forget the mile-wide smile of Cito Gaston running out to join the celebration, the experienced respect from Dave Winfield exchanging hugs with Jack Morris, who was now partying with the team he'd beaten a year earlier, and the innocence of Carter and Maldonado, who were dancing around like little boys.

Budding superstar John Olerud looked overjoyed but also overwhelmed. Series MVP Robbie Alomar was being embraced, and I'm sure thanked, by nearly everyone on the field. If it weren't for Alomar's lightning bolt in Oakland, there was a chance the Blue Jays might have been watching the A's celebrating a championship.

Fireworks and smoke filled the dome as the players bolted into the dressing room to uncork the champagne. At long last, the wait was over. The ghosts of '85, '89, and '91 had left the building. The Toronto Blue Jays were *finally* American League champions and were partying like they had just won the World Series.

But oh, wait, that was still to come.

Where were you in '92?

Now, I realize that some of you may not have been born yet in 1992, to which I say too bad for you because 1992 was a historic year in Canadian sport.

If you weren't living on the planet at that time, were part of a witness protection program, or were perhaps living under a rock in the Canadian Shield, I would encourage you to tap into YouTube, or even better, jump into my "Rod Black to the Future time machine," where we can set the flux capacitor to overdrive and take you back to a year that saw stuff happen that had never happened before, at least in most of our lifetimes.

Every time Canada competed at the Summer or the Winter Olympics, it was a dream come true for sports fans. The summer games in Barcelona was a good Olympics for Canada. That year Canada won eighteen medals, including seven gold, the country's second-best showing at the time.

It wasn't just the Olympics in 1992 that was special. It was everything, every sport, in every way possible.

It was a smorgasbord, or should I say, smorga-sport. And it was mind-boggling.

My broadcast world was spinning like a figure skater after a triple espresso, and while I got very little sleep trying to cover it all, I felt so lucky to be wide awake and right in the eye of that '92 sports hurricane.

So many athletes and teams to cover. So many amazing stories to tell. So many magical moments to witness, and I was privileged to have a front-row seat for most of them—and best of all, once again, I was getting paid to be there.

The highlight of the year came in October, when I had the opportunity to go to a place I had only ever dreamed of: the annual Fall Classic, the World Series.

With the Toronto Blue Jays becoming the first Canadian-based team to ever advance to the Fall Classic, a nation known for ice hockey was suddenly bursting with baseball pride, especially with the possibility of becoming the champions of America's pastime.

It didn't matter to the average Canadian that the Blue Jays were made up of players born and bred in the US and Latin America, or that the Series only pitted one city against another—Toronto against the National League champions from Atlanta.

No, to most Canadians, this was more. Much more. This was country against country—this was us versus them, Canada and the United States—a baseball battle of the border. The War of 1812 on the basepaths.

Frankly, the hype was a little contrived, but we all bought in, and why not? This was uncharted territory for so many of us, especially most of the players.

The Jays were a confident bunch and deserved to be exactly where they were. They had been built for success. They had the highest payroll in baseball, and they made believers of everyone who doubted them from their previous playoff failures by capturing the American League championship.

Despite all of the positive Blue Jay mojo, though, there was still some trepidation around the team heading into Game 1 in Atlanta, and for good reason.

While Toronto shared the best record with Oakland in the American League during the regular season, 96–66, the Braves owned the best mark in all of baseball at 98–64 and were coming off a Game 7 thriller over the Pittsburgh Pirates in the National League Championship Series.

Like their visitors from the north, the hometown team also had a bounce in its step.

Managed by former Blue Jays skipper Bobby Cox, the Braves were a determined but bitter bunch, carrying a huge Georgian pine on their shoulders, having gone from worst to first in 1991, only to lose to Minnesota in Game 7 of the World Series.

They not only had unfinished business on their minds, but also had one of the deadliest pitching staffs in baseball, led by John Smoltz, Steve Avery, and lefty ace Tom Glavine, who would get the start in the opener. If future Hall of Famers Glavine and Smoltz got hot, there was little chance to extinguish the fire. They were that good.

Atlanta's biggest advantage, however, was its home field, Fulton County Stadium.

It was my first trip to the home of the Braves, and while it didn't seem to be anything extraordinary, a number of Jays players had mentioned to me during batting practice that what made the place special was not what you saw but what you heard.

I remember a number of the veteran players, like Dave Winfield, taking some of the newbies who had never played in this National

League park aside and warning them to be ready for the sound, or as Winfield put it, "the chop shop."

Honestly, I was confused as shit by all the chatter. I mean, any arena or stadium can get loud, and I had already been to a number of eardrum-splitting venues. It's the World Series, for chrissakes; of course it was going to be loud.

All that noise about the noise still wasn't resonating with me as we prepared to go live to air across the CTV network. As with the previous playoff series, we were forced to simulcast the games with CBS, taking their American broadcast and supplementing their coverage throughout the game by inserting our Canadian stories during the odd commercial breaks, which in my mind just seemed so cheap and so wrong.

Dammit, I constantly lamented, we should be doing our own broadcast for our own country. How can we give proper perspective if we aren't actually doing the game for our viewers? How could Major League Baseball be so tone-deaf to their fans north of the border? How could CTV just roll over and let the American TV army march in? Who the hell made any of these decisions?

Many questions, very few good answers.

CBS, with its years of experience and financial girth, still put on a good show, for the most part playing it straight and showing very little favouritism to either side. As you would expect, they showed why they are a network superpower.

Even though we were lean, our CTV crew went above and beyond to bring the best possible coverage to a dramatic World Series that had a little bit of everything and a whole lot of something I did not expect.

That whole lot of something was exactly what Winfield was talking about in warm-ups—the noise, which wasn't just the stereotypical roar from the stadium crowd but a chant called the "Tomahawk Chop," which Atlanta fans had started doing a year earlier at the '91 World Series.

I remembered watching and listening to the series on TV, as Braves fans stood in unison, chanting the war cry at the top of their lungs while simultaneously waving one arm in a tomahawk-throwing motion. It was loud, it was intimidating, and of course it was controversial, especially with its racially insensitive overtones. Over the years, the tradition would become widely criticized by many Native American groups, but back in 1992, despite the backlash, it was part of the emotional soundtrack to the Series.

To me, it was haunting. The game hadn't even started yet, and the chant was already echoing throughout the stadium, cascading in a crescendo as the players were introduced one by one. I could feel the sound pounding through my entire body as I looked down from our broadcast perch, barely able to hear myself think. The only time it stopped was when the colour guard marched onto the field and national anthems were played.

Canadian tenor and *Les Misérables* actor Michael Burgess was selected to sing "O Canada" for the first time at a World Series and sang it beautifully, in both English and French, and was greeted with warm polite applause. Country music star Billy Ray Cyrus then performed "The Star-Spangled Banner" wearing blue jeans and a cut-off T-shirt, and though he looked like he wanted to break into a chorus of "Achy Breaky Heart," he pulled it off nicely, hitting the last line—*And the home of the brave*—perfectly, bringing a roar from the Fulton County crowd and setting the tone for an epic six-game tug-of-war.

The atmosphere was electric, and Game 1 lived up to the hype, especially the matchup of two superstar pitchers in Atlanta's Glavine and Toronto's "Black Jack" Morris, who had dashed the Braves' World Series hopes in a brilliant Game 7 performance with Minnesota a year earlier.

Each team got only four hits off the future Hall of Famers, but two of those hits were home runs. Joe Carter silenced the "chop house" when he opened the scoring with a solo shot in the top of the fourth inning. But unsung hero Damon Berryhill answered in the bottom of the sixth with a three-run home run that proved to be the difference in the Braves' 3–1 series-opening victory.

Yes, it was only one game, but I have to admit I was a little less optimistic about the Blue Jays' chances when heading back to the hotel after wrapping up the post-game show and doing some locker room interviews. The players said all the right things, but I could smell the disappointment and frustration from top to bottom. They knew they had played a terrific game, but they also recognized that all of that momentum they had flown into Atlanta might have just disappeared into the Georgian night.

The pressure was back on. The team needed a big turnaround in Game 2.

And things did turn around—or should I say, they turned upside down. Unbelievably, prior to the start of Game 2, the US Marine colour guard marched into the stadium—and the Canadian flag was flying upside down.

Conspiracy theorists still think it wasn't an accident, but American officials were deeply embarrassed by the gaffe.

The flag mishap wasn't bad luck for the Blue Jays, though. In the ninth inning, Toronto was trailing 4–3 when pinch hitter Ed Sprague stepped to the plate. Only a few months earlier, Sprague's wife, Kristen Babb, won a gold medal for the US at the Summer Olympics after a controversial judging error cost Canada's Sylvie Fréchette a victory. This time, it was Babb's husband striking gold for Canada, hitting a two-run home run that helped send the Jays back to Toronto with the series tied at 1.

Flag-gate was far from over. Scores of Blue Jays fans showed up wearing shirts with the American flag upside down, and several signs displayed the maple leaf with the words "This Side Up." It was all in jest, though Canadian baseball fans were still pissed.

They were much happier after Joe Carter and Kelly Gruber homered to give the Jays a 2–1 series lead.

Jimmy Key was brilliant as the Blue Jays won Game 4 by a score of 2–1. In Game 5, the Braves beat the Blues Jays in Toronto 7–2 to send the series back to Atlanta with the Jays on the edge of history. And then . . .

On October 24, 1992, the Toronto Blue Jays finished off the Braves in six games to become the first Canadian team to win the World Series. The winning pitcher, again, was Jimmy Key, and Joe Carter caught the final out in the bottom of the eleventh inning.

I'll never forget that night of October 24 for many reasons—both good and bad.

I was moments away from hosting the Game 6 pregame show from the right-field bleachers, sitting alongside the beautiful World Series trophy, when suddenly, a baseball bounced off the trophy with a *thud*. Horrified, I looked down to the field, and there was reliever David Wells grinning from ear to ear after using the trophy as target practice. Thankfully, he didn't break anything, but I could only imagine if he had, and I came on live with a damaged trophy. It might have been a worse situation than the upside-down flag.

The game itself was an October classic. With the Jays holding a 2–1 lead to the ninth, I was sent down to the locker room for the potential celebration interviews. When I walked into the Jays' clubhouse, people were busy taping plastic around the lockers and gearing up for the champagne showers.

We watched the ninth inning on the television monitor. Team president Paul Beeston was nervously chomping on his unlit cigar, and starting pitcher David Cone was taking a drag on a cigarette. That's when the

Braves tied the score to send it to extra innings. Beeston almost choked on his cigar. He motioned for all of us to "Get the fuck out."

Two innings later, we were shuffled back in when Dave Winfield hit a double down the line to give the Jays the lead.

I had one foot out the door in the bottom of the eleventh when the Braves pulled within one run, but then with two outs, Otis Nixon inexplicably laid down a bunt that reliever Mike Timlin fielded and shoveled over to Joe Carter for the final out. Joe started jumping and was joined by his ecstatic teammates in a dogpile for the ages.

The Blue Jays were bringing the World Series trophy north of the border for the first time, and the celebration on the field and in the locker room could be felt all the way back to the SkyDome in Toronto, where forty thousand people were watching on the Jumbotron.

Our postgame interviews in the locker room were priceless. Half-naked players hugging it out like they were little boys. Champagne spraying everywhere, stinging my eyes, but we kept broadcasting live back to Canada until we heard from all of the new champions.

It was a weird feeling walking back to the hotel after the Blue Jays won the World Series. The streets of Atlanta were so quiet. We got to our hotel, and there was a party taking place to celebrate the World Series win. But everyone was so exhausted that the party wasn't too crazy. I flew back home the next day, wondering what the reaction had been like back in Canada. It was a little underwhelming to experience winning the championship on the road.

Our flight landed, and we went straight to SkyDome for the parade. When I got to the stadium, it hit me how big of a deal it was. I had heard about the people celebrating the night before, but now we were able to experience it first-hand. The players realized that they hadn't just won a World Series for the city of Toronto, they'd won it for all of Canada. For the next year, I hosted a lot of events with the players, and I would interview them everywhere from Sears to a charity golf tournament.

During the 1992 World Series, I came up with an idea for a story to show people why it was so important that Toronto had a domed stadium. In the third inning of the third game, back in Toronto, I did my live hit from home plate at the old Exhibition Stadium. I was a few kilometres from the Dome, and it was a miserable day of cold rain and wet snow. I was frozen stiff. I realized at that point that the Blue Jays would have never been in a World Series if it weren't for SkyDome.

One year later, on October 23, 1993, Joe Carter hit one of the most famous home runs in baseball post-season history as the Blue Jays repeated as World Series champions.

Throughout the entire 1993 season, the Blue Jays were incredible. The season didn't feel like a celebration tour; the team had a back-to-business mindset. Coming off the win in 1992, Paul Beeston and Pat Gillick did a great job of reloading, acquiring veterans like Paul Molitor and Rickey Henderson. Both players were key components that year and were on base when Joe Carter hit the series-winning home run. The 1992 team was good, but the 1993 team was a powerhouse, with the famous WAMCO group—Devon White, Robbie Alomar, Paul Molitor, Joe Carter, and John Olerud—at the top of the batting order. Olerud really stepped up in 1993; he flirted with hitting .400.

There was a perfect balance in the clubhouse of fiery and emotional players and cool, calm, and collected players. If you ever had to design a team, the 1993 Jays were the team you would want to put together. Rickey Henderson was thirty-four years old when he played for the Blue Jays, and he was like a little kid every time you spoke to him. He loved baseball so much.

When the Jays got back to the post-season, they were on a mission. I know people talk about Joe Carter's home run, but an equally important home run for the Jays was Robbie Alomar's in the 1992 ALCS against the Oakland A's. Ed Sprague's homer in the 1992 Series was also very important. In 1993, they defeated the Chicago White Sox in six games in the American League Championship Series and faced the Philadelphia Phillies in the World Series.

In 1992, CTV Sports had simulcast the American feed of the World Series. In 1993, the network had a bigger role. We were doing live reports and fan interviews throughout the series from Barrie, Ontario, to Calgary, Alberta. Every CTV affiliate and the network led with the Blue Jays every day, all day.

That was the year that Rob Butler, from East York, was a member of the Blue Jays, and we did many stories about his Canadian connection.

Years later, I developed a deep friendship with Rob. I don't know if my sons would have ever been pro baseball players if it weren't for Rob Butler. When they were young, I took them to the baseball camps put on by Rob and his brother Rich.

In Game 4, the Jays were trailing and Rob came into the game and helped spark a comeback. In the end, the Jays won the game, 15–14.

In Game 6, I did the pre-game and the post-game. Before the game, I did a hit from the bowels of SkyDome. Near the entrance to the Blue Jays' clubhouse, there was this big cement wall covered with pictures and posters and letters from Canadians from coast to coast. Live on the air, I started reading one of the notes from an eleven-year-old girl from Pembroke, Ontario. It read, "Robbie Alomar, will you marry me?" The entire country was in love with the Blue Jays in 1993. I spoke to Joe Carter at the batting cage before the start of Game 6. He looked at me, winked, and said, "Rodney, we got this."

The game went on and I was upstairs, doing the opening of the broadcast. I was going to be reporting from the clubhouse at the end of the game. In the seventh inning, I headed down to the lower level, in the tunnel before the entrance to dugout. I was standing with Buck Martinez, who was reporting for TSN that night. Jays pitcher Dave Stewart came out of the game after giving up a three-run homerun to Lenny Dykstra, and he almost hit Buck and me as he threw his glove. Stewart had a high-pitched voice, but he had a menacing stare. I looked into the dugout and I could see Rob Butler sitting there with his head in his hands, like he was in a trance.

In the bottom of the ninth, with the Jays trailing 6–5, Rickey Henderson got on base; two batters later, Paul Molitor singled. Now, Phillies reliever Mitch Williams had never used the slide step before in his career. But he was so worried about Henderson and what he would do at second base. Williams kept slipping off the mound as he made his slide step. Then he threw that fateful pitch to Joe Carter, who was always a good bad-ball hitter, didn't miss, and the rest was history.

Because Buck and I were not totally in the dugout; we were watching the video feed of the game on a monitor. What people don't realize is that TV broadcasts are on a slight delay. And all of a sudden, I heard a thunderous boom from the crowd; it felt like an earthquake had hit the stadium. I hustled into the dugout, and everyone was running everywhere, and it was pandemonium on the field. To win the World Series at home was unreal.

It was so joyous in the clubhouse afterwards. I was able to interview Henderson and others after the game. One of my all-time favourite interviews was with Rob Butler. He was giddy. And he wasn't just a token Canadian on the team; he had contributed to the team's success and had a couple of hits. "I'm so happy!" he said. "I love everyone in East York, and I love everyone in Canada!" He had tears in his eyes. "My brother Rich, this is for you. I love you, man!" Then he took a can of beer and poured it all over my head and ruined my brand-new suit. But it was all worth it.

The 1992 and 1993 World Series wins were two of the greatest things I have ever witnessed. I have been at the Olympics and called gold medal wins. I have called the hockey World Championships, and I have been to the Stanley Cup Final. I was at the Masters when Mike Weir won, for goodness' sake. But to be a part of the back-to-back World Series, to me it is at the top of my list of things that I have covered. It was unbelievable to cover, and it was unbelievable the way the city of Toronto and all of Canada reacted. It was great to see a Canadian team defeat an American team. It was the first major championship that I had been around. The Blue Jays in 1992 were good, but they were not favoured to win the World Series. In 1993, the Jays were the definite favourites.

Fast-forward to 1998, and Joe Carter had retired from baseball. Sportsnet had a press conference to announce that they had purchased the rights to broadcast forty Blue Jays games.

Baseball holds a special place in my life. I played baseball as a kid, and I loved it. I followed the stories; I loved the fact that it was great theatre. I loved that baseball had no score clock. I loved the stories about the players: where they came from, how they got to the big leagues. I loved the poetry of baseball and all of the stats that came with the game. I followed all of the announcers. I loved Dave Van Horne, the voice of the Expos, and the long-time voice of the Dodgers, Vin Scully. I used to mimic all of the great announcers while I was playing baseball. But I didn't think I would ever call play-by-play of a baseball game.

Up until the late 1990s, I had hosted baseball broadcasts, but I had not done any play-by-play. I was at Sportsnet in the late '90s when network president Scott Moore called me and said, "How would you like to do baseball? And I have a partner for you, too. His name is Joe Carter."

That was an easy thing to say yes to. I called twenty to thirty games a year, and then Sportsnet lost the rights. I moved to TSN and started calling twenty to thirty games a year there. One year, we did close to fifty Blue Jays games, which was great. I loved being on the field before the game; I loved that every night you went to the ballpark, you could see something that you'd never seen before. This is the beauty of baseball. That is a broadcaster's dream.

I was doing these Jays games after their glory days of winning back-to-back World Series titles. I was also hosting Montreal Expos games, and I knew about the importance of baseball to Canadians. I closely followed all of the Canadian-born players when they came into Toronto or Montreal. Guys like Éric Gagné, Jason Bay, Kirk McCaskill, and others. When I was a kid, Fergie Jenkins and Terry Puhl were the only prominent Canadians in the big leagues. But suddenly, the list was growing. And I could only imagine how many more would be on their way to the show after being inspired by the Blue Jays' World Series wins. I got to work with Joe Carter. Joe and I became great friends over time. Because we not only loved baseball, but we also shared the same passion for another sport.

Joe and I both loved to golf. The thing with Joe Carter is it didn't matter what city we were in, he could get on any golf course. On an off day Joe would call the clubhouse: "Hi, I'm Joe Carter." And these were elite golf courses I am talking about. It didn't matter what course, we would get a tee time, and usually it was for a great price: free.

Joe was a very generous guy with all of the crew. Whenever he was in Toronto, he never had to buy a drink or food because of that World Series–winning home run. He would talk to the catering staff and make sure there was a food cart with enough treats for everyone.

Our last year working together was 2000. But it was my most memorable. On July 26, I was scheduled to call a noon Blue Jays game. The night before, my wife, Nancy, went into labour. I tried to call for a replacement and couldn't find anyone, so I was going to have to call the game no matter what happened. I'd told Joe that I didn't know what was going to happen, and he replied, "Rodney, don't worry about it. I am at the SkyDome hotel, and I have an extra bed. Don't worry."

Nancy was induced, and Tyler Alexander arrived at 3:21 a.m. We were all excited. I tried to sleep in the corner of Nancy's room at the hospital before saying goodbye to her and Tyler to get some rest before the Jays game. I went to the hotel and arrived at Joe's room around six in the morning. I knocked on his door, and he gave me a big hug and congratulated me. I walked into his room, and there weren't two beds—there was only one. So, Joe Carter and I recreated the famous scene in *Planes, Trains, and Automobiles*. Two guys, one bed, and a pillow in between us. The upside is that I got to sleep with Joe Carter, a World Series hero.

After a few hours' rest, we went to the ballpark and called the game. In the middle of it, the Blue Jays put a notice on the Jumbotron that Tyler had been born, and they congratulated us. I was sky high, and the Blue Jays won. Afterwards, I had the scorecard signed as a memento for Tyler. On that scorecard were a number of players who would later help Tyler on his path to the major leagues—guys like Robbie Alomar, Rob Butler, and Paul Spoljaric. Eighteen years to the day that he was born, Tyler got a chance to play in the East Coast Pro Classic, held at what had been SkyDome but was now called Rogers Centre. It was almost as if Tyler was born to play baseball. I had grown so close to Joe that we had considered calling him Carter. Then I thought it would be too much pressure on him. As it turned out, Tyler was the perfect name.

One year, Joe and I were at the Masters. I was there working with TSN, and Joe and a friend of his were going to join us at the house we were renting. I'd told Joe we had lots of room. He was arriving late at night, around two in the morning. It turned out the couch didn't turn into a bed, so we found a mattress, and Joe and his friend slept on it in the dining room. The thing is, I hadn't told any of the crew that Joe was arriving. So, around six in the morning, a crew member nudged me awake because we had to head over to Augusta National. Then he said, "Hey, there is a Black guy and white guy sleeping in the dining room, and the Black guy looks like Joe Carter. What is going on here, man?"

Now, if you ask Joe about his memories of what happened, he has a slightly different version of the events:

"Rod is not always the best with instructions. Rod and I were talking about going to the Masters. Not only had I never been there, but I also didn't have a place to stay. Rod tells me, 'Oh, you guys can stay with me at our rental house.' This is in February, two months before the Masters. I took Rod at his word, and when the Masters rolled around, I called him up and said, 'Rod, where is the house located?' He had no clue what I was talking about. I said, 'You know, Rod, you said we could stay at the house with the production crew.' Rod had forgotten about it.

"My buddy Terry Jarvis and I arrived at the house at night, and I ended up sleeping on the couch. When the guys woke up to leave for the golf course to interview Mike Weir, they found me sleeping on the couch. My buddy Terry was in the other room. The next night, we got our hands on a blow-up mattress that we set up in the dining room. It was a queen-size inflatable mattress, and Terry and I slept on that. I came from humble beginnings and I was never too proud where I couldn't sleep on a couch or an inflatable mattress. The crew loved having me there because I made them my pecan pie. Every day, they couldn't wait to eat my pecan pie. They said it was the best they ever had."

Yes, the pie was great, and unfortunately, I did forget about telling Joe that he could stay with us in Augusta. Hey, it happens. In my defence, I thought we had plenty of room for Joe. Despite the fact that he had to sleep on the floor, he doesn't hold grudges and we are still buddies. To this day, I host the Joe Carter Classic celebrity golf event in the Toronto area, which has raised millions of dollars for charity over the years. Joe Carter touched them all, but he has touched a lot of people's lives as well. It's a friendship that has lasted beyond baseball.

I also covered the Montreal Expos during my time at CTV. As with the Blue Jays, I hosted the Expos broadcasts. I did the same job that Fergie Olver did for the Blue Jays: I would sit in the dugout with the players, working as a host and a reporter. As I discovered, crazy things would happen in the dugout, from pranks to sudden breaking news. During a game in August 1993, veteran Expos pitcher Dennis Martinez came over to me and shook my hand, and said, "I'm out of here." He had been claimed on waivers by the Atlanta Braves. This all took place in the middle of the game. I reported the news of the deal from the dugout during the broadcast. One day later, Martinez used his 10-5 veteran player rights as per the collective bargaining agreement and vetoed the move, and he ended up staying put in Montreal. The next time I saw him in a dugout, I shook his hand and said, "Welcome back." Dennis laughed at that.

Another time, we came close to losing our broadcast licence. Dave Van Horne was doing play-by-play, and Ken Singleton was the colour analyst, and during a pre-game hit for local news, they threw down to me in the dugout with Ivan Calderón. Calderón was from Venezuela, and I asked him about his off-season trade from the White Sox. "What did you think about when you got traded to Montreal?"

He answered, "Oh, it shocked me. I was in the backyard, playing with my cock." He said this live on the air!

I jumped in: "You mean your roosters?"

Calderón was emphatic: "Yes, I play with my cock."

I kept trying to say "rooster." As I turned red, I threw back to the studio, knowing full well that Dave and Kenny were laughing upstairs in the booth. I was so relieved that social media had not been invented yet.

This was the kind of moment as a broadcaster that I loved. It was totally unplanned, and without knowing it, Calderón had given me one of the funniest moments of my career.

9

"SORRY ABOUT THAT"—JACK NICKLAUS, MIKE WEIR, CHARLES BARKLEY, AND TALES FROM THE GOLF COURSE

GOLF HAS ALWAYS HELD A SPECIAL PLACE IN MY HEART. I USED TO PLAY IN MY BACKyard growing up, dreaming I was Jack Nicklaus. He was a hero of mine. We had a small yard, and I would chip golf balls into one of my dad's old tobacco tins. I had found an old wooden-shafted left-handed golf club, and that is what I learned with. When I was ten years old, I would chip and pretend I was on the tour. I had five balls that I would chip, each named after a golf legend: Nicklaus, Gary Player, Tom Watson, Tom Weiskopf, and Arnold Palmer. I was such a Jack Nicklaus fan that if I thought one of my other imaginary golf legends was going to win, I would miss on purpose so that Nicklaus could prevail! To think that years later, I had a chance to chat with Nicklaus and to be around him.

Jack Nicklaus is the reason that I started playing golf. I used to read the little comic strip in the newspaper where Nicklaus gave lessons. I am a lefty, and I would take everything that he said in his lessons and reverse it to fit my swing. He was such an icon throughout my childhood, into my teens, and on into adulthood.

Nicklaus was the first person I ever felt nervous being around. He was at Glen Abbey during the 1995 Canadian Open, as he was being inducted into the Canadian Golf Hall of Fame. I was hosting that week and looking forward to finally meeting my idol. Gary McCord was on our broadcast team. Earlier in the week, McCord, a veteran broadcaster, criticized the course—which Nicklaus had designed. "The seventeenth green looks like Salvador Dalí on acid," he sarcastically told a reporter.

After the Pro-Am on Wednesday, I had to interview Jack Nicklaus. He couldn't have been nicer. Meanwhile, I was a nervous wreck; my hand holding the microphone was shaking. The interview ended, and he looked at me right in the eye.

"Look, I have to ask you something," he said in his classic squeaky Nicklaus voice.

"What's that, Jack?"

"Why did Gary McCord say that about my seventeenth green?" Maybe Jack thought I was the commissioner of Canadian golf or something. "Listen, Rod, I am going to take you out right now and let you check it out."

And then, Jack Nicklaus made me ride with him on a golf cart to the green on seventeen. He walked around the funky green and showed me all the nuances. I just nodded my head and tried to listen to what he was saying, though I don't think I absorbed a word. All I was thinking was that the first chance I got, I was going to call my dad in Winnipeg.

I was scheduled to attend the Hall of Fame dinner that night. So, we finished on the seventeenth hole and I went down to the locker room to get changed—at that time, the broadcast crew were able to use the same locker room as the players. My locker was next to Fred Couples's, which was really cool. I wish I had a photo of it, to be honest. I was by myself in the locker room, and guess who walks in? Jack Nicklaus.

So, there we were, just the two of us in the locker room.

Jack was around fifty-five at the time and was on this fitness kick. As I was getting changed, he said, "Hey, Rod, come over here." He started showing me his new line of golf clubs and telling me why they were so special. Once he was done, I decided to get in the hot tub before my shower. I closed my eyes, and as I opened them, Jack Nicklaus was hopping into the hot tub with me! And still talking to me.

After that, I went to take a shower. At Glen Abbey, there were around thirty shower heads in the locker room. I had shampoo on my head, and I was startled because Nicklaus was in the shower stall right beside me. We were the only ones there. And Jack was still talking to me—about Canada and the near misses he'd had at the Canadian Open.

I went back to my locker and started putting my suit on. I looked over, and Jack was across from me. Not just across from me—he was on the floor of the locker room. I was so confused at this point. Jack was in his underwear and an undershirt, and he was doing crunches. And the whole time, still talking to me. After a few reps, Jack was in mid-crunch when he let go of the biggest fart I have ever heard in my life. I was startled, and as I looked over, Nicklaus met my gaze. "Sorry about that!" I had to put my head in my locker because I was laughing so hard.

Later on, I told David Feherty the story of what had happened. Feherty was crying from laughter. From then on, every time I talked to Feherty, the second he picked up the phone, I would say to him, "Sorry about that!" in my best Jack Nicklaus voice.

Here was my ultimate hero, and I was in a hot tub with him and showering next to him. He was sharing time with me like we were best buddies. That experience also taught me never to be intimidated by anybody. Everyone is human. Even the Golden Bear, Jack Nicklaus, will fart.

Later on, I told Tiger Woods the Jack Nicklaus story, and he thought it was hilarious. It turns out that Tiger can fart on command. Tiger has a great sense of humour, and he loves to be one of the guys.

They say never meet your heroes, but I met Jack Nicklaus, and it felt like I was hanging out with my dad or my uncle.

The Golden Bear was everything I thought he was, and even more.

MIKE WEIR

In addition to the Canadian Open, I hosted a lot of events on the Canadian golf tour. Even during my days at CKY in Winnipeg, we covered stops on the Canadian Tour. In fact, in 1989, Dale Hawerchuk was my colour commentator at the Manitoba Open—Stuart Hendley won it that year. As I covered these tournaments, I got to know all the guys on the tour, and one guy I kept hearing about was a Canadian by the name of Mike Weir.

In the summer of 1997, Weir was one of the leaders of the Canadian Tour's Order of Merit. I got to know him through Bell Mobility, as I was hosting a lot of their events at the time. I was called to host Wayne Gretzky's golf event at Redtail, an exclusive private course south of St. Thomas, Ontario. Before GPS was invented, it was impossible to find and almost as impossible to book a tee time. A lot of rich people are members. Around seventy people were taking part in this Gretzky event, and each one was richer than the last. On the way to the course, everyone stopped at Wayne's childhood home in Brantford, where his dad, Walter, would give them a tour of the trophy room in the basement.

Molson Brewery was also a major sponsor of the event. They had me make some announcements and outline the rules, and then I said, "Hey, we are about an hour from teeing off; if anybody wants to get a free lesson down on the range, we have Order of Merit winner on the Canadian Tour, Mike Weir, from nearby Brights Grove, Ontario, here." Weir is a little guy, and he was wearing glasses.

I knew Mike fairly well at this point. I went down to the driving range, and my brother Ryan was there helping out. There were only three of us there. Not one person taking part in the tournament came up and said hi to Mike or asked for a lesson. Later that day, after the tournament was over, we were in the clubhouse. At this course, you had to wear a suit jacket and a tie. Well, Gretzky didn't have a jacket and tie with him. So, my brother had go to London to get one of his jackets and ties and give them to Wayne Gretzky. To this day, Ryan still has that jacket and tie. I am sure he still has it in a trophy case.

Here is an example of the kind of person Wayne Gretzky is: Weir was a rising star, and Wayne knew about him. But Wayne felt badly that nobody was talking to Mike earlier. So, he made sure that Mike sat right beside him at the dinner table that night. Once that happened, five or six of these rich guys were ready to offer up sponsorship money for Mike. After that, he ended up as a client of the powerful IMG sports agency.

Fast-forward to 1998, Mike Weir got his PGA Tour card. A year and a half later, Mike won his first PGA Tour event at the 1999 Air Canada Championship in Surrey, British Columba. I was broadcasting the event, and I was convinced that Mike was on the path to something special. Well, four years later, he won the Masters. I swear to you, of the seventy guys who were at the Redtail event back in 1997, all of them watched Mike win the Masters and bragged to their family and friends that they got a lesson from him! If they were not on it already, everybody jumped on the Mike Weir bandwagon after he won that tournament.

It isn't a new story, but years before he was at Augusta, Mike Weir wrote a letter to Jack Nicklaus. Mike is a lefty, and he asked Jack if he should change and golf right-handed. Jack told him no, don't do it. As a fellow left-handed golfer, I was so happy that Mike took Jack's advice.

I was covering the Masters when he won in 2003. Jim Nelford was my broadcast partner. On Saturday, the day before the final round, I said to Nelford, "Weir is going to win." That night, Weir had a barbecue at his rented house. IMG and Molson took care of everything and made sure there was plenty of food and beer. We didn't see much of Mike that night because he had business to take care of the next morning. I later heard from his brother that Mike was practising his putts on the linoleum floor in his kitchen. He knew the greens were going to be very fast on Sunday, and he felt that putting on the smooth surface would help him get ready.

On Sunday, I was with NHL legend Paul Coffey, following Mike around the course. Here was a guy who'd won everything in his hockey career, and he was as excited as a little kid, watching Mike in that final round. Everyone was so pro-Canadian that day. Mike Weir's pitching wedge was magical. After he won, I was brought to the clubhouse in the famed Butler Cabin to interview Mike. I didn't have a jacket with me, and you had to wear a jacket and a tie to get into the cabin. I found a jacket, and Mike gave me a Masters tie to wear. I don't keep many souvenirs. I still have that tie to this day. Mike was so excited when I interviewed him he could barely contain himself. We both knew that his life had changed forever.

Mike has done so much foundational charity work over the years. And he has inspired a generation of Canadian golfers, including the current crop of Canadians on the PGA Tour—Nick Taylor, Mackenzie Hughes, Corey Conners, and everyone else, including LPGA star Brooke Henderson. Mike passed the torch to the new generation, and they ran with it. Just as Steve Nash made Canadian kids believe they could play basketball at the highest level, Mike Weir made Canadian golfers believe they could play and excel on the PGA Tour. He taught me a lot about the game of golf, and he taught me a lot about being a pro.

To go to Augusta National, to be at the Masters, to see Butler Cabin, it was surreal. It was a magical time in my career. One year, on the Tuesday of Masters week around seven in the morning, I was having breakfast in the clubhouse with long-time golf reporter Bob Weeks. All of sudden, we heard a voice: "Hey, boys, can I join you?" It was Arnold Palmer! He sat with us and had breakfast and talked to the entire crew for almost an hour. It was such a humbling experience. I never in a million years believed I would even be around these PGA legends, let alone watch a Canadian win the Masters. Every time I was there, I thought of that little ten-year-old kid, chipping balls in my backyard.

Doing those Canadian Tour events when I worked at CKY helped me with my golf coverage. We did only four holes of local coverage, but I gained some invaluable experience. And it made me realize how much I loved calling golf and announcing golf events. The little steps you take along the way are what make the complete package. I always felt that every time you have the opportunity to do something, you never say no. It is bound to help you in some way down the road. Being a pro golfer is like being a broadcaster, prep, reps and a mentality to refine your game.

Along the way at CTV, and TSN, and Sportsnet, we did so many golf events—the skins game, the senior tour, the ladies' tour, amateur events, and the Canadian Open. Reporting on, broadcasting, and playing golf has been a big part of my life. I met some of my best friends through that great game.

CHARLES BARKLEY—FRIEND FOR LIFE

My friendship with Charles Barkley was forged on the golf course. He used to come to Toronto, and I would play with him a lot.

I was there when the infamous hitch in his golf swing started. He was a good golfer, and still is. That weird hitch in his swing started around the time of my honeymoon. I mean, not too many guys get to go on their honeymoon and end up in Las Vegas as a guest of Charles Barkley.

My wife, Nancy, and I got married in 1998. Charles was supposed to come to the wedding, and he couldn't make it. We were on our honeymoon in Mont-Tremblant on Labour Day weekend—the weather was terrible, or as Charles Barkley would call it, "turrible," and Nancy and I were hanging out in the room when the phone rang. The operator told me there was a phone call for me. Charles came on the line and started swearing. "What kind of language are they speaking there? What is that?" He wished us the best, then said, "I want you and Nancy to come down to Las Vegas with me and Tiger and Michael and play some golf and celebrate." I remember thinking there was no way in the world my wife was going to want to do this on our honeymoon. But Nancy looked at me and said, "Yeah, come on. Let's go to Vegas."

So, there we were, in Las Vegas with Charles Barkley and some of his buddies: Michael Jordan, a young Tiger Woods, the Wayans brothers, and many other celebrities. He invited Nancy and me to golf with him, and I witnessed that hitch in his swing. I was stunned. I asked him what the heck he was doing. Charles told me to shut up and said he was taking lessons. I said, "Lessons on what, becoming a shitty golfer?" As I said, Charles is a good golfer. But he had so much information in his head about how to be a better golfer, it changed his swing.

Jordan was on the course in a foursome ahead of us. We were on the back nine, and we could hear these young college guys partying in the backyard of a condo that backed onto the golf course. They were chanting, "Michael! Michael!" Jordan was smoking this big cigar, and he smiled and waved at them and kept going. Then we got close, and they saw Charles Barkley. Sure enough, these guys started chanting, "Charles! Charles!" We teed off, and on our way to our second shot, we stopped by that condo. There must have been fifty guys there for a stag. We stayed for about fifteen minutes and had a beer, and these guys couldn't believe what was happening.

In the meantime, I'd forgotten about Nancy, who'd played out the hole and was wondering where we'd got to. Suddenly, there she was, opening the back gate, and she decided to join the party. Later that night, we went out to a nightclub, and Charles was dancing and wearing one of the Bob's Stag T-shirts the guys had given him. Charles Barkley is one of a kind.

When you are with Charles Barkley in Vegas, you golf around nine in the morning, then you take a nap in the afternoon. After one of our rounds, I was taking a shower, and I heard some golf spikes echoing off the bathroom floor. Then a tub full of ice was poured on me by Sir Charles. He laughed and said, "Happy honeymoon, motherfucker."

With Charles, you watch him gamble a lot. I witnessed him losing hundreds of thousands of dollars, and I saw him win hundreds of thousands of dollars. And then we would go for dinner and party until five in the morning. Then we would get up a few hours later and go golfing again. And watch him gamble again. It was wild. What a honeymoon. I doubt many people had a better honeymoon in Vegas than we did.

Charles is so genuinely nice; he is generous, and he will talk to everybody. He taught me a lot about being a normal dude and having no ego, no matter who you are. There is no one like Charles Barkley. I have never met anyone who better represents how to live in the spotlight, and how to give back. To this day, I get text messages from people who are watching Charles on TV, giving me a "Rod Black shout-out." I always giggle and say, "That's Charles for you—he is larger than life."

WAYNE GRETZKY, GUY LAFLEUR, AND OTHER NHL LEGENDS

My relationship with Wayne Gretzky is a special one. I don't know why, but most of that comes from my friendship with Gus Badali. We started to get to know each other during the 1980s, when I was working with the Winnipeg Jets. In 1987, there was a seven-year-old kid who was ill and, through the Rainbow Society, which granted wishes to terminally ill children, he was at the rink. The CKY studio was right next to the visitors' dressing room in the Winnipeg Arena. I brought the kid and his parents down to our studio. The kid was battling cancer, and he was wearing this little toque to cover his head. The young man hardly said a word; the whole scene just broke my heart. Keep in mind, I didn't promise them anything, but I took him out to the bench during the pregame skate. As the kid was standing there, Wayne Gretzky suddenly skated over and ruffled his toque. Wayne said hi and started talking to the kid. He went out of his way to make this kid feel like he was his best friend. He didn't have to do that; Wayne did it all on his own. Then he asked the Oilers trainer to get some photos from the dressing room. The kid was beaming from ear to ear. After Wayne skated over, all of the other Oilers also skated by and said hi and gave him a high-five. It just reinforced the power of athletes when they do things the right way.

To me, living and working in Winnipeg, Wayne was sort of the enemy. He and the Oilers would break the hearts of the Jets and their fans every year in the playoffs. But as I got to know Wayne, I really grew to admire him.

Over time, I started to host some of Wayne's charity events. And every Saturday afternoon, I hosted the *Live from Gretzky's* radio show from the old Wayne Gretzky's restaurant in Toronto. I hosted a few events for TD Bank, and whenever Wayne was invited to appear, he would ask for me to emcee. Wayne didn't like public speaking, but he loved it when someone was asking him questions. The funny thing is, you could ask Wayne one question and he wouldn't stop talking!

One time, we were both flying back to Canada after a speaking engagement. Well, Wayne Gretzky almost always flies on a private jet, and this time, we both had to fly commercial. Because of all my travel with work, I had elite flight status. Since he usually flies privately, Wayne has virtually no status on any airline. That meant I had to get Wayne into the Air Canada lounge before the flight. Trust me, that is the only time a broadcaster ever gave 99 an assist.

When you see the way Wayne is with people, it teaches you a lot. When people recognize you and they want to say hi, it costs nothing to be nice and say hi back. To anyone who thinks Wayne Gretzky is fake nice, he is not—he is the real deal. Wayne is human, and there are days he doesn't want to see anyone. I get it because no athlete has signed more autographs than him. He continues to do it, and it all goes back to the way he was raised by his dad, Walter, and his mom, Phyllis. He is a classic Canadian, almost a hoser. He is just one of the guys.

I took my son Jesse to an event I was hosting in Toronto, and Wayne was there. Jesse was eight at the time, and he wore number 99 when he played hockey for the Markham Waxers. Wayne was sitting at our table, and he went out of his way to be so nice to Jesse, who brought over his number 99 Waxers jersey for him to sign. Wayne said, "Oh, that's so nice. You wear number 99." Jesse looked at him. "Actually, that's not because of you." Wayne started laughing and asked why he wore the number. I told Wayne that Jesse is a perfectionist, and he always wants to give 100 percent. But since you can't use the number 100, he went with 99. Wayne just howled with laughter.

There is no doubt that Wayne is one of the greatest athletes of all time. But he is not the only great one I have been around.

I have dealt with so many famous athletes and famous people who are really nice. Jeremy Roenick is near the top of the list, and to me, he is the Charles Barkley of hockey. When I first met him, he was full of bravado, but he has a kind and genuine heart. I was with J. R. a few weeks before he got the call telling him he would be inducted into the Hockey Hall of Fame. He thought it would never happen because of his outspokenness. I told him it would happen, and it did. When he got the news, J. R. was in tears. He has rubbed some people the wrong way, especially NHL commissioner Gary Bettman. But if you get to know the real Jeremy Roenick, you understand why he is the way he is. Little-known fact: J. R. is the best dancer that I know, both on and off the ice.

The media's portrayal of so many athletes as miscreants or bad people is often inaccurate. Social media these days has created a huge wall between athletes and fans. That is why broadcasters and journalists are jaded, and we base our assessments not on a person's true character, but on how they treat us. We are in the media, and we have to ask them questions they might not like. I prefer to judge them on how they treat other people. There are just so many great ones who are ridiculously nice. CFL players are wholesome dudes, and they are nice as they come. Pinball Clemons is probably the nicest person that you will ever meet. You meet Pinball and you think, *Come on, he can't be that nice*. And in reality, he is nicer.

As a kid, I loved Jean Béliveau and Guy Lafleur and the Montreal Canadiens. I idolized them growing up in Winnipeg, when the Montreal

Canadiens were on every Saturday night. A big reason for that is that Manitoba has the second-highest French population in Canada outside of Quebec. Béliveau was actually the first pro hockey player that I met, even before Bobby Hull. Early in the 1970s, Esso ran a promotion for hockey cards that you got when you filled up. What a surprise it was to me when my dad took me and my bother Derrick to the corner gas station in Transcona. And there, looking like a hockey god in a suit, in the middle of summer, was the captain of the Montreal Canadiens, Jean Béliveau. It was such a thrill. I cherish the picture I have of him to this day. What made this story even harder to believe is that years later, I got to work with Béliveau at several speaking engagements. He was nicer than nice, living up to his legend, and like every Montreal Canadiens great, he passed the torch to other superstars.

Players like Guy Lafleur carried that fire. And over the course of my career, I was a part of a number of events with the Flower. I had a chance to go overseas with him because I hosted a number of winter shows for the Canadian Armed Forces. We went on a friendship tour that included Guy, bands, and other celebrities, and I hosted the things. I went to Kuwait, Crete, and Ukraine with Guy. Even though a lot of the men and women serving in the military were so young, and some of them might not even know who Guy Lafleur was unless they googled him, he was a magnet wherever we went. He talked to everybody, and he was a genuinely nice man. I would often see him standing around with all these people, having a smoke and chatting away. We went to Ukraine, and it was bad situation, as it was during the crisis in Crimea in 2016. We didn't realize what we were getting into until we got there. When we arrived, the organizer was stressed and worried that we hadn't come at a good time. The Canadian soldiers seemed so young, and a little scared about their future. Guy still did his thing: He lit up their day and made them feel happy for a short period of time. At the end of the show, Guy had tears in his eyes looking at these young Canadian soldiers who were helping to train members of the Ukrainian armed forces. Later, Guy played ball hockey and Ping-Pong with them and had a laugh with everyone. To me, Guy Lafleur was the real deal. He was beyond what everyone thought of him and his persona. The Flower was such a true gentleman.

THE LEGENDS TOUR

I hosted the NHL Legends/Oldtimers Tour for around ten years. I also hosted NHL alumni games, and I would play in them as well. It was an awakening for me, as I really got to know the players on the tour. It was a thrill, too, because I got to play with a lot of my heroes—guys like Bryan Trottier, Billy Smith, Dale Hawerchuk, and Steve Shutt. Maurice "The Rocket" Richard would coach on occasion. Guy Lafleur joined us at times. It is sad to me that both Hawerchuk and Lafleur have passed away. They were the two best numbers 10s that I ever met.

It was an incredible event to be a part of. Think of it as the Harlem Globetrotters on ice. The lead organizer of the tour was a woman named Cathy Sproule. A former broadcaster, Cathy was amazing at putting events like this together, and she got me involved to help add some colour to the games. At first, there was just a hockey game, but we made it something bigger and took it across Canada. A few games were played in front of over fifteen thousand people. We did this all across Canada, and I took part in some of the hijinks during the games.

There was one skit where I took part in a shootout in slow motion to the theme from *Chariots of Fire*. I often skated on the same line as Chris "Knuckles" Nilan and Bob Probert. Former NHL official Ron Hoggarth would often referee the games, and he would ask everyone how many goals they'd scored in the NHL. They would get to me, and I would say, "None." That is when I would break into my slow-motion shootout attempt, and we would add some special effects while I did it. It was a lot of fun.

Being on the road with these guys was fascinating. It gave me a great insight into how much they all still loved the game. It also taught me how much they missed playing. Some of the guys, quite frankly, needed the money. I was a little worried about Nilan because he was still battling addiction at the time. And Probert, who had previously had some addiction issues.

Mainly, we played our games against police officers and firefighters, with the main charity being the Special Olympics. I would worry about Knuckles and Probie because there were times when opposing players would take a run at them. I told Cathy one time that we had to be careful—there could be a fight, and that would end the tour. I wanted to make sure there were no problems. Fortunately, there were never any issues on the ice, and we would all get together after the game for a social.

One week, the tour was in Ottawa, and I couldn't make it. Gus Badali, who was at the event, called me up and said, "Rod, you were so right." I asked him what he meant. Gus said, "Well, Nilan and Probert did fight." I asked who they'd fought. "Each other!" They were in a bar and Probert had had enough of Knuckles, so he slugged him. It started a little dust-up. Generally, though, it was a trouble-free event.

We were in Leamington, Ontario, one time, and I had the thrill of a lifetime. The Hanson brothers from *Slap Shot* often joined us, and it was a lot of fun. Well, in Leamington, Cathy came up to me and said, "Rod, Steve Carlson couldn't get over the border. There was a problem." Then she looked at me and said, "Listen, I can get a wig. Would you like to be the third Hanson brother?" I said sure, and I put on some fake glasses and a wig, and for that night, I was one of the Hanson brothers.

I took part in all of their shenanigans, and nobody knew it was me. I started the game as myself and introduced everyone, then went back to the dressing room to change into my Hanson brothers outfit. What a night. I had always dreamed of being a pro hockey player, and here I was, starring in my own version of *Slap Shot.*

BOB PROBERT

As tough and feared as he was during his playing days, Bob Probert was one of the nicest men I have ever met. I spent a lot of time with Bob and got to know him. Because I was a media guy when I first joined the tour, he was a little standoffish, but we got to hang out on the road. Like most people, I loved his personality. I knew he had fought some inner demons. Physically, he was a huge man, but he was so kind and so gentle. Not long after I joined the tour, I recommended Bob for a speaking engagement in Halifax. It was part of a dinner that I do annually with the Canadian Progress Club, which is easily one of the best charity events in Canada. The money raised goes to support individuals with developmental or intellectual disabilities. They consistently have the best guests. Everyone who is anyone has been a part of the dinner, from Joe Montana to Georges St-Pierre, George Foreman to Mark Messier and Carey Price.

Bob Probert met the people we were raising money for at a luncheon the day before, and he was so great with everyone. Then, an hour before the big event, he looked at me. "Blackie, I have never done one of these things before. I don't even know what to talk about. What should I do?" This was an hour before the show, and he was standing outside, smoking a cigarette. I just told him to be himself. Paul Coffey was with him, and he told Bob to tell one or two good stories. Sure enough, Bob gave one of the most memorable speeches I have ever heard. He was so emotional, and he didn't hold back at all. He talked about his previous troubles, and how he was coming back. It gave me an appreciation of what the real Bob Probert was all about. Bob was an amazing dude, and I miss him dearly.

At the same time, I got to know Chris Nilan. Soon after the tour, Knuckles turned his life around. And I believe a big reason for that was Bob Probert's death in 2010. Nilan figured out a way to get off his addiction to painkillers.

During that tour, I would get calls at my hotel room, and as soon as I answered, they would hang up. I was so confused. We were in Nova Scotia, and I would see some guys hanging around, and I didn't know who they were. I was on the team bus one day, and Chris Nilan asked me, "Blackie, have you been getting some phone calls?" I said yes, what is going on? He told me, "Dude, they call me all the time."

It turned out the FBI had been tailing Nilan for a long time and following his every move. Nilan's partner at the time was the stepdaughter of infamous Boston gangster Whitey Bulger. We were on this hockey tour, playing against police officers, and now this was going on. I had a long conversation with Chris one day, and he told me all about what happened and how he knew Whitey. Knuckles said he hadn't talked to him or seen him in years. The FBI wanted to know if Chris had any contact with Whitey because, at the time, he was the most wanted man in the United States after Osama bin Laden.

Those years were crazy. The NHL alumni never lost. And they were facing some good teams. It taught me about the beauty of hockey and how these guys could still pass the puck. Younger players would try to skate around the former NHLers, and that never turned out well. Former Islanders goalie Billy Smith played with us, and like in his playing days he would chop at players who got too close to the crease. In the warm-up, if you took a shot up high, Billy would get angry at you. At the same time, he was always the last guy to leave the bar. He loved first responders, and he would tell stories until two or three in the morning. What I thought I knew about Billy Smith from my broadcasting days was completely different than the real person. He still had an edge, but Billy was the nicest man. He had a kind heart, and he had time for everybody. Just don't go near him in the crease!

There were times when we would be sitting in these tiny dressing rooms in small-town arenas across Canada. But because of the love the game, and the love of the camaraderie that comes with hockey, these NHL legends never complained. Everybody on the tour got along so well. It was one of the greatest experiences I had over the years. Yes, they were the greatest hockey players in the game, but they were even greater guys. And even though they played hockey at the highest level, I realized that their sweaty equipment stank just as much as mine.

10

PRESIDENTS, PRIME MINISTERS, AND HOLLYWOOD STARS

THROUGHOUT MY CAREER, I HAVE HAD THE OPPORTUNITY TO SPEAK WITH PRESIdents, prime ministers, and future presidents.

I met President Barack Obama at an NCAA basketball regional tournament. I was working courtside, and I shook his hand, and we had a nice conversation. He loves basketball. I was able to interview Joe Biden back in 2010. I also got a chance to meet Bill Clinton. Canadian Prime Minister Jean Chrétien, for whatever reason, took a liking to me. He was like a great-uncle; a nice guy, and he was a big guy in stature as well—he was taller than you'd think.

Chrétien would look at me and say, "Hey, handsome guy." That is what he called me. I don't care what you think of his politics, he was a likeable guy. I played golf with him once, and it was the fastest round

I had ever been a part of. We played at the Ottawa Hunt Club, and we played nine holes in just over forty-five minutes. Chrétien golfed so fast. Later, I caddied in the group with the prime minister when he played with Tiger Woods. Tiger and the prime minister got along well. They laughed and joked, and Tiger even gave Chrétien a couple of tips. I later did an event for Prime Minister Stephen Harper on Parliament Hill. I also got to know Prime Minister Brian Mulroney.

Later, I interviewed Israeli Prime Ministers Benjamin Netanyahu and Ehud Barak and British Prime Minister Tony Blair while I was working at *Canada AM*.

This little old sports guy from Winnipeg, talking to all of these world leaders. I never thought that would ever happen.

I met former US President Jimmy Carter when I went to Ghana for Plan Canada. President Carter was the ultimate hero, and he and his wife, Rosalynn, were so nice. He was there working for Habitat for Humanity.

All of them, they are as human as they come. They are just like you and me, except that they are in an incredible position of power.

I interviewed Donald Trump a few times, long before he became president, when he was doing his show *The Apprentice*. I also interviewed him at a number of golf events. He was a great interview, and he always called me Roderick. He was a larger-than-life used-car salesman. You never knew what was going to come out of his mouth next. But never in a million years did I ever think he would become president. I asked him one time if he was going to get into politics, and he said something like "I can't take the pay cut." I have friends who know Trump and golf with him. They swear that everyone who gets around him, even those who despise him, comes away loving the guy. Trump has this sort of charm and charisma about him.

Meeting these kinds of leaders has given me a great perspective on the world and how, no matter who you are, everyone is the same. One trait all leaders have is that they are masters of communication; they know how to talk to people. But they don't waste words. That is not the way it works in the media world. Like most broadcasters, I can be the enemy of silence.

I will talk to anyone about anything, anytime. It has made me a better broadcaster and a better person. When I first started in the business, I was still young. I put on a brave face early on, and I didn't go out and seek new people right away. Once I got around some of the people I have come to know over the years, I realized you should never miss an opportunity to meet somebody and never miss the opportunity to shake someone's hand and find out what they are all about. Even now, I get asked questions. If I am golfing, usually around the fourth hole, I get asked how I got into the business. I answer these questions, but I want to know about the people I am with and where they are from and what they are all about. That is the art of communication. It just pays to be curious.

Meeting all of these people has given me a proper perspective on my own life. Everyone is going through something, good and bad. The key is to find balance in life. And balance in our industry is tough to find. I didn't have a lot of it when I was younger. My wife and my family gave that to me. Before that, I was 100 percent focused on work. It did well for me and allowed me to get to where I did, but it goes back to the triangle of life: work, family, and leisure. If you take too much of one, the triangle is going to stretch and turn into a flatline. I still struggle to find balance to this day.

Trust me, finding balance in work and in life isn't easy. It gets even harder when you end up covering one of the most tragic events of our lifetime.

11

CANADA AM AND 9/11

THE MORNING OF TUESDAY, SEPTEMBER 11, 2001, WAS MY SECOND DAY ON THE JOB at *Canada AM*. I had been filling in at the show for a while. I am a workaholic, and whenever there weren't many sports events taking place, I would fill in. Plus, I found that working there helped build my broadcast skills. I worked with Keith Morrison, John Roberts, Pamela Wallin, Valerie Pringle, Dan Matheson, and Lisa LaFlamme. Jeff Hutcheson was also part of the team.

In the summer of 2001, network president Ivan Fecan tried to convince me to stay on more permanently at *Canada AM*. He thought Lisa and I had good chemistry, and we did, and I liked working with her. I was still doing sports at night, and I would come in the morning to do *Canada AM*. Though I was having fun doing the show, I had zero intention of taking the job. Fecan kept trying to convince me, though, so I sat down with my wife, Nancy, and my agent, Elliott Kerr, and we talked it over. We eventually said yes, and I joined *Canada AM* in August 2001.

Even though I am a sports guy, I really liked working on the show. I had the opportunity to interview politicians and world leaders and all kinds of amazing people. I used to joke that I could interview former Prime Minister Joe Clark, hockey legend Wendel Clark, and country singer Terri Clark all in the same hour. Yes, you get "Clarked." Not to mention talking to most of the Hollywood stars while I was there.

Our first official day as a team was on Monday, September 10, 2001, one day after I'd hosted the Canadian Open in Montreal. We had a great show. And on Tuesday, we started off fine, and it seemed like a normal show. I interviewed a TV critic about the fall programming lineup. Then we got word that a plane had flown into the World Trade Center in New York. So, we started to interview someone who used to work at the US Federal Aviation Administration, when, all of a sudden, another plane flew into the second tower. Lisa thought it was a replay, but I said on the air, "That's no replay, that is live. This is no longer an accident." We had to pivot from an accident to a potential act of terrorism.

This was at the time when we couldn't get information instantly the way you can now. We contacted security expert Allan Bell. Bell happened to be close to CTV, and he immediately joined us in studio. Allan, a specialist in international counterterrorism, already had his finger on the pulse on what was happening. We were on the air, and Allan confidently said, "This is the work of Osama bin Laden."

Here was this show that I'd enjoyed doing, and wanted to do because it seemed like it would be fun. You know, talking to all of the Clarks. Now, two days into the job, we were dealing with a terrorist attack that had taken place while we were on the air. From then on, for months, every day we were talking about terrorism and the Middle East and the hatred that was going on in the world.

That day, 9/11, we were on the air for eight hours. Lloyd Robertson came in around two in the afternoon—he ended up getting nominated for a Gemini Award for his coverage of the day's events. Meanwhile, we were on the air all day! We had a band that was supposed to perform, and they joined at least fifty people standing behind the cameras, watching how everything was unfolding. Thankfully, because of my sports background, I was able to navigate throughout the day without a script. But while I was on the air and doing the show, I was still not processing everything that was happening. I was trying to find out information about topics that I didn't know much about. CTV News anchor Sandie Rinaldo is a warrior. She wasn't even on the air, but she spent the morning handing me wire copy of the latest updates from New York.

My head still hurts just thinking about that morning. When the second tower collapsed, all of those people who were watching what was going on started sobbing. Camera operators and members of the crew were crying. It certainly wasn't what I had signed up for, and it was something I never want to have to go through again. It did give me a new-found appreciation for what news correspondents go through and how they have to report on events like that. It was then that I understood why Lisa LaFlamme loves news so much.

Though we would eventually have bands come in and perform live to lighten things up in the last hour of the show, the heaviness of it all started to beat me down mentally and emotionally. I was still doing sports at night, and then I'd have to read my research for the next morning's show, which was sent to my house. I would finally go to sleep around midnight, then I'd have to get up around four in the morning and be back on the air by six thirty. I was so tired during that time. Oh, and my wife and I were having another kid. Our first son had been born in 2000, and our second was born in 2002. (We later had two more kids, in 2003 and 2005.) After four kids in five years, my wife, Nancy, was the real champion in the family.

When I finally got off the air on 9/11, our boss, Trina McQueen, came in and told us we had done an amazing job. I went into my office and I just broke down. I was thinking of our one-year-old son, and the second on the way, wondering what kind of world they were coming into. I could not talk about that morning for a long time. I worked on 9/11 so much, I had to compartmentalize to cope with it.

Then, one week later, I had to go to New York to interview Lenny Kravitz. There was still smoke smouldering at the crash site, and the whole interview was taken up by talk about 9/11. I loved working on *Canada AM*, and we had so much fun together. We still would have fun, but it became a different show after 9/11. It is tough to have fun when so many lives were being lost and Canada was sending troops to Afghanistan.

I'd worked around a month a year at *Canada AM* throughout the 1990s. After I started full time, I lasted around eighteen months. Eventually, I got too busy with sports and I had a lot going on. It was for the best for everyone that I returned to sports full time. Don't get me wrong: I loved *Canada AM*. I just wish it was during a better time.

12

GAME-A-DAY BLACK

IF THERE IS ONE THING PEOPLE MENTION WHEN THEY TALK ABOUT MY BROADCAST career, it is my flexibility. You name the sport, and I have likely hosted it or called the play-by-play. It is something I am proud of. I don't think a lot of people realize the work that went into being able to call all of those different sports. Beyond the fact that I really have no social life, I love sports and I watch every game. I know one thing: I have watched more sports than any other human being on the planet. That is not something I am proud of, but I watched them all to be prepared.

When I started calling games, there were often scheduling conflicts between sports. I might call a CFL game one night, then a Blue Jays game the next. One week, I called a Blue Jays game, a CFL game, a golf event, and then a boxing match at the Royal York hotel in Toronto—four events in five days. At one point, people called me "Game-a-Day" Black. I felt so lucky to be able to do it all. I was happy people were asking me to do it, and best of all, I was being paid to do it.

If the Jays were playing and I was working a CFL game, it meant I couldn't watch the baseball game live to prepare for the next Jays broadcast. I would have someone send me a video copy of the game via a taxi, and it would arrive at my house around midnight. Then I would stay up until three in the morning and go through all of my prep.

It did take me a few years to learn that whatever prep work I was doing, it wasn't ever enough. After that, I would over-prepare for everything. If I ever felt a little skittish before the start of an event I was calling, it was because I hadn't prepared enough. My files are always full of stories that I keep on hand for future broadcasts. I may never use them, but I like having them in case I need them. And I like to think that I have a good memory for that stuff. I can't remember where my car keys are, but I can tell you every Stanley Cup champion and every NFL rushing leader. It all goes back to my youth. To this day, I can remember all of the numbers of everyone who played on the Winnipeg Jets or for Team Canada. These days, technology has changed my preparation for everything I do. What used to take days and weeks to research and memorize can now be pulled up in a few seconds because of AI technology. The ability to get all of this lightning-fast information so quickly now allows a broadcaster to concentrate more on the stories than the statistics. Some people are afraid of AI. I am not. I embrace it. But I also realize that all of these AI platforms are not human. And they can make mistakes sometimes.

I just love calling sports, all of them. I like being versatile, and I like calling different events and different games. Moving from one game to another, and one arena to the next, I might have made a whole lot more money had I concentrated on just one sport, but I liked them all, and to this day, I like the sights and smells that come with covering a sporting event. It doesn't matter to me if it is a pro event or amateur; I've never said no to anything. I was always ready to call a game. I didn't care what the sport or what the event, I loved it all. I always learned something along the way.

I treat a high school competition with the same respect that I would give to covering the Stanley Cup Final. That's because I have kids, and I have watched online streams of some of their events and hated how little work went into calling them. It drives me crazy if a name is mispronounced or a fact is wrong. I am stickler for making sure I get all of that right. Especially if it is an amateur or high school sport—I feel I am broadcasting for the parents, and I want to tell their stories right. I received a text message not long ago from the brother of a coach of a game I called, and he was so happy that we told their story. As a father who has two sons playing pro sports, I appreciate those stories. Preparation and repetition are huge for me.

There are times when I feel that television today doesn't do a good job of telling the stories we need to hear. How can we get to know the athletes if we don't tell their stories? That is why coverage of local sports is so important.

Because of all of the sports I called over the years, nobody has worked with more colour commentators or analysts. More than colleagues, they became teammates. And in many cases close friends. Calling a game is never a solo act. The best broadcasts are conversations. You listen, you react, you set up, you challenge each other, and you build something together in real time.

Sometimes I have had to call a game by myself, which is a lonely proposition. I have always loved to lean on my analyst's perspective. To this day, I am still learning about the games, the players, and the stories that bring it all to life.

In May 2025, I hosted an event for the Heart and Stroke Foundation with Carey Price. I thought I knew everything about him. I knew he was shy, but I didn't know how soft-spoken and interesting he was. I honestly didn't know how much I was going to get out of him. Then I did the event, and I ended up learning so much about him. The audience was captivated by Carey, and so was I. It was an incredible interview. His dad was in the audience, and I watched Carey go through every story, and his dad was in tears throughout. The experience taught me that it's what you say, not how you say it, that matters. Carey captivated the crowd. It was an incredible interview—candid, colourful, and deeply real. His dad, Jerry, sat in the audience, in tears throughout an emotional conversation that traced every peak and valley of his incredible career.

It wasn't just about wins and losses. Carey spoke openly about the weight of expectations, his relentless quest for perfection, the toll it took on his mental health, and the grounding force of family that helped pull him through. He also understood—and embraced—the responsibility he carries as a role model, particularly within the First Nations community, where his voice and visibility mean far more than hockey.

I'll admit, at first, I wondered if someone so soft-spoken could reach a sold-out crowd. I couldn't have been more wrong. Yes, he was quiet, but he could have whispered and people still would have hung on every word.

It was a powerful reminder that authenticity carries its own volume, and that what you have to say will always matter more than how loudly you say it.

After the event, Carey made time for every person there. The lineup went on forever, and he took pictures with everyone. Carey Price is a special person.

Moments like that night with Carey stay with you. They remind you that sometimes the most powerful thing you can do is know when to speak—and when not to. Kind of like announcing games. Because every sport has its own rhythm, its own volume, and its own truth. And learning to respect that is one of the great challenges and the great joys of broadcasting.

Calling baseball and football and golf all take a different set a of skills. The same goes when you are calling figure skating. There is a unique nuance to calling this sport. I was thrown into it, and I quickly learned to love calling the special rhythm that comes with figure skating. One thing I noticed was that the American announcers would talk over every moment in the routine. I decided I was going to let the routine breathe, and we could talk about it after the skaters were finished. I always considered figure skating to be a sport where we let the viewer know what is about to happen—I would tell them a jump was coming, or mention that the skater had just performed a certain move. But while I had to frame stories, I didn't see a need to overly talk about it.

The greatest adjustment as an announcer that I ever had to make was at the 2010 Winter Olympics in Vancouver. I was calling figure skating and short-track speed skating, which was held at the same venue. You go from this sublime, artistic skating event to what is basically roller derby on ice. I loved the differences in the two sports.

There is a certain sophistication that comes with calling figure skating. When I started, I didn't like how all of our broadcast openings were poetic and soft. I urged the producers to put a little pizzazz into the broadcasts. We were in the glory days of Elvis Stojko and Kurt Browning, who were rock stars. Heck, even as announcers at these events, we were treated like rock stars. The arenas were full, and for some Saturday night figure skating events, the TV ratings would often beat *Hockey Night in Canada*. It was the most incredible time to be a part of the sport. Everybody knew all of the skaters and all of their stories. We were so lucky. It was the most incredible time to be part of the sport. Skating could have easily had its own TV channel. Then I would go from that and call the rock-and-roll short-track speed skating.

Similarly, the week I called the Blue Jays, the CFL, golf, and boxing, each sport required its own pacing and cadence. At the same time, you have to meet the moment in every event you call.

When I first came to Toronto to work at CTV, I was skeptical about figure skating. At the time, I had never really watched it. One of my first events was the McCain World Cup of Figure Skating in Kitchener. I immediately fell in love with it—I loved the music, and everything else involved with it. I had people like Tracy Wilson and Debbi Wilkes who helped me understand the sport.

Over time, an interesting change occurred in my personal life. Especially when I was hanging out with my buddies. I had always played a lot of hockey, and I was a part of this league where we would play on Sunday mornings. At first, guys would always ask me about hockey and players like Doug Gilmour and Mark Messier. After about three years of covering figure skating, I started to get questions like: "What do you think about Elvis Stojko's routine this year?" "How is Kurt Browning doing?" "Is there anyone else landing the quad?" "What is with these judges?" That's when I knew that figure skating was making inroads in Canada.

The sport of figure skating owes a great deal to Johnny Esaw. He was a driving force in putting figure skating on Canadian television. He made it a viewer-worthy sport, highlighting the drama and intrigue and politics of figure skating—especially when it came to the judging. But it was a blessing and a curse that figure skating was on television so much. I really believe that it ended up getting overexposed. And the judging scandals also hurt the sport. I always wanted to maintain a level of integrity in the sport, but some of my superiors didn't want me to talk about the judges. And I knew there were a number of judges who hated me, because if they made a horrible error in evaluating a skater, I would say on the air that it was awful. I found a lot of people in the skating world were afraid to complain. I wasn't an expert, but I wasn't a fool either. But, I mean, the viewers had questions as well.

I will never forget the time we were in Helsinki, Finland, in 1999 for the World Figure Skating Championships. One of our camera operators,

Alf Carboni, came up to me after one of the routines and said, "Hey, listen, these judges are tapping each other and talking to each other." I told him to start filming it. Then we looked back at the video Alf shot and saw the judges giving coded messages to each other during the gold medal pairs routine of Elena Berezhnaya and Anton Sikharulidze. The integrity of the competition had been compromised. I showed the video to officials, and they tried to downplay it. Then I showed the video to Dick Button from ABC, and he said it was nothing. Well, sorry, there was a lot to this judging scandal. I was so upset that neither one of those judges was ever sanctioned, and everyone tried to sweep it under the rug. Whatever happened to any of the judges, the consequences were not stiff enough. If an American team had been affected and a reporter like Christine Brennan from *USA Today* had seen the video, it would have been a different story.

Sure enough, a few years later, those same judges were communicating again, currying favors, and actually fixing the final result that cost Canada's Jamie Salé and David Pelletier a gold medal in pairs. The scandal rocked the sports world, and Jamie and David would eventually receive their medals, but not before the sport of skating had been shredded to its bones.

As the years went by, TSN and CTV dropped figure skating. Quite frankly, my bosses were not big fans of the sport and didn't want anything to do with it. Johnny Esaw, the man who brought figure skating to Canadian television, would have rolled over in his grave. But at its peak, it was a very popular sport. It just doesn't get the TV coverage that it once did.

Like everything else, change was inevitable. Make no mistake, skating is still must-see Olympic TV, but unfortunately, the sport that at one time was on almost every television every weekend can now barely be found on any channel. Like many people, I miss it.

13

A SHARP-DRESSED MAN AND THE LEGENDARY MOUSTACHE

WHEN YOU HAVE AS MANY EVENTS ON THE GO AS I HAD THROUGHOUT MY CAREER, there are times when you run into problems with your wardrobe. I know basically every sports stat there is, but I often can't find my laundry.

One time, I was working with hockey player turned broadcaster Cheryl Pounder, and I forgot my dress pants, so I went out to see if I could find some. This was a Sunday in Quebec City, and I couldn't find anywhere to buy a pair, so I ended up wearing blue jeans for the broadcast. I just told the producer to film me only from the waist up. Later on, I was calling a CFL game in Ottawa with Duane Forde. We were scheduled to call a game in Winnipeg at three o'clock the following afternoon, and I did something stupid, a real rookie mistake: I checked my baggage. I was planning on staying in Winnipeg for a couple of days, so I had packed some more clothes than usual. I got to the Ottawa airport around five in the morning for the flight to Winnipeg, and when I landed at about eight thirty, my bag didn't. The airline said my baggage would arrive on the next flight, but it didn't. Then they told me it was going to be in Winnipeg by two. Duane met me in the lobby of the hotel around twelve thirty, and I was wearing sweatpants. I ended up going to Marshalls and spent a total of ten minutes in there. I grabbed a suit off the rack, a dress shirt, a tie, and some dress shoes. The whole outfit came to just over $140. The ties that TSN gave us to wear on the broadcast cost more than my entire outfit. Nobody would have known, but then Duane had to tell everyone what I was wearing. And Duane let everyone know about my cheap suit, which would have been a safety hazard around an open flame. I still own that suit.

That experience showed me you don't have to worry too much about the quality of the clothing when you are on TV. When I was working at *Canada AM*, I had a deal with Hugo Boss: I would get fifty thousand dollars' worth of clothing every year. It was crazy how much money they spent to make us look good. But really, did it make a difference? A case in point, after the Winnipeg game, Duane and I decided to conduct an experiment. We called four games in a row, and we both wore the exact same clothes for each game. And do you know what? Nobody noticed.

Another time, I was in Yankee Stadium for a Blue Jays game. It was one of the hottest days in the history of New York City, unspeakably hot. I was calling the game with Pat Tabler, and we decided not to take the subway to the stadium because it was just too hot. We took a limo instead. One block from the hotel, the driver turned back towards us and said, "I am so sorry, but my air conditioning is not working." We were both sweating like pigs. I was really pissed off at our bosses that day. I'd asked if we could wear golf shirts because of the incredible heat, but we were told we had to wear our suits. It was so hot that for the first time ever at Yankee Stadium, they gave away free water to the fans. We got to the stadium, and we were sweating so hard it had soaked through our suits. We got into the booth and I said, "Fuck this," and took my pants off. Scott Carson, our statistician, ended up taking his shirt off. It wasn't a pretty scene, but we desperately needed to cool down.

I had a good relationship with Bob Sheppard, the iconic Yankee Stadium PA announcer. I would always say hi to him, and he would come to our booth to ask about pronunciations. He was such a nice man. Just before the start of the broadcast, old Bob came into our booth and said, "Mr. Black." I turned around, and he was greeted by the sight of me sitting there in my sweat-soaked, soggy underwear. I thought he was going to have a heart attack as he asked me, "How do you say 'Encarnación'?" He stared at me for a second, looking like he'd seen a naked ghost, and then sprinted out of our booth.

Because I called so many sports in so many locations and in such different weather conditions, I had to have clothes for every occasion. I have called events when it was forty Celsius, and others when it was minus-forty. I've had so many clothing mishaps over the years. Sometimes an article of clothing is sponsored, so you have to wear it. Then you put it on, and it is shocking how bad it is. Joe Carter once asked me, "Rodney, did you dress in the dark?" It was that bad.

When I called CFL games and I was driving to Hamilton, or downtown Toronto, or even to Ottawa, I wouldn't change into my suit until I got to the stadium. I often would change in the broadcast booth or the bathroom. CFL legend Angelo Mosca walked in on me one time as I was changing. He looked at me and said, "I have been around a lot of wrestlers, and you ain't one of them!"

THE MOUSTACHE

I had my moustache for a long time, but I shaved it off because of my kids.

Moustaches were in when I was young, and everyone had one. And I grew up with not much money, so we didn't have spare razors. In the beginning, it was a cheesy little moustache. I had it all through high school and even when I got older. It was a cool thing to have at the time, then I kept it out of comfort, because I only had to shave half of my face. Over the years, a few producers asked me to shave it off, and out of defiance, I kept it. Scott Moore once said to me, "You are a pretty good-looking guy. Why don't you shave that moustache off?" Because I was upset that he said that, I kept it out of spite. Our production crew shaved off my moustache as a goodbye gift on the air during my last day at *Canada AM*. But I grew it back.

When Tyler was four and his brother Brody was two, they started asking questions about my moustache. Brody said to me, "Daddy, I have never kissed you without a moustache." So, that is why I shaved it off. I would shave it off occasionally on vacation, but I always grew it back before I went back on the air. People tell me to this day, "I don't recognize you without the moustache." Meanwhile, I haven't had one for twenty years. This is a great example of how people have strong memories of great sporting events that I covered—Olympics, World Series, and so on. Either that, or they confuse me with Ron Burgundy.

It is all good. I only hope that people also remember me for the quality of my work. I always wanted to be remembered for what came out of my lips, not what was on top of them.

14

MY WORK FAMILY

I HAVE HAD THE PRIVILEGE OF WORKING WITH SOME AMAZING PEOPLE OVER THE course of my career. Many of them were more than just my colour analyst, and more like a part of my extended family.

One of them is David Feherty, and the other is Jim Nelford. For years, Nelford was *the* voice of Canadian golf. He was a big part of my life while we worked together. We were the Canadian version of Jim Nantz and Johnny Miller. Not in the same ballpark in terms of TV stature, or salary, but Nellie and I did all of the Canadian golf events. I learned a lot from him. To many, Feherty is the most entertaining analyst in golf. David was like a brother to me, and little-known fact, one of his first TV broadcasts was with our crew in Canada. The Royal Canadian Golf Association brought him in to be a part of the broadcast at Tiger Woods's first appearance at the Canadian Open, back in 1996. We hit it off right away. David was unpredictable, and he was so real.

The first time I worked with him, he was the on-course reporter. I was working in the booth with Jim Nelford, and I threw down to him. I said, "David, come in. Can you hear me?" David, in his famous Irish lilt, answered, "Rod, I would like to talk to you, but right now I am in the porta-potty." After that event, David was promoted to work in the booth with Jim and me, and he was such a natural at it. During the broadcast, whenever I threw to a commercial break, they would play this soft symphonic music with the camera operator focusing on a shot of some Canada geese walking across the fairway on the eighteenth hole. I said, "We will be back with more opening-round coverage in a moment from Glen Abbey." We still had ten seconds to fill, so I motioned to David, and he said, "Well, there they are, some Canada geese. Fancy that. You see a lot of them when you don't have a gun."

One time, David said to me, "Rod, that green is kind of like you, shallow and hard to hit." All I could do was laugh. David Nelly and I spent a lot of time together after the rounds as well. Golf is very social, and we would always go out for dinner after we were done with work for the day. When you went out for a drink with David, you went hard; it was always a late night.

I once hosted a corporate event for Pfizer in Prince Edward Island. The celebrities were Pat Quinn, Sandra Post, David Feherty, Tom Watson, and Jack Nicklaus. The night before the event, we were at the Links at Crowbush Cove. David loved hockey, and we were watching the Stanley Cup Final and drinking hard. Feherty drank so much that night that he ended up with his head lying on the bar. I helped him get to his room and into bed. The next morning, we were lining up for pictures with all the celebrities, and after the photos were done, Tom Watson pulled David aside. After their talk, David quit drinking and stayed sober for more than a decade. During that time, he turned to cycling as therapy, a way to clear his mind, steady his life, and stay on the right path. A couple of years into that sobriety, he was nearly killed in a serious bike accident. Feherty broke numerous bones throughout his body. Yet another brutal reminder of how fragile life can be.

Then tragedy struck in 2017, when his son died of an overdose. The loss was unimaginable, and David fell off the wagon. Somehow, he kept going. He battled his own addictions, continued to broadcast, and once again found his way back.

Feherty wrote a bestselling book, hosted his own award-winning talk show, and now shares his story around the world while doing remarkable work for mental health foundations. He's still broadcasting. Still razor sharp. Still one of the funniest men I've ever met, and one of the greatest dudes I've ever worked with.

DUANE FORDE

While he has a completely different personality than Feherty, I became just as close to Duane Forde during my years calling CFL games for TSN. I can't say enough good things about Duane. He is a quiet guy, and I had met him a few times after I started doing Canadian football with Leif Pettersen. Eventually, I was paired with Duane and we started calling games together. We had an instantaneous connection.

Duane is one of the smartest guys I know. Nobody knows the Canadian-born players in the CFL better than him. We got to the point on the air where we could finish each other's sentences. We travelled all over Canada together, including to exhibition games in Moncton, New Brunswick. I learned a lot about football and the strategy behind it from working with him. We worked together when it was minus-thirty Celsius and plus-thirty. We also called Canadian university football games together. We covered a game at Laval University in a snowstorm. We couldn't even see the players; it was snowing so hard our commentary deteriorated to "We think that is a first down," or "We think that is a catch." It was chaotic and a beautiful experience all at the same time. One of my greatest memories working with Duane was the 2011 Vanier Cup at BC Place in Vancouver. This was the game between McMaster and Laval. The two of us had called hundreds of football games in our careers, but we both agree that the 2011 Vanier Cup was the wildest, craziest roller-coaster ride of a game that we had ever called. At one point, we both blurted out at the same time, "This is the greatest game ever." To this day, many people still agree with us.

We shared a lot of time together. We would have breakfast every day, and we talked a lot about our families. Our crew had a favourite spectator sport: watching Duane eat. The guy could devour a cow on his own. One time, in Vancouver, he came so close to finishing a six-pound hamburger in record time. The dude could eat. I once joked that one of our crew members was missing, because Duane ate him. Duane and I lived by the same motto—we stick together. If we were getting off a flight, we would wait until the last member of the crew had joined us. Not all crews did that. I hated hearing about broadcast teams that would take five different cabs to the hotel. We were never like that. We were brothers in arms. And stomachs!

CHERYL POUNDER

For many reasons, I loved hosting and calling women's hockey over the years. One of the main reasons was the opportunity to work with two-time Olympic gold medal–winning hockey player Cheryl Pounder. Cheryl ended up becoming like a sister to me. I'd first met her years earlier, when I was covering women's hockey, and there wasn't the same interest in the game that there is now. I was broadcasting NHL games as well at this time, but I liked women's hockey.

At first, I thought it was over-hyped. There were people comparing the top women's players to the top men's players. You can't do that; they are two different styles of the same game. The sport grew, and the stars of the game, such as Hayley Wickenheiser and Cammi Granato, became legends. I was lucky to be involved in an era when women's hockey made great strides.

Then I was teamed with Cheryl, who had just finished her Olympic career. She is so fun to work with, and she has great passion for the game. Cheryl had a lot to learn at first, and she would ask me questions. I'd never worked with an analyst who regularly asked me what they should do. She became a great researcher and did a ton of homework before each broadcast. We travelled around the world together, and she became a star. I had more laughs working with Cheryl than almost anyone else I ever worked with. Cheryl had this crazy laugh where she ended up snorting. Sometimes you could hear her laugh on the broadcast.

Whenever a tournament ended and we had a wrap party, Cheryl loved to dance. One time, we were in Malmo, Sweden, and everyone on the crew ended up dancing on the tables. It sounded like it was a lot of fun for everyone. Until the next morning, when we had to pick wood chips out of our scalps from hitting our heads on the ceiling the night before. One of the first trips I ever took with Cheryl was to Zurich for the 2011 World Championships. Our rental car had a standard transmission, and I hadn't driven a stick shift in a while. It was a Mercedes-Benz, and the shifter was a little sticky. I almost put poor Cheryl into traction by damaging her vertebrae as I tried to change gears driving through the mountains of Switzerland—a hard thing at the best times, let alone with a tricky stick shift. The drive was no more than twenty minutes each way, but to Cheryl, I am sure it felt like hours.

Out of anybody I ever met, I could tell how she became an Olympian and a champion. Her work ethic was extraordinary. And her quest to be great was unwavering. She put the time in and she put the work in, and she wanted to be better with every game she called. She knows the game of hockey like few people I have worked with. Cheryl is a pro's pro, and she is a friend for life.

PAT TABLER

I put Pat Tabler right up there with my favourite people I have ever worked with. Tabbie and I didn't do that many games together, usually anywhere from twenty to thirty-five a year. We worked together for close to a decade. The two of us had a great time together. We called the last home opener at old Yankee Stadium, and we called the last Blue Jays game ever at the stadium. Along with Pat, I was able to call the famous Carlos Delgado four-home-run game. That was a real thrill for me, as it was such a remarkable feat. Hitting four home runs in a single game is just as rare as throwing a perfect game.

Pat and I are close in age, and both of us come from big families. He is a good-hearted man, and he was one of the bench players on the 1992 Blue Jays World Series team. That was when I got to know him first. Back then, if I needed to put a story together, I could always rely on Tabler and the guys on the bench. The two of us had so many laughs along with Scott Carson, the long-time stats guy on Blue Jays broadcasts.

Pat Tabler is a nice man and great to work with, and he had a slight drawl to his voice. I was notorious for bringing my kids to the stadium, and Pat never minded; he loved that my family was around. He was so proud when my son Tyler made it to the big leagues, because he remembers Tyler as a seven-year-old visiting the booth with his younger brother Brody every time we broadcast a game. Pat watched as Tyler grew up to be a great baseball player.

I took pride in the fact that I built friendships with the people I worked with in the broadcast booth. Some were less of a friend than others—that happens. But Pat Tabler was all class. Pat and I would either call games on the West Coast or call big games against the Red Sox and Yankees. We got a chance to call games at all of the great ballparks—we were in Yankee Stadium and Fenway Park a lot. At that time, the Blue Jays should have been better than they were. Paul Godfrey, a former Toronto politician and CEO of Sun Media, was president of the team, and they had Roy Halladay and other great players, but they just couldn't win during that time. But there was one date that will always stay with me: September 25, 2003—the date of those four home runs, one of the greatest individual achievements I have ever witnessed, never mind called.

Carlos Delgado was one of my favourite Blue Jays of all time, not just because of his Hall of Fame–calibre talent but because of his infectious personality. His smile lit up a stadium, and he never said no to a charity request.

So, it was a little awkward for me when Carlos looked me in the eye after batting practice that day and unsmilingly asked, "Blackie, are you on our team or against us?"

I asked him what he meant, and I guess he'd heard that I had used that old, tired cliché the night before on our broadcast about his teammate Kevin Cash not hitting his weight. I didn't think it was such a cheap shot, but Delgado thought otherwise, so I told him, "Hey, Carlos, I don't get paid to be a cheerleader." We chatted a little longer, each making our points, and even though Cash's batting average *was* below his poundage, I admitted that perhaps I'd been a little harsh and likely could have worded it differently.

Tabbie heard the whole conversation, and I could tell by his reaction as a former player that he understood how teammates stood up for one another—and how players hear everything.

Yep, words can hurt, but we also have to be fair and objective to the fan base and call it like is. But I told him I'd be careful with those words in future. Carlos smiled. Said no problem. Dabbed me up. Gave me a half hug. Went back to the locker room, put his jersey on, and then had one of the greatest nights in Blue Jay history, belting four home runs against Tampa Bay.

As Carlos Delgado was with his teammates, Pat Tabler was the same kind of teammate with our broadcast crew.

JACK ARMSTRONG

American sportscaster Jack Armstrong is a good man. Jack liked to stay up late, drink beer, and then wake up and run every day. Once, we were in Portland, and it was someone's birthday party. Usually, the night before a game, the entire crew goes out, and we often watch a game on TV. Later that evening, Leo Rautins saw Jack and me standing in the street, singing, *Alice, Alice, who the fuck is Alice?* No matter what happened, we would always end the night with Jack Armstrong. His Irish eyes were always smiling, or they were bloodshot. And we almost always ended up in a bar, where Jack would get up, grab a microphone, and sing. During the Toronto Raptors' NBA championship run in 2019, Jack sang every night. Jack is a crooner, and he's pretty good—he can carry a tune. Jack even released his own Christmas album in 2022.

Another classic night took place in New Orleans around the NBA All-Star Game in 2017. Every morning, Jack and I had to do TV hits back to the network. Every night, we shut down Bourbon Street. One drink became two, and then the next thing you knew it was four thirty in the morning. I would beg him, "Jack, can we just go?" I had never heard of a dive bar until I met Jack. We ended up in a bar and Jack would feed quarters into the jukebox and grab the mic from the stage and sing along to every song. We got into a rickshaw to get back to the hotel. We finally made it back at five, and I knew we had to be back in the lobby at eight thirty to start our day. I was so tired, and I had had way too much to drink. I fell asleep at five thirty, my alarm went off at eight, and I went to the lobby—and there was no Jack. At 8:31, Jack came running into the lobby. "Roddy, sorry, I just had to go for a jog." Even after a late night, Jack still ran at least five kilometres that day. He was fresh as a daisy!

Another time, we were at the 2018 All-Star Game in Los Angeles. That was so much fun. We did all of our hits on the beach, wearing beach shorts with our suits. Our producer, Michael Hamarneh, was so good; he wanted us to have fun. We all affectionately called him "the Hammer," and he allowed us to shine on the air. Not all producers think like that, and as a result, so many panels you see on various sports networks are so boring. It was a fun week at the arena and at the beach.

Jack is a great guy to work with, and he is a great storyteller. You can throw anything at him, and he is colourful and entertaining. But he is also thoughtful, and he thinks of the game differently than others. Leo Rautins thinks like a player, but Jack thinks like a coach.

Jack would often tease me for being late and always running a little behind. And he would say I looked like Pig-Pen from the *Peanuts* comic strip when I got to the arena. Hey, I don't like to get dressed up until I'm about to go on air. Why would I drive to the game with a suit on? I have a long way to go. And I am notorious for running late. It was the schedule I was keeping. I am married and we have four kids; I wanted to get everything out of my twenty-four hours every day.

Before the internet, it was even worse. I would read all the newspapers every morning. I wanted to get a good perspective of all sides of a story. I would get *The Toronto Sun*, *The Toronto Star*, *The Globe and Mail*, the *National Post*, *USA Today*, and *The New York Times*. And all of those papers would get delivered to my place every day. I would wake up around six and try to read all six papers from cover to cover before ten in the morning. On the road, I would take them with me. I liked to fly with nobody sitting beside me because I would bring all of these newspapers along—it was the only way to get all the information I needed before the internet took off. It was a different time, but it was a fun time, and it forced you to keep on top of things. I had so many papers piled up on my seat that I am sure Jack would have given me his trademark call: "Get that garbage out of here!"

LEO RAUTINS: MY BROTHER FROM ANOTHER MOTHER

Hockey is my first love, and baseball is my passion, but basketball is my obsession. Covering the Raptors and the NBA meant so much to me. That is why I still love calling games for the Canadian Elite Basketball League. Of all the people I have worked with over the years that I consider a friend, Leo Rautins is the person I am closest to. He isn't only like a brother—he's like my twin brother.

I first met Leo in 1983, the year he was drafted in the first round by the Philadelphia 76ers. Leo and the Sixers were to play an NBA exhibition game against the Denver Nuggets in my hometown of Winnipeg. Upon their arrival at the airport, I had a chance to interview Leo and my boyhood idol, Sixers legend Julius Erving. They both were great interviews, but I also had another mini mission.

The day before the Sixers arrived, I got a phone call at my desk at CKY from a young basketball fan coincidentally named Jay, who like me was a Dr. J fan. Jay told me he was sick in the hospital and couldn't make it to the game but wondered if I might be able to get him a Julius Erving autograph. Now, the cardinal rule as a broadcaster is never to ask for an autograph at any time, but I told Jay I'd try. I didn't feel comfortable asking for the autograph, but when I finished the interview with Doc, I handed him a piece of paper with Jay's phone number and told him that this kid was sick, and that he was Dr. J's biggest fan. Maybe he could give him a call.

I went back to the station to cut my story and cover the game later that night. Leo had a big game, scoring thirty-plus points, but the Doc did not. In fact, he didn't even play, which was a big downer for all of those who bought tickets. The next day, I was sitting at my desk when my phone rang, and it was Jay. "Hey, Rod, how are you? I just wanted to thank you for what you did for me with Dr. J." I wasn't sure what he was talking about, and like most Winnipeggers I was still disappointed that Erving didn't play the night before.

As it turned out, after our interview, the Doc got in the cab by himself and ended up visiting Jay in the hospital, spending a good hour with him, and giving him an autographed basketball. Young Jay couldn't say thank you enough, and I always remembered the last words he said to me: "Listen, Rod, I hope we can see each other again someday."

Unfortunately, we never did. Jay lost his battle with cancer a few months later. Such a sad story, but I couldn't help but think how a visit from a different doctor, Dr. J, not only helped make Jay's day but also gave him one of the best moments of his life.

I also couldn't help but think about how much in life is all about timing.

That never would have happened had I not met Leo, who had introduced me to the Doc. A few years later, we would become broadcast buddies.

In 1994, we found out Toronto was getting an NBA expansion team. From the start, CTV signed a national deal to broadcast the Raptors' and Vancouver Grizzlies' games. I was expecting to be the host of our broadcasts. Before any of that started, I went to Secaucus, New Jersey, to cover the expansion draft with Bob Costas of NBC. Clearly, Bob did not think this was one of the highlights of his esteemed broadcasting career. At the end, he said, "Transcripts of this show are UNAVAILABLE." To his credit, Bob did chuckle after he said that.

A little later, I went to Burkina Faso with Plan Canada. I got a phone call at the hotel, and I was so confused as to who might be calling me. I picked up the phone, and the line was crackling and full of static. "Rod, it's Doug Beeforth here." That was my boss at CTV, so now I was really confused. "Rod, I need to talk to you for a second. Listen, we were wondering if you would like to call the basketball games for the NBA." I had done some play-by-play, but I was mainly a host. Doug said, "When can you come back? I want to take you and Leo to Secaucus and do a trial run and a rehearsal."

I was dead tired when I got back home from my trip to Africa. We then flew to Secaucus and went into a little studio. The NBA commissioner, David Stern, wasn't there, but his little-known assistant Adam Silver was. Hard to believe, but back then, Silver was helping us get coffee and snacks. We called a game off tape, and I thought the rehearsal went pretty well. I got home, and they called me and told me I was their guy. Now I was calling games with Leo Rautins. We became inseparable, and Leo knows so much about the game and all the players in the NBA. We became known as the *Miami Vice* guys because we took advantage of our clothing allowance and always dressed well. We had so much fun doing the games, and he was so easy to work with.

However, he would wear me out on the road. I would get into my room, and Leo would call right away: "Rod, what are doing? Do you want to go for a walk? Do want to go to lunch? Do you want to work out?" He would just hammer me with these questions. When we did go out, we were out late every night. It was insane. Leo had just stopped playing, and he loved the lifestyle of a pro basketball player. We did the season opener for the Raptors, then flew to Vancouver to call the opener for the Grizzlies. Leo Rautins was a machine; this guy just wouldn't sleep!

Charles Barkley was in Vancouver one night as a member of the Houston Rockets. He joined Leo and me the night before the game and we all went out. I tapped out at about four in the morning; I couldn't keep up with those two. Of course, the clocks moved ahead one hour that day, and we had a production meeting at nine in the morning. We still ended up having a great broadcast.

We were with Charles during the warm-up, and he was hurting. TV star David Duchovny was sitting courtside with his then wife, Téa Leoni. Charles had just missed a shot, and he walked over to our broadcast table just as we were going to break and looked at Duchovny and Leoni. "Hey, folks! You see those two guys right there? They kept me up all night!" He giggled as he walked away. It was hilarious. Even hungover, Charles went off and ended up scoring twenty-eight points and grabbing thirteen rebounds.

Post-game, our courtside reporter, Sandra Neil, started to ask Charles a question. He cut her off, said sorry, and jumped over the broadcast table. He joined Leo and me and said, "I haven't seen you guys in a long time." That was classic Charles Barkley. He wasn't trying to be rude to Sandra; he just wanted to spend time with Leo and me. Plus, once Charles is your friend, you have a friend for life.

Leo and I had so many moments like that working together. In every town on every night, there was a story that involved Leo. He was a father of four boys, and I am the father of four kids. Even though his first marriage fell apart, Leo was one of the best fathers I have ever been around. He was so good with the boys, and he was always guiding them, but not interfering.

We called the Raptors' game where they beat the Chicago Bulls before a packed SkyDome. There were thirty-six thousand people at that game. The Raptors were not good back then, so our storylines involved the stars of the visiting teams, and I was lucky enough to interview all of these star players when they came to town. Before the Raptors tipped off against the Bulls, we knew that Michael Jordan and Scottie Pippen had been out all night enjoying the Toronto nightlife. With its world-class restaurants offering every kind of food you can imagine and vibrant nightlife, Toronto was quickly becoming the favourite road city for teams in the NBA. It has everything wealthy athletes are looking for, and much more. When there was an afternoon game in Toronto, the Raptors always had a distinct advantage.

I got to know Kobe Bryant because Leo Rautins had played with his dad in Italy. Thanks to him, I have my favourite photo from my broadcast career—it's a shot of me interviewing Kobe courtside at a Raptors game. The film *Reservoir Dogs* had come out just before Kobe joined the NBA. He always called me Mr. Black, and I called him Mr. Purple as a reference to the characters in the movie. Interestingly enough, his nickname was the "Black Mamba," and he was ruthless on the court. He scored eighty-one points one night against the Raptors in 2006.

Leo and I were together for all of the great Raptors playoff runs as the team became contenders. Then, in 2019, they went on their incredible championship run. I had tears in my eyes at the end, when the Raptors won Game 6 in Oakland. It had nothing to do with me; it was for Leo. His dream was always to win the NBA championship. I could see how much the Raptors' win meant to my best friend. He never had a chance to see his dream come true because of injuries. When healthy, he was a fantastic player, but by the time he retired, Leo had undergone fourteen knee surgeries.

The night the Raptors won, we all went out late. I left the party at 4 a.m. because I had to call a CFL pre-season game in Edmonton the next night. All anyone asked me about at the football game was the Raptors' win. Much like the Blue Jays in 1992 and 1993, the Raptors were Canada's team and had loyal fans from coast to coast and, because of the internet, around the world.

Basketball isn't the only thing that Leo is known for.

There is a video on YouTube that went viral, and it is still played to this day. What people have to realize is that Leo farts all the time. We all tease him about it, and Leo still farts. In November 2019, I was in studio, hosting a Raptors game against New Orleans with Sam Mitchell and Leo. In the fourth quarter, just before we came back from a break, Leo let a big fart bomb go. My nostrils were burning—it was brutal. On the air, I said, "I apologize profusely. There was a gas leak in the studio." After that, the three of us laughed non-stop for close to a minute. We couldn't talk; we just kept laughing. Leo said, "What is wrong with you people?" The next day, I got a call from our executive producer, Paul Graham, and I thought I was going to be in trouble. Instead, he said, "That might have been the best analysis from you guys!"

More stories have come out of basketball than any other sport I covered. Thanks to basketball and the Raptors, I developed life-long friendships with Leo, Jack Armstrong, Matt Devlin, and Paul Jones. And in all of my dreams as a kid growing up in Winnipeg, I could have never imagined what basketball has given me. All the money in the world can't buy the experiences I have had during my career. My favourite picture is from an interview I did with Magic Johnson and Charles Barkley. All three of us were laughing our heads off, and it probably had something to do with one of Leo Rautins's farts!

I was also lucky enough to be around Tiger Woods and host a number of his golfing clinics—we hosted *Canada AM* from a clinic he ran on Toronto Island. I loved working with him, and I hosted a number of his Nike golf clinics, where I got to know him even better. I was covering the 1996 Canadian Open, and Tiger was becoming good friends with Charles Barkley at the time. This was Tiger's second-ever PGA Tour event, and Barkley told me straight out, "Look after my boy Tiger." Tiger wasn't a diva; he was just shy. We took him out for dinner a couple of times, and believe or not, he always wanted to go to Boston Pizza in Oakville. Tiger loved it because nobody bugged him there and he could eat in peace. And one more tidbit about Tiger: Like Leo, Tiger Woods—and David Feherty, for that matter—is notorious for farting!

The relationships I have had in sports are invaluable. I was never a millionaire during my career, but I was living like one. And I never took it for granted. The athletes knew they could trust me. I would not betray a friendship, ever. That was more important to me than some scoop. Unless the friend did something egregious, I wouldn't say anything. Those relationships last forever. Even though there are many of these people I haven't seen in years, if I ran into them tomorrow, it would be like we were never apart.

After the Raptors won the championship, we were on the air until midnight California time. It was such a wild night. They asked all of us to do a post-game show on Raptors TV. They had all this wine set up and we were drinking it on the air. Jack Armstrong was so pumped up; while we were live, he shouted, "We won it! Can you guys believe it? We fucking won a championship!" Once the post-game show wrapped up, Matt Devlin joined us and we took a photo with the Canadian flag at centre court. All the money in the world couldn't buy a moment and a memory like that. And I have been so lucky to have had many moments like that throughout my career.

15

THE CODE OF THE ROAD: TRAVEL DOS AND DON'TS WITH ROD BLACK

BY NOW, ANYONE READING THIS BOOK WILL REALIZE THAT I TRAVEL A LOT FOR work. And when I mean a lot, I mean that I have well over two million travel miles with Air Canada. And that is no exaggeration. Since I broke into the business in the early 1980s, there are few countries left that I have not been to at least one time.

In June 2025, I hosted a corporate conference in TD Bank in San Diego. As a proud Winnipegger, I am happy to say that the entertainment was music legend Burton Cummings. Magician Darcy Oake (son of CBC's Scott Oake and a boy from Winnipeg) was also there. I have been so lucky throughout my career. I have been able to see every part of Canada, from Iqaluit, to St. John's, to Vancouver and Victoria, and up to Yukon and Churchill, Manitoba. And in all that time, I grew to realize just how great our country is and that you don't have to travel elsewhere. I've hosted a huge sports banquet every year in Halifax for two decades. I love Halifax, and I have been even luckier to spend all that time in the Maritimes.

When I do have to travel to the United States, I love Chicago—one of my favourite cities. In my mind, Chicago is the greatest sports town in America, especially the way they support their hometown teams and get into the rivalries. In Chicago, everyone is so passionate about the Bulls and the Bears and the Cubs and the Blackhawks. New York City is great, but there is something about Chicago that I really like.

I also like small towns in America. I've visited a lot of minor-league ballparks, and I have called many games at various NCAA arenas and stadiums. Culturally, when it comes to sports, Canadians are so different than Americans. In Canada, generally speaking, we love our pro sports. In America, they love every sport, no matter what level.

When it comes to Europe, I love Prague, in Czechia. I loved all the Olympic cities that I worked in. I loved London and Barcelona, but I really loved Lillehammer in Norway. I fell in love with the place. What I love about Europe is that you can travel five kilometres and everything is so different.

I have travelled so much—way too much, actually—but I found out there is one constant in every place I've been to: the love of sport. You can be somewhere that there is war or civil unrest, but there is nothing like sport that unites people.

When it comes to packing for a road trip, I learned how to pack properly from *CFL on TSN* buddy Duane Forde. The trick is to roll everything before you pack it. I try to pack light, but I struggle with it. I never want to leave out one thing I might need, and comfortable clothes as well.

I know all the shortcuts when going to the airport. I always make sure that I get in the right line and the right place at the right time. I am notorious for getting to the airport late, but I don't call it late; I call it getting there on time. I don't like to waste time at the airport. If I have time to kill, I am in the lounge and I am working. I try to be as efficient as possible when I travel. If I have a flight at nine in the morning to Montreal, I will get dropped off at the airport at eight. I don't check any bags, and I just go and get on the plane. I know I cut it way too close, but that is what works for me. Thank goodness that I have a NEXUS card.

I was also notorious for using a lot of printer paper to prepare my game notes. I would go into an airline lounge to print all of my hundreds of pages of notes. One time, I printed so many pages that the guy in line behind me angrily shouted, "What the hell do you think this is? A Kinko's?"

I love Air Canada, and I still like to fly with them. I liked British Airways, too, and I like flying Delta in the United States. I have always found Air Canada to be the best. I have flown so much that some pilots got to know me.

I found out early in my career that FedEx flew at night. I got to know some people at a shipping and cargo company, and the flight crew would invite me on some of their cargo flights. We would leave at one in the morning because I had a game to call the next day. I would end up in one of their little jump seats because the cargo flights have only a few spare seats. On two of my cargo flights, they were transporting not only hundreds of bags of FedEx cargo, but also deceased bodies. Here I was, sitting on a plane filled with deceased bodies being flown to another city so they could be laid to rest by their loved ones. That freaked me out a little bit.

I am notorious for taking red-eye flights. Duane Forde and I both had young families and both wanted to get home as soon as possible. So, we always made sure to get on overnight flights. A few times, we would get on the late-night flight out of Edmonton with all of the oil workers from Fort McMurray. They all seemed like such great guys. They would see us, give us a high-five, and ask us about the game. Little did we know, they had been drinking all night while waiting for their flight. Often, one of the oil workers would end up getting hauled off the flight by police for excessive drinking or for smoking in the bathroom.

Traveling was always an adventure, especially if you traveled with me.

16

GIVING BACK, CHARITY, AND TENNIS WITH PETER GABRIEL

IN 2013, I WAS AWARDED THE QUEEN ELIZABETH II DIAMOND JUBILEE MEDAL FOR the charity and volunteer work I've done over the years, especially my work with Plan Canada. Originally called the Foster Parents Plan, the organization was started during the Second World War to help displaced children throughout Europe. From there, it grew to help children around the world and eventually evolved into what it is called today.

I didn't do charity work to win any awards. I always thought I had a responsibility as a young broadcaster to do work in the community. At the start of my career, I was asked to do a lot of community and charity events, and I never said no. To this day, I still don't. When I was a young roller-rink DJ in Winnipeg, my heroes were radio stars like Brother Jake Edwards, Lee Marshall, and Steve Jackson. I would ask them to come out to the roller rink for a community event, and they would come out and support the event. I never forgot that, and I thought it was so cool that they would take the time to be a part of it. I told myself that if I were ever in the same position as them, I would do the same thing.

Little charities led to bigger charities, and the bigger ones led to even bigger ones.

I came back from the Winter Olympics in Lillehammer in 1994 and got a phone call from Foster Parents Plan of Canada. I didn't know much about them, to be honest. I had seen some of their commercials, and they were kind of like World Vision. I wasn't interested in the whole idea. I told them I would get back to them and hung up the phone. I told my then girlfriend—now my wife, Nancy—"I don't know about this. I think it is bogus." She looked at me and said, "You never say no to anything. I am surprised you are thinking of saying no." Clearly, I phoned them back and said that I was in.

On my first trip in 1995, they sent me to Burkina Faso. After that, we went to Senegal. It ended up being a trip of a lifetime. I had no idea where I was going with this production crew. I told them at the start that no matter what, I would not do anything scripted. I went to these places in Africa, and I saw the need. I saw people who didn't have anything, and sports became irrelevant, and it really put my life into focus. It became this awakening, witnessing these people on the other side of the world who had absolutely nothing. But they had great joy, and the kids were so generous and loving. I am still an ambassador. I witnessed first-hand that the donations were working, and I saw what the generosity did for these communities. I did so many infomercials, and I went to nearly every African country. I went to Sri Lanka after the tsunami. I went to Nepal, and I went to Central America. I went to Brazil and everywhere else. Because of my sports schedule, I would travel to these places for a few days and do all of my on-camera work. Then I would have to come back to North America to call or host a sporting event. It had a profound effect on me. One time, we arrived in Sierra Leone as they were in the midst of a civil war that I didn't know about. It was a very dangerous experience, and I couldn't talk about what I witnessed for a couple of years afterwards. I had PTSD from my time there, it was that bad.

It was a beautiful country, and the rebels were trying to take over and take the diamonds. It was like the movie *Blood Diamond.* As a matter of fact, I was there at the time the events in that story were taking place. I didn't even realize it until I saw the movie years later. The movie and the memories of that time gave me nightmares. There were guns everywhere, and we arrived at this field outside of a town called Bo. We were told that we had to leave by sunset for our own safety. One of our cameramen continued to keep filming as the day got shorter. I frantically told him that we had to get on this plane. We all sprinted to get on board while the sun was setting. As we were taking off, I looked down and I could see the rebels coming into town. They knew we were there, and they were coming for us. They were converging at the end of the runway. Here I am, a sports guy who reads scores, and I was in the middle of these countries that were at war. I saw kids who had been hacked and mutilated by rebels. It was a turning point in my life. It made me realize just how lucky we are. I have bad days; everyone has bad days. But after those experiences, I never complained or got angry about little things ever again. It was a gift given to me by Plan Canada. They keep thanking me for helping them. I want to say thank you to them, because it was an eye-opener.

Through these experiences, I had a chance to interview rock star Peter Gabriel.

In 1995, I was in Dakar, Senegal, for my thirty-third birthday. I was with our tour guide, Edwin, and we were scheduled to do an interview with Gabriel. Peter was known for his humanitarian work around the world. I had just come from covering the US Open tennis tournament. I was never the biggest fan of Genesis and all that. But on the way to meet Peter for the interview, I listened to a bunch of his music on a Walkman. I think Peter sensed that I wasn't a big fan, and he kind of liked that. We were sitting down at his place in Dakar, and he was such a good interview. He was performing on behalf of numerous music charities to support Africa. I enjoyed the interview, and I was getting ready to leave when he asked me, "Do you want to play some tennis?"

I said yes, of course, and I ended up hitting tennis balls with Peter Gabriel on the court on his property. I figured I was never going to have a chance to do this ever again, so it was an easy thing to say yes to. He gave me a tin of black tea, and I had that tin for years. And I never drank the tea.

Later, my buddy Edwin called me at midnight, and he told me we were going out to this bar to celebrate my birthday. I was getting ready for bed—I had a shoot at eight the next morning. Well, he talked me into it, and the bar was packed when we got there. There were more than a thousand people in the bar. I had a great time, and I was drinking Tusker beer. Around two in the morning, I was ready to go, and Peter Gabriel walked in with his wife. Peter and I ended up talking for a few hours. He loves sports, and he had a lot of tennis questions. Now it was five in the morning; I said goodnight to Peter and his wife, and when we walked outside, all of the cars were blocked in. Edwin got this guy to go onstage, and the plan was to announce the licence plate number so the car's owner would move it, allowing us to get out. All of a sudden, the guy says, "Ladies and gentlemen, please welcome my good friend, Mr. Peter Gabriel!" Peter performed a full ninety-minute concert. He sang "Biko," "Red Rain," "Solsbury Hill," and "Shock the Monkey." As he was wrapping up, the sun started to rise. We finally made it out of there and back to the hotel. I got on a pay phone and called my wife.

"You are not going to believe this!"

When you give a little, you get gifts back. I was in the right place at the right time, and it was a special night. What a day, what a night, what a birthday gift. I would never have met Peter Gabriel if it weren't for his love of charity and my growing love of what I was going to do for charity. Peter did it for nothing; he did it out of the goodness of his heart. He saw pain and suffering and he wanted to do something. It is humanity, and he felt that people shouldn't suffer. Needless to say, I became a huge fan of Peter Gabriel for many reasons.

While I did a lot of work with Special Olympics during my time at TSN, I first started working with them back in Winnipeg. I grew up in a neighbourhood where a couple of kids had Down's syndrome. Back in the 1960s, people with developmental disabilities never left the house, and the parents rarely brought them out in public. When they did come out, we would invite them to play with us, and they were no different than any of us. When I was at CKY in Winnipeg and doing some community work, I saw the work that Special Olympics Manitoba was doing. I got to meet some of the Special Olympics athletes, and it was great. More than just great, these athletes had an impact on me. When I moved to Toronto, I started to get more involved, especially during my time at TSN, where network president Jim Thompson was a huge champion of the Special Olympics movement. I started to host some of TSN's Special Olympic events, and from there, it became a life-long love affair.

I was seeing the evidence of how Special Olympics worked. I met two young men, Arthur and Troy. At first, they never said a word. Then, when they started to play ball hockey and participated in Special Olympic events, they blossomed. Years later, I found out that one of them was working as a manager at Staples and another was climbing the ladder with a major Toronto business. Because Special Olympics believed in them, they truly rose to the occasion. I saw the true power of it, and it was incredible.

I had the privilege of getting to be around people like Dr. Frank Hayden, who started the Special Olympics movement back in the 1960s with Eunice Kennedy Shriver. To me, Dr. Hayden is a true Canadian hero.

A lot of people with developmental and intellectual disabilities would never have had an opportunity to shine if it weren't for sports, which was a great outlet for them, and in the end, that is what sports is all about. Working with Special Olympics gave me a great perspective on life. I had been working on all kinds of pro events, and there is so much love and adulation for the athletes. People fawn over and deify the athletes one day, then tear them down the next. Pro sports are filled with money and scandals and everything else. Then you get to the purity of Special Olympics. It was such a breath of fresh air.

People ask me all the time about the greatest golf shot I have ever witnessed. I called the famous Tiger Woods shot from the eighteenth hole at Glen Abbey. I was there with Mike Weir at the Masters. However, the greatest shot I have ever seen was in 2015 at the Streamsong Golf Resort just outside of Tampa, Florida. I was hosting a big-money corporate event, the Northern Lights Golf Invitational, where people come down to Florida and raise money for Special Olympics.

That year, the organization brought in a young woman, Tess Trojan, who was an aspiring golfer. Golf was just becoming a part of Special Olympics. People got a chance to meet with Tess and talk to her about her start in golf. Her dad had taught her how to play, and she was pretty good. We were at one of the par-3 holes on the course. I had met Tess before because she was a part of the Special Olympics Limitless gala. She is an engaging and empowering athlete. People always use the term *disability*; no, it is just a different kind of ability.

I played my shot first, and honestly, it was one of my best golf shots I ever hit. I ended up three inches from the cup. I made a joke and said, "Come on, Tess, you have to beat that." Tess then hit the ball, and it landed around fifty yards short of the green. But it started rolling, and it kept rolling until it went into the hole. Tess had just hit a hole-in-one! I will never forget her reaction. I was jumping up and down, all excited—"Tess, a hole-in-one!" She looked and me and said, "Yes," in a matter-of-fact voice. I asked her if she'd ever had one before. She looked at me. "I don't think so." It was so charming and sweet. It was probably the first hole-in-one by a Special Olympics athlete. There is a great photo of me giving her a hug after her shot. The shot made my job easier as an emcee for the rest of the week, because all anyone wanted to talk about was Tess's hole-in-one.

Often at this event, the corporate golfers donate their prizes back to the charity. That year, the big prize was a trip to Portugal, and the winner gave it to Tess and her family. I talked to Tess's dad, and I asked for the ball from the hole-in-one. I put it in a frame with her scorecard and our picture, and I gave it to her at the Limitless gala later that year.

Fast-forward two months, and for the first time ever, golf was a part of the Special Olympics' summer games in Los Angeles. Tess won the gold medal for Canada.

Tess is now on the board of directors of the Special Olympics foundation. When I was growing up, something like that never would have happened. Special Olympics has given these athletes an opportunity to succeed, and sports has done that. Tess calls me her good-luck charm. It is not even close: Tess is my angel and good-luck charm. She is unbelievable. She is the epitome of the Special Olympics motto: Let me win, but if I cannot win, let me be brave in the attempt.

I have my own motto: Never miss an opportunity to meet somebody.

There are times when I say yes to something, and I question why I did. But every time I have a feeling like that, I end up enjoying the event and having a great time. I often say, "I am so glad I did it." There are so many people you get to meet just by chance. And those people end up becoming contacts or acquaintances or great friends. Never miss your opportunity.

17

FAMILY IS EVERYTHING

MY WIFE, NANCY, AND I HAVE THREE SONS: TYLER, BRODY, AND JESSE. AND WE have one daughter, Sienna. Sienna is our miracle girl. My wife was tired of having all this testosterone in the house when they were young. We had the three boys in a four-year span, and it wasn't planned when she got pregnant again in 2005. She had a rough pregnancy in the early months, and at one point, we thought we had lost the baby. It was traumatic.

One night, we had to rush Nancy to the hospital. I was resigned to the idea that this was not going to happen. At first, the medical team was preparing as if she was going to miscarry. Leafs play-by-play voice Joe Bowen's wife at the time was working in the natal ward at the hospital we were at, and she walked in and asked what we were doing there. After we told her, she took her stethoscope and she could hear a faint heartbeat. Nancy had to get tests done, but the baby was still there and the heart was still beating. After that, she was on bed rest for the remainder of her pregnancy. She also underwent more testing, and that is when we found out that not only was the baby fine, but we were having a girl. The rest of the pregnancy went well, and not only that, to this day Sienna is fine. She is my little miracle girl for sure.

I love my kids so much. Then they grow older, and the next thing you know, they are people. I still think of them as little kids. Sienna is so talented—she sings and acts, and I think that will be her future. She is fearless; she can stand up in front of anybody and sing.

My family is everything to me. I need their support because I find it hard to shut it off. There are times that I go to bed, and I can't shut it off. Especially if I am editing a lot of content. I will lie in bed and see the material, the games, everything I need to do. I also get FOMO, the Fear of Missing Out.

I like to keep busy and cover games. I ended up finding ways to make work for myself. Once you are involved in the broadcast world, it is hard to shut it off. It is not just sports; I know Lisa LaFlamme is the same way—she can't turn her news motor off. Even after leaving TSN, I work more now than I did before because of my freelance broadcast work and all of my speaking engagements. After a couple of days without working, I start to get antsy.

Over the years, I have learned to use my spare time to prepare for my next event. And I am getting pretty good at shutting it off for family time—going from 120 miles an hour to 10. If my wife and I have stuff to do with the kids, I am better. But my wife will tell you, the day after family time, I am up at five in the morning to start working again. Because I don't go to work; I go to fun. I don't go to work; I go to excitement. I don't go to work; I go to thrills and games. There are people in our business who do treat it like work, and I don't think they have as fulfilling an experience as I do. The people who have a real passion for it, they end up standing out because you can't fake that passion.

When I broadcast late-night sports, I would sometimes take a week off and go away, and I found myself wanting to get back to work so much because I didn't want to miss a big story. I had six weeks of holiday time, but I don't think I took more than one week for years. I treated it like I had a responsibility to the job. And I had an obsession as well. It was something I felt that I had to do. My longest vacation was two weeks, max, when the kids were young. I just love being around the games. I love the smells and the sights and the sounds and the thrills of it. I love the camaraderie that comes with covering sports. I never thought I was going to work. I was always going to have fun.

18

THE CRUEL BUSINESS OF SPORTS BROADCASTING

WHAT I DIDN'T LOVE WAS HOW MY CAREER AT TSN AND ITS PARENT COMPANY, BELL Media, ended. First off, I never wanted to do a farewell tour; it isn't about me. And I kind of had an inkling that something was up because TSN/Bell Media was beginning to make cuts—always the people making the biggest money with the biggest contracts. Lisa LaFlamme was let go from CTV News, also owned by Bell Media, one year to the day that they got rid of me. When I was let go, I warned Lisa to watch out, because I knew they were making cuts like crazy. They were getting rid of anyone who made more money than the managers, and they didn't care who they were. I also knew my contract was due to expire in two years. I was let go during COVID, and to this day, I haven't had a conversation about it with anyone at TSN/Bell Media.

I was busy during the pandemic. In the spring of 2021, I hosted the men's World Hockey Championship from the studio in Toronto.

My son Tyler was scheduled to take part in the NCAA regional baseball playoffs. At that point, it was the biggest tournament in his lifetime, and I didn't want to miss it. I had a travel exemption that allowed me to enter the United States, so I looked at one of the days on the schedule and said to my boss, Paul Graham, who months earlier had told me he had my back, that I needed a day off to watch Tyler play. Up until then, I had never seen him play in person while he was at college.

The game was in Knoxville, Tennessee, on a Saturday, a day that Canada wasn't playing at the World Championships. So, I thought that was perfect timing for me to go see Tyler play. Paul then told me, "You can't go. Laura Diakun can't work a triple shift." I was incredulous. I had just worked seven triple shifts in a row, and I only wanted one day off. But TSN said no. Tyler had a great game, and I watched it from the studio with my analyst, former NHLer Marc Methot. I was kind of pissed off about what had happened. I saw my wife, Nancy, on TV; she was there, but I wasn't. I was at a TV studio in Toronto, cheering my kid on and upset that I couldn't be in Tennessee.

Then a few weeks later, and just a few days before the MLB draft in July, I travelled with Tyler to Tampa for a workout because the Rays were thinking of taking him. I used my travel exemption to go to Tampa to watch his workout. The next day, I went to the gym and got a phone call while I was there. It was Stewart Johnston, the president of TSN. "This is an uncomfortable call. I just wanted to have a discussion about TSN's plan without Rod Black." I was floored by what he said. Stewart added, "As you know, this is a challenging time in our business."

I said to him, "First of all, Stewart, you are doing this on the phone. Are you serious, for all that I have done for this company over the last thirty years?" I was so angry. It wasn't so much at what he was telling me—it was the fact that he told me the news over the phone that made me so upset. He started stammering after that. I cut him off and said: "Here is what we are going to do, Stew: I am going to talk to Elliott, my agent, and we will get back to you about what is going to happen from our end."

I didn't tell anybody what had taken place. My son was about to get drafted into the major leagues, and I had all this shit going on at TSN. Elliott got back to me and said it was all about cost-cutting. People who were not sports people or broadcasters were making decisions that were all about money. But I had a legacy to protect, and I wasn't prepared to leave on TSN's terms. I was so angry with Stewart that I vowed to never speak to him again. The whole thing made me even angrier because I hadn't been able to see Tyler play in the NCAA regionals two weeks earlier.

Management asked me how I wanted to leave TSN. I told them that I wanted to call the Women's World Hockey Championship in Calgary in August, and I wanted to call one game in every CFL city. It wasn't a farewell tour; it was just something that I wanted to. At this point, the only one outside of TSN who knew what was happening was my agent. I didn't tell my wife or anyone else. None of my colour commentators knew. Tyler was about to get drafted, and I didn't want to do anything to take away from his day. I wanted to wait until that excitement had died down. Which meant I had another four months to think about things before my last day.

As the date got closer, I didn't want some big announcement. I wasn't retiring; I was still going to be working as a broadcaster. Some people in management were worried that I might go rogue and say something on the air. They sent me some sample news releases for my approval. One of them made me livid. It said, "Rod Black has decided to retire to spend more time watching his son pursue his professional baseball career." I was irate. None of this had anything to do with my son. Finally, in August, I told my wife what was happening. She couldn't understand how I was able to call all those games, knowing what I did.

I didn't want any fanfare on my final day. I did my final broadcast, and I said goodnight at the end. I called the game as I would any other game. Because to me, all the games are important. I never shed one tear over what happened at TSN. Two days later, the announcement was set to be released. I posted the news on X/Twitter before the news was sent out. It was a stressful time in my life.

I was a CTV guy who ended up at TSN. I felt comfortable, but at the same time, I never felt totally comfortable with management at TSN. I had an agent, and management hated agents.

It was a real shock to me when it all happened. The first month after everything ended, I didn't know what was going on. It was then that it really dawned on me what a cruel fucking business it is. I'd given my heart and soul to the network, with no regrets. I felt that I had a CTV/TSN tattoo emblazoned on my heart and on my ass, but one of the good things about tattoos is that they can be removed.

The anger lingered for a while. If it could happen to me, it could happen to anybody. After I was let go, I told everyone who asked, "Do not put this job ahead of your family." And I had. I'd missed funerals, weddings, birthdays, and my kids' regional championship because I cared about doing my job. I'd missed so many things in my life, working for that company.

After the news broke, so many people reached out to me. Just before I announced the news on social media, I called the commentators I was closest to. The first call I made was to Duane Forde, then Leo Rautins, and finally I talked to Cheryl Pounder. I went down the list of everyone and anyone I had worked with over the years. I called Charles Barkley and told him as well. I didn't want them to find out from anyone else but me. After I sent out the post, I received a lot of calls and messages. A lot of people I worked with, including some of my producers, were crying on the phone as we spoke. There were some people I couldn't talk to—I was too emotional at the time.

But I was so angry at the way it had all happened. I felt that I deserved better than that. I gave CTV/TSN thirty years of my life. That is the problem in Canada: We don't celebrate our announcers until they are gone. Look at Dave Hodge, one of the greatest announcers Canada has ever produced, and TSN mistreated him. One day, Hodgie said he had just had enough, and he quit. In the modern era, we replace the veterans with AI or young kids who make no money. That is fine; I was one of those young kids once.

I reached out to all of the charities that I worked with and assured them that I was not retiring. I am never retiring. It is the only thing that I know, and that is what I do.

It took a few months, but leaving TSN opened up some real doors for me. It was the best thing to happen to me, honestly. I like being my own boss. I can do my own thing, and be happy doing it. And if I am not happy, I will fire myself.

MY MENTAL HEALTH

After everything ended at TSN, I needed to spend more time working on my mental health. I didn't sleep much during the bulk of my career. Like most men, I compartmentalized everything and pushed things aside. I was very good at staying in focus when the red light was on and I was looking at the camera. It was the periphery that would get to me sometimes. Things would hit me after the fact. Like anyone, there are times that you are down and dealing with life's challenges. The birth of a child, the death of a loved one. You have bills to pay;

you have to fix things that are broken. My attitude has always been to just try to do one thing before the other. I find if I get one little thing done, one positive thing, one step in the right direction, that always helps. The other thing is that I will call someone and talk to them. I am eternally optimistic, but the business can get to you.

As much as everyone called me the hardest-working guy and all of that stuff, I never took it too seriously. I never took sports as if it were life or death. It also made me understand how important charity work was, because working in sports is like working in the toy department. Working with charities keeps me grounded. Balance in life is so hard, and I always had a theory about the triangle. Work is one point, play and recreation are one point, and family is one point. Those are three big things in my life. Whenever one point got to be too much, it pulled at the triangle and distorted it. If you get too involved in work, which I have in the past, it distorts the triangle. People ask me why I still play so much hockey. Trust me, I don't think I am going to play in the NHL. I do it because it is a great way to relieve stress. On game days, I would work out. I am not a runner, because of my knees. But I would get a workout in. In the past few years, I have been doing a lot of meditation. It helps calm me and it helps me when the days are not good. Being a broadcaster can be an intoxicating business.

I still get FOMO a lot when I'm not around games. I want to be around the game, and I want to call a game. I started so young in the business that going to and covering games has been a part of my daily routine my entire adult life.

I would have been quite content to keep working at CKY and talking sports. What a great way to make a living. I loved it. I treated everything I did at CKY the same way that I did at the national level. The longer I was there and the more events I covered, I would think, *Maybe I could do* this. *Or maybe I could* that. The more I was around the stars of sports, people like Jack Nicklaus and Charles Barkley, it made me believe I was just like them. I would spend time with them and carry on a conversation with them. They are just human, and they have the same faults and frailties as everyone else. They might be elite athletes performing at the highest level, but they have the same fears and challenges as the rest of us. What makes the great athletes better than the rest is that they hate losing more than they love winning. They hate losing more than anybody else you will meet.

I was never afraid of the next assignment. My bosses would ask me to do something or cover a sport, and I would say sure. If I was given an assignment and I had a chance to cover a sports event, I never turned it down because I wanted the weekend off. It would drive me crazy whenever a young reporter turned down a great opportunity. One time, I had another assignment, and I couldn't work one of the Raptors games. A young reporter was asked to fill in for me, and he said no because he was about to go on a holiday. I couldn't believe that someone would choose a holiday over a dream job like hosting a Raptors game on TV. Finding a job in Canadian sports broadcasting is getting harder every year. That is why you don't say no to any opportunity that comes along.

At one time, I was close to taking a job in Tampa, Florida. I wanted to work in the United States because all of my broadcast heroes worked there, and let's face it, the money is way better. But frankly, I am so proudly Canadian, I didn't want to leave. I wanted to change the culture in Canada and bring some of that American pride over here. I wanted everyone to know that it is cool to be Canadian, and it is cool to be proud of that fact.

When you have been doing this as long as I have, people come up to you to say hi or, for the most part, say something nice. In the old days, I would receive letters from people. Sometimes famous people. I certainly don't do what I do for compliments. Even to this day, I will host an event, and someone will come up to me and say, "Can you say hi to my mom or my dad?" I will tape a video for them, and they really appreciate it. I also get this: "You were the voice of my generation." I always smile at that one.

In 2024, at the Canadian Baseball Hall of Fame, a guy came up to me and said, "I saw you with your son Tyler at his major league debut." Tyler is an infielder in the Milwaukee Brewers organization. On April 30, 2024, he made his major league debut in a game against the Tampa Bay Rays. This was also his mother's birthday. In his first at-bat, he hit a double to centre field. Then, thankfully, his proud dad and mom were there that night. During his second at-bat, I was being interviewed by a local Milwaukee reporter, and while we were live on the air, Tyler got his second major league hit. I blurted out in my best baseball voice, "There is a base hit to right field by my boy, Tyler Black. Oh, there you go! Happy birthday, Nancy." I called a lot of important events in my time, but to me, that was the greatest call of them all.

As this older gentleman spoke to me about that day, he had tears in his eyes. That moment meant so much to me. That is what sports and humanity are all about.

It has been great to meet so many people, shake their hands, and listen to them tell me a story about watching something that I have done. When I cover an event or call a game, I can't afford to think about anybody watching me. I am totally focused on calling the game or the event I am at. Years later, though, people will come up to me and talk about the Olympics or the Blue Jays or the Raptors. I meet adults now, people in their forties, who say they watched me when they were ten years old. I like hearing those stories. But shit, it makes me feel old.

ANOTHER ROD BLACK?

Will there be another Rod Black type of sportscaster, who can call every sport you can think of? I sure hope there is. I hope that somebody can do it. They have tried to do that with certain sportscasters, but with the current state of the broadcast industry in Canada, I am not sure they could. The only announcers who come close to doing what I have done work in the United States. Based on the number of different sports they have called, you are talking about people like Bob Costas and Jim Nantz. Generally speaking, they call three or four different sports. I have called everything. Give me a sport, I am sure I have called it. And that includes pickleball, which I called off a stream. I am not the only person to have done it—I just don't think the industry would take the time to develop another broadcaster with the same kind of versatility. It has become a very cheap industry now. Having said that, it wasn't exactly lucrative for me to call some of those sports!

I was this adopted orphan who came over to TSN from Sportsnet. This was because the CRTC ruled that CTV had to sell Sportsnet so that they could buy TSN. I had great bosses who believed in me and trusted me. I always said, if you trust me, I will trust you right back. It wasn't long before they realized I could do it all. I loved calling the Canada Winter Games. I would wake up in the morning and call curling. From there, I would move over to short-track speed skating in the afternoon and then cap off my night by calling boxing. I loved covering three different sports in a day—it was a lot of work, but I loved it.

At a network level, we should have more coverage of amateur sports in Canada. To me, that has always been an issue in this country: the lack of coverage of anything that isn't professional. I think anybody can do what I did and call as many sports as I did. But to do it at the national level and get the kind of exposure that I had, that will be tough. Mainly because broadcasters don't cover as many sports as they used to, because they don't want to spend the money.

My versatility has a lot to do with the fact that I did so many voices as a kid. I had to understand cadences to do those voices. I never changed my voice, but I would adapt my cadence to suit the sport that I was calling. And I learned that because I watched so many different announcers growing up. And the only way to learn from them is to watch them and to mimic them. I did that when I was a kid.

Any time I was asked to cover or call a sport, I would always say, "Yes, let's do this, let's go." It always seemed like something I should do. As a kid, I never had a dream that I would become a sports announcer because I didn't even think it was possible. I was this teenager with a huge head of curly hair and a cheesy moustache. When things started to fall into place when I worked at CKY, it became this natural progression. It is all because the people above me believed in me. People like Ralph Mellanby and Doug Beeforth and Rick Chisholm and Jim Marshall and Peter Sisam and Scott Moore and all of my bosses put me in a position to call those different sports and to succeed. Let's face it, I saved a lot of companies a lot of money over the years. When I left TSN, even though I was well paid at the time, they ended up hiring four people to fill all the roles I used to fill. In the end, did they really save any money by getting rid of me? Who knows?

Bottom line, I really hope there is someone else who ends up calling all the different sports I did, but it likely will come from a streaming service or maybe AI. Television is never going to be the same as it was during my heyday. But then again, change is inevitable. You have just got to be able to jump on the boat and ride the waves.

19

THE FUTURE

A SPORTSCASTER CAN FAKE A LOT OF THINGS, BUT THEY CAN'T FAKE A GENUINE love and appreciation for the sport they are covering. I have always believed that, and I still do to this day. More than anything, that is why people come up to me, because they just want to thank me for covering their favourite sport or interviewing a family member and treating everyone like a star. That is the way it should be: A broadcaster must treat every story and sport and event and athlete like they are special.

That is why I get excited doing play-by-play for a Canadian Elite Basketball League game. I get that same enjoyment hosting a charity hockey heroes' event. I love it all. It doesn't matter what game it is or what league it is, I love calling live sports. In the last chapter I wrote about about calling three sports in one day at the Canada Winter Games. To me, that was one of the most fun events that I was a part of. I went to Whitehorse, Yukon, and even to Bathurst, New Brunswick.

A good number of the athletes I covered at the Canada Winter Games went on to become stars. I called a game that Sidney Crosby played in when he was only fourteen years old. Even back then, you could tell he was going to be special.

Moments like that have inspired me over the course of my career. I still get inspired every day. I find that, at this stage in my life, little things inspire me. I have always believed in living the "dash." I am talking about the dash between when you are born and when you die. On your tombstone, it will read: *Rod Black, 1962–whatever*. It isn't the years at either end, it is that dash in the middle that matters. That is what you have to do: Live the dash between the beginning and the end. Get the best out of your dash.

I am inspired by my kids and how they are finding their way in life. To this day, I still get inspired by athletes. I hosted the Joe Carter Golf Classic in 2025, and I spent time with former Jays catcher Russell Martin. Russell inspires me. His dad helped pay for his sports by playing the saxophone in the Montreal subway. I am inspired by Shai Gilgeous-Alexander. I was there when he was a young athlete taking part in the BioSteel All Canadian Games, a series of all-star basketball games involving high schoolers. Shai didn't do much in that game, and I would have never believed he would be the NBA's MVP one day. Or have one of the greatest seasons in the history of basketball. But like all the great ones that I have been around, SGA put in the work. And he continues to put in the work every day.

I am still fascinated to watch the development of great athletes. And I am really inspired by good people who do good things. It costs nothing to be nice, or to make a difference when nobody is watching.

I am still a big believer that anything is possible in life. The unpredictability of sports still fascinates me. You can't write the ending to a sporting event before it happens. And over the course of my career, every week something would happen that would make me think, *You can't make this shit up!*

In 1980, I was working at the roller rink in Winnipeg. I got off the bus I was riding from college to the roller rink and went straight to the TV section in a Woolco store to watch Team USA beat Russia in men's Olympic hockey. It was something I will never forget. Every time I think I have seen it all in sports, I end up seeing something else happen.

A perfect example was the unpredictable roller-coaster ride of the Blue Jays and the Dodgers in the 2025 World Series. Even in the new world of sports betting, there was never a sure bet in any of the seven games. Once again, you can't write endings like that.

I will say that one of the great things I like about golf is that we mere mortals can, on a very rare occasion, make a putt or take a shot that is just like something Nick Taylor or Tiger Woods or Jack Nicklaus did. You can't do that same thing in hockey, but you can in golf.

Winning in sports, especially in hockey, is hard. I believe that Connor McDavid will win a Stanley Cup one day. But it isn't that easy to win one. When a team finally does win the Stanley Cup, that is why it is so special: because it is so hard to win one.

Doing what I do keeps me young. I am in my sixties, and I still feel like I am in my twenties. John Shannon once said that I am like Peter Pan—I have never grown up. There is no drug like the feeling you get covering sports.

I have had a full-circle life, and it continues to be that way. I believe that stuff happens for a reason because you make it happen for a reason.

My entire life has been about sports. From my childhood to the present day. To this day, I will cover and announce for whatever sport and whatever game comes up. Because I love them all. Have microphone, will travel!

While my family, as I've said, is my number-one priority, I've also started to think about how the next few chapters in my life are going to play out. Make no mistake: I have not retired. I'm not ready to, and I will not retire until I have a mic drop into a coffin. My retirement plan is pretty much Freedom 95. By then, I'll probably be calling bingo games at the Legion.

But that doesn't mean I'm not going to change my game plan, either. As John Shannon once said, you've got to evolve or you will die.

So, evolution it is.

I've really enjoyed getting to know the business side of sports—becoming a minority owner in the Toronto Maple Leafs, a baseball team in the Canadian Baseball League (formerly the Intercounty League). I also sit on several boards, including Special Olympics, AMJ Moving, and the Pinball Clemons Foundation, and I'm branching out and have started my own production company, which includes everything from broadcasting to podcasting to Rod-casting.

I've been lucky enough to be asked to speak at many dinners, galas, corporate events, and business sessions, and while I always like to design my "Rod Talks" around the group I'm speaking to—telling a lot of stories, cracking a few jokes, and doing a number of voices—the one theme that is always a constant for me is the "seven-letter rule." My speeches usually come down to the seven-letter words that can transform lives.

I don't want to give my whole speech away here, but take a look at these words and how they impact all of us:

First off, it starts with the *journey*, where everyone of us is a *dreamer* with a *purpose*. To move *forward*, we need *purpose* and *courage*, not to mention patience, because along the way we will encounter a lot of *failure*, which means we need *balance*.

And that's where the most important seven-letter word comes into play: *believe*.

Do yourself a favour and listen to the conversations around you today. Listen to the newscasts, podcasts, and interviews, especially in sports, and you will be hearing that word more than any other.

I believe that because it's true. I still see and hear that word every day in the games I cover, the teams that reach incredible highs and fascinate not only a city but a country, like the 2025 Toronto Blue Jays.

If you don't have that word *believe* on your lips and in your heart, you will never get to the ultimate seven letter word: *success*.

What I love about life is that there are so many great things and great people to believe in.

I look back on how I got into the business, how I grew as a broadcaster, how I was able to cover events around the world, how I was able to meet so many great people, and ultimately how privileged I've been to be part of so many games and events. The crazy thing is, even though I'm a little older and the hair is much thinner, I still get the same excitement and juice that I had when I first started broadcasting over four decades ago.

I may not have as many assignments now, but I still get pumped for whatever freelance broadcast that I have upcoming on my calendar. As I said earlier, have microphone, will travel. I still get stoked when producing documentaries and features and creating content for a number of corporations around North America. I still have a secret dream of someday directing an Oscar-winning sports documentary.

I still get jacked for all the speaking engagements that I do. Special thanks to Andrew Jackson and the Jackson Events team for keeping me running from gig to gig with their relentless desire to always make events bigger and better. I still love contributing articles to the *Toronto Star*. I love acting, doing some stage work and appearing in a number of films—usually playing a sports announcer. Most of all, I still love paying it forward and getting a chance to make a difference in someone's life.

After reading this book, it is obvious that I still never say no. But that dash needs to be filled up, and why not fill it with the stuff that you *love* and *believe* in?

Oh yes, and I still love to play. That little boy in me will never grow old.

Today's game may be over, but there's always another one tomorrow. And there is as good a chance I'll be at that game.

Thanks for watching. Thanks for reading. And most of all, thanks for believing.

Acknowledgements

ROD BLACK

And now, the end is near . . .

But only for this book and this last chapter. Because believe me, this story is far from over. I'm not sure what the sequel will be like, but if you've been following along, you've probably come to the same conclusion that I have through this absolutely wild but fulfilling ride: *You can't make this shit up.*

Actually, that would have made a good title for this book. But none of it has been made up and no names have been changed to protect the innocent, although there are many stories that we left on the cutting-room floor.

If there's one thing I've learned over the years, it's this: Nobody does this alone. Not a career. Not a life. Not a story worth telling. This book exists because a lot of people believed, sometimes before I did.

Brian Wood was one of those people. The publishing super-agent was the first person to say, "You should write a memoir." To which I immediately replied, "I don't want a *me*-moir." Because this was never meant to be about *me*. It's about moments. About people. About the noise, the chaos, the beauty, the misses, the miracles—and everything in between. Brian saw the story before I did, and sometimes that's all it takes.

Jim Gifford is another believer. He pushed me like no other coach or producer I've ever had, even when I had to extend many deadlines because of my ridiculous schedule. Jim and the Simon & Schuster team constantly encouraged me to do what I always do—keep grinding and trust the process.

Jim Lang helped take this story to another level. The über-broadcaster/writer hopped aboard midgame, helped put the pieces of this crazy puzzle together, and became the best teammate anyone can have.

And as you've discovered in this book, I've had so many amazing teammates through the years and to this day.

People like Andrew Jackson, who keeps running me out to events, stages, rinks, ballrooms, locker rooms, back halls, and front doors because he also believes in what he sees and what he's hearing. Andrew doesn't just book events—he fuels passion and momentum. And when someone like that keeps betting on you, you don't stop moving.

People like my great friends, many of whom aren't in the broadcast industry and who know that as much as I don't take myself seriously, I take my business seriously. I loved the shit.

Although I've made more than a few mistakes, I offer no apologies. Except maybe to Ryan Bonne.

If you don't recognize the name, you certainly know who he is. Ryan is a former competitive gymnast, a fellow Winnipegger most famous for being the long-time mascot of the Toronto Raptors. If you've seen Ryan in costume and in action, you know he's an incredible talent who always has the crowd in claws. He's also a great friend who donates a ton of time to charity, including my own celebrity golf tournament, which we held for years in Winnipeg.

He's also one very lucky Raptor.

Over a decade ago, Ryan came to perform as he always did at the tournament, running around in costume on the course, entertaining everybody and generally doing mascot things. But on this particular year, Ryan also came out and played an early-morning round with a small group of friends just before my tournament was about to start.

We were about seven holes into the round when I did what I usually do and sliced a ball down into the woods on the left side of the fairway at Elmhurst Golf & Country Club. Hockey stars Dale Hawerchuk and Kirk Muller were also in our group, as well as my great buddies Stan Vasilakos and singer Michael Burgess.

I found my ball and decided to punch it back out to the fairway, but just before I did, I realized that I actually could take a full swing and had a narrow opening to advance the ball even farther. About fifty yards ahead of me in the trees was Ryan, who was also looking for his ball.

"Hey, Ry, heads up, I'm going to punch out," I hollered over as he ducked for cover behind a tree. Well, this story writes itself. Because you know what happened next.

I took my swing. Ryan bobbed his head out at the last second, and my ball smacked into the side of his melon like a missile.

We were all in shock. Ryan was jumping around like he was doing his mascot routine, only this time there was blood squirting out everywhere like the famous knight scene in the movie *Monty Python and the Holy Grail.* Ryan fell to the ground, telling us to keep him awake and make sure that we told his family he was going to be all right. The blood was still gushing from his skull when both Dale and I applied pressure to the wound, but it was now actually leaking through our fingers. This wasn't good. As bad as Ryan was, I was as white as a zombie, and quickly we all got him back to the clubhouse. Guests for my tournament were already arriving as Ryan was being wheeled into an ambulance.

The good news came later when we learned Ryan would be okay. No concussion and he only needed a few stitches, but he was so mad that he had missed the tournament. He did show up for the dinner ceremony, where we told everyone the whole bloody story. Ryan had everyone howling when he said, "Rod was concerned, but then again, he came up and said that he needed to play his next shot where it lies—in my skull."

I countered with "Worse than anything—I got a double bogey on the hole."

As much as we laughed, it wasn't funny when it happened, and like so many times, you realize that life can sometimes flash before your eyes.

So, Ryan, I'm sorry for almost killing you, and I'm so happy that we've stayed friends all these years.

Oh, but karma is a bitch.

A few years ago, the golf gods—or perhaps the Raptors—got their revenge when a ball unexpectedly plunked me on the head at Michael "Pinball" Clemons's golf tournament. Same spot. No stitches required, but man it hurt like hell, and like Ryan, I was leaking like a faucet.

The lessons never stop.

What goes around does come around, or what goes around does come back around to hit you. But the best thing to do in a bad situation is to laugh, and so we did when the next year, Pinball gave me a gift before we teed off: an autographed Toronto Argos football helmet. Thankfully, I didn't need it.

But that's the way the ball has bounced my entire life. From that kid who was on stage as an emcee in grade 3, when the principal introduced him as the next Ed Sullivan, to the guy who was the "man for all seasons."

Things change, but some things never do.

Sport was the original obsession. To this day, it still is. As a kid, it was calling games to nobody. Timers, stats, imaginary crowds. That love affair never cooled. It evolved—but it never left. I still get the same buzz before the lights come on. Still feel the same nerves. Still think, *How lucky am I to be here?*

Then charity changed everything. It gave me perspective I didn't know I was missing. It introduced me to courage that makes scoreboards irrelevant. To families who redefine strength. To athletes, kids, and communities who remind you what really matters. Charity didn't slow me down—it deepened the meaning of the ride.

And family? That's the baseline. That's the anchor. They're the constant when everything else is variable. The ones who see the real version—after the applause, after the travel, after the noise. Nothing works without them. Nothing matters more.

The last few years—losing my parents, COVID, job changes, unpredictability, curveballs I never saw coming—taught me something essential: You have to stay ready for the next moment. The next chapter. The next opportunity. The next reinvention. Nothing is permanent except change—and authenticity.

Which makes me want to repeat: I'm not retiring. Not now. Not ever. I'm evolving. Adjusting. Listening. Learning. And doing what I've always done—showing up as myself. Because the only thing you can truly control in this business, and in life, is who you are when the mic is on . . . and when it's off.

This book isn't an ending. It's a breath between plays.

It started with a kid obsessed with sports. Shaped by stories. Grounded by family. Defined by gratitude. Still driven by curiosity.

I have always been a believer that anything is possible. From the bottom of my heart, thank you to all of you who have been part of my dream.

Time to CUT TO BLACK . . .

For now.

JIM LANG

I was thrilled when my agent, Brian Wood, called me out of the blue in the spring of 2025 with a proposal. He had a client who was always on the go and always working. This person wanted a helping hand finishing his book. The second I found out it was Rod Black, I was thrilled. Even though we are close in age, Rod was already a bona fide Canadian broadcasting star when I started moving up through the ranks. Over the years, I have had the good fortune to get to know Rod both personally and professionally. Trust me, he is even nicer than you think. To echo the words of Jack Armstrong, Rod is the real deal. Rod is a true pro in everything he does, and he is a genuinely good person. That is a tough combination to find in life.

Which leads me to a number of people I would like to thank in finishing this project. First and foremost, thanks to my wife, kids, dog, and cat. They keep me grounded and provide invaluable emotional support.

Even though he constantly reminds me of the pain that comes from cheering for my favourite hockey team, I am legally obligated to thank my agent, Brian Wood—thanks, Brian. I kid—Brian is the best! Thanks to all-star editor Jim Gifford and the entire team at Simon & Schuster Canada.

Thank you to Joe Carter, Jack Armstrong, Eric Smith, Cheryl Pounder, and Andrew Jackson of Jackson Events.

And finally, thank you, Rod Black. It will be a long time before we find another sportscaster in Canada who is able to call four different sports in five days and make them all sound great. Thank you, my friend—it was a pleasure to work with you.